S0-CMW-176

BRISBANE

Also by Oliver Carlson

(with Ernest Sutherland Bates)

HEARST: LORD OF SAN SIMEON

BRISBANE

A CANDID BIOGRAPHY

OLIVER CARLSON

•

1937

STACKPOLE SONS NEW YORK

Manufactured Entirely in U. S. A. by
The Telegraph Press in Harrisburg
Pennsylvania

To

PATRICIA ANN

FOREWORD

Writing a biography of Arthur Brisbane bears at least one resemblance to the Biblical concept of Creation: "In the beginning was the Word." With Brisbane, "the word" was multiplied twenty-five million times over.

Few men, in this or any other age, have put on paper so semmingly endless an array of words, dealing with so seemingly endless a variety of topics. No man in the long history of journalism has been more widely and continuously read. No columnist ever enjoyed such a nationwide vogue, or was more unsuccessfully imitated.

The record of the man has presented certain obstacles to the biographer:

The sheer mass of wordage piled up by Arthur Brisbane in his fifty-three years of journalistic activity was overwhelming. To read and to select in such a way as to give what seemed to be a developing picture of the man and his opinions was in itself a difficult task. I have preferred to quote him directly more frequently than I might have if his whole life had not been consecrated to—words.

In the second place, Brisbane was in the service of William Randolph Hearst for two score years. The two names are inevitably bound together, and Brisbane, as editorial mouthpiece and political go-between for his employer, cannot be understood or explained except in that relationship. Hearst, in his personal life, his spectacular actions, his regal manner of living, his flouting of established traditions and moral codes reminds one of Henry the Eighth. And if Hearst assumes the character of the self-indulgent, brazen British monarch, Brisbane seems to be his Wolsey, whose every word and action, no matter how questionable, is covered by a smoke screen of moral and religious precepts.

FOREWORD

My discussion of Hearst in this book has been confined to those incidents which involved or affected Arthur Brisbane.

Arthur Brisbane is worthy of a biography only with respect to his public life. His personal life, except for his childhood and adolescence, was commonplace and of interest only to his family and friends. His home and family, though generously provided for, were secondary to his career, and both wife and children were considerately self-effacing so that the spotlight of attention might focus wholly and completely upon the father.

The extended discussion in this book of Albert Brisbane, Arthur's father, is due not only to the fact of Albert's own importance, but to the contrast between father and son in outlook and achievement.

The author takes this opportunity to acknowledge the assistance given him by members of the staff of the New York Public Library, the Carpenter Memorial Library of Manchester, New Hampshire, the University of Pennsylvania Library and especially the Public Library of Los Angeles, California. Thanks are also due for use of the files and libraries of the *New York Times*, *New York World-Telegram*, and *Time, Inc.*

Of the many persons who assisted me only a few can be mentioned, but to each one I give thanks. Special mention must be made of Henry F. Pringle, Oswald Garrison Villard, Stanley Walker, Henry H. Klein, Idwal Jones, Charles Edward Russell, Harry Bressler, Jesse and Isabel Mayers. To my wife, Beatrice Hunter Carlson, whose active assistance from first to last made this book possible, I owe unending gratitude.

O. C.

Los Angeles, July 22, 1937.

THE CONTENTS

LIST OF ILLUSTRATIONS

INTRODUCTION

The last of New York's Christmas Eve revelers were returning to their homes in the dawn of December 25, 1936 when screaming headlines announced that Arthur Brisbane had died. The news came as a shock to his millions of readers as well as to his newspaper associates, for his illness had been kept a closely guarded secret. His daily output had continued without interruption to the very end; and the Hearst papers which blazoned the news of his death to the world also carried his last column:

"Another Christmas has come, a birthday that means kindness and hope for so many millions of human beings . . ."

Expressions of sympathy poured in upon the family from all over the world. Prelates and politicians, Wall Street financiers, captains of industry, editors, publishers, and common folk (to whom Brisbane's daily column was considered as natural and as necessary as the morning alarm clock) joined in tribute to the man.

The telegrams, letters, articles and editorials were, with one or two exceptions, paeans of praise to the deceased:

"I took keen delight . . . in exploring with him the teachings of history and the philosophy of our civilization."—Franklin D. Roosevelt.

"Mr. Brisbane's editorials were an inspiration to me."—Mayor Fiorello LaGuardia.

"A personality and a genius which contributed important developments to the art of journalism and many significant thoughts to the science of business administration."—Alfred E. Smith.

"The War Department and the millions of citizens who believe in peace have lost a friend."—Secretary of War Woodring.

"An accurate and painstaking historian."—Senator Ashurst.

"Mr. Brisbane was a genius."—Senator Borah.

"The oppressed peoples of the world have lost their sincerest friend."—Walter Winchell.

"He was at home in any society and with any type of mind. He had the greatest gift of all—Humanity"—Bernard Gimbel.

"A bench mark in the ever-changing scene of his profession, he brought such freshness and vitality to his work that even those who had reason to differ with his point of view were impressed by his dynamic force and homely philosophy."—A. H. Sulzberger, *New York Times.*

The encomiums were so many and so flattering that the irreparable loss the country had suffered should have been obvious to even the most sceptical. But the loss was undoubtedly greatest (except for Mr. Brisbane's own family) to William Randolph Hearst. Brisbane was not only one of his oldest, as well as his most highly paid employees. He was also his trusted lieutenant, business adviser, political weathercock, ace editorial writer and columnist, newspaper doctor, advertising expert and chief manipulator of public opinion.

"I grieve inconsolably," Hearst wrote, "that the long, long friendship, uninterrupted by a single quarrel or definite difference of opinion of any kind, is ended—that I will no longer knew his enjoyable and helpful companionship, and that the world in which I must spend my few remaining years will hold for me a blank space, which had been so unforgettably filled by my more than friend and more than brother, Arthur Brisbane."

INTRODUCTION

The sands of time were running low, even for the Lord of San Simeon. One by one his galaxy of devil-may-care reporters, sob-sisters and editors had passed away. Arthur Brisbane, alone of them all, had seemed ageless and unchanging. Dynasties fell, wars, famines, periods of frenzied speculation followed by panic and disaster came and went, but Arthur Brisbane's daily stint continued its uninterrupted flow. Now it was ended. Ended at a time when his facile pen, his sound advice, was more needed than ever before. For the mighty Hearst Newspaper Empire was beginning to crack up. Like one of those prehistoric dinosaurs—big of body but small of brain—about which Arthur Brisbane so loved to write editorials, it lurched about clumsily and helplessly as pigmy rivals sank their fangs into its organs of circulation and advertising.

Was Arthur Brisbane aware of what was happening? It is doubtful. He was too close to the canvas to see the picture as a whole. Furthermore, being by nature and habit a perennial optimist as well as a confirmed believer in the greatness of himself and his employer, he no doubt viewed the growing hostility to all things Hearstian as one of the vagaries of public opinion—a temporary abberation—which would in due time be corrected. After all, he had seen such periods before. And after each such setback, he and Mr. Hearst had risen to attain new heights of power, circulation, and wealth. Why shouldn't it happen again!

Was Brisbane a great man?

The answer depends upon the yardstick used. If greatness be measured in terms of mass appeal—then Brisbane was truly great. If it be measured in terms of financial success—again the answer must be in the affirmative. If it be measured in terms of achievement within his profession—then too, he is great, for his innovations in the field of journalism were pioneer efforts in creating the "yellow press." But if the yardstick be an intangible something such as truth, integrity, consistency or humanity, the answer must be in the negative.

Early in his career, Brisbane determined that he would follow no will-o'-the-wisp radical theorists. The pattern of his father's life, to which in later years he gave such devoted lip-service, was not for Arthur. He craved power, popular success, and, above all, money, though he knew full well what would happen to his ideas on socialism and humanitarianism once wealth and affluence touched him. His was no life to be spent in the contemplation of his own navel or in quest of eternal verities. His philosophy of life, if such it may be called, was a vulgarized pragmatism which belived that any means used in attaining the end sought was proper and justifiable, provided that it was adequately seasoned with ripe old moral and religious precepts plucked for the occasion.

And his perpetual advice to his readers to THINK, while it was, perhaps, well meant, and fed his own ego, certainly didn't improve his own powers of cognition. His active mind, had it been harnessed to some important problem for more than a few consecutive moments, could have made important contributions to any field he had chosen to explore. He read widely, but not well. He thought quickly, but superficially. These qualities, which fitted him so well as a newspaper editor appealing to the mass mind, at the same time unfitted him for a more profound and worthwhile contribution to American thought and letters. But the fact of his great influence and appeal makes even his mediocrity important. In an age in which manipulation of public opinion has become the fulcrum of the political lever, Arthur Brisbane's strange career is an astonishing document.

1

THE TRUTH-SEEKER

THE NAME *Brisbane*, according to genealogist E. Haviland Hillman, is derived from the village of Brespan, in the commune of Lemerzel, arrondissement of Vannes, department of Morbihan in Brittany, "not far from the original home of the Stewarts at Dol, with whom the Brisbane's were early associated." He adds, "There is absolutely no ground for assuming a Saxon origin for the family, while there is every reason for believing a Breton or Norman one."

These early Brisbanes first settled in England in the wake of the Norman invasion, but soon moved to the west of Scotland sometime between 1124 and 1153. In the course of the centuries, the name has undergone various changes.

For more than five hundred years the Brisbanes remained in Scotland, where as defenders of kirk and covenant and clan they fought a long, losing fight against the English. Thrift and hard work could not overcome the double handicap of a thin, worn-out soil and invasion from the south. So, as the Brisbanes kept slipping rung by rung, down the ladder of security and success, even their strong ties to the land which had given them birth and from which they had eked out their livelihood could no longer hold them.

Tales of strange lands across the Atlantic were seeping back into Scotland: lands so vast, so rich as to beggar description; lands to be had for the taking, where religious freedom was assured and where English interference with one's life was very small indeed.

Colonial America was beckoning to the adventurous and the hard-working. At least two of the Brisbanes cast their lot with other Scotsmen and reached the shores of their new homeland soon after the eighteenth century was under way. One, a Doctor William Brisbane, went to Charleston, South Carolina, in 1730-31; while another, Captain John Brisbane, settled in New York, acquired land, raised a family, and continued clinging sternly to the faith of John Calvin.

The War for Independence found all Brisbanes of fighting age ready and willing to do their bit in driving the redcoats from American soil. In doing this they felt that they not only were helping to assure greater freedom for themselves and their offspring, but that they were helping to avenge the insults and oppression which they had had to accept from the English.

The Brisbanes multiplied. Some of them prospered. When the Federal Census of 1790 appeared, there were numerous Brisbanes in New York, Pennsylvania, New Jersey, South Carolina and elsewhere.

The grandfather of Arthur Brisbane was James Brisbane, born in Philadelphia, October 12, 1776. At the age of twenty-two, on April 18, 1798, young James, together with John Thompson and others, left Philadelphia with a supply of stores for the Holland Purchase—a vast tract of land comprising some four million acres which had been acquired from the Indians by representatives of Robert Morris a year or two earlier. This land had been turned over to a Dutch syndicate and was known for the next hundred years as the Holland Purchase. The company was one of the many which were then swallowing up vast strips of virgin land in the interior and laying the foundation for many of America's great fortunes.

Young Brisbane was a hard worker, a good farmer, and a

shrewd judge of land. He decided that this was a logical place to settle down and raise a family. The land was rich and the crops were good. The westward urge was increasing, and the slight population trickle of the 1790's became a steady stream after the turn of the century. The Hudson River and the Mohawk offered a cheap and easy method of travel into the west. Some continued their journey out into what was then the Northwest Territory, but many remained to settle on the fertile soil belonging to the Holland Land Company.

Batavia became a village in 1801. The next year, James Brisbane erected its first store. He continued to function as a merchant there until 1819. He was also the first postmaster of the community. In 1807 he married Mary Lucy Stevens, an English girl of unusual ability. She was an ardent student of history and science and she must have seemed a queer figure to the wives of the backwoodsmen.

James Brisbane was fairly well educated in terms of his times. He had long since broken with the faith of his fathers and developed a strong repugnance to religious doctrine and dogma. His scepticism grew with the years. An ardent Adventist accosted him on the street one day in 1843. It was, in fact, the very eve of the world's destruction, according to the prophesy of the Millerites. "Mr. Brisbane," said the Adventist, with mingled joy and terror, "Mr. Brisbane, do you know that the world is coming to an end tomorrow!?" To his great consternation, came the immediate reply: "Damned glad of it, sir! Damn glad of it! This experiment of the human race is a total failure."

James Brisbane went to New York City in 1806, where, for two years, he engaged in the book business. Then, returning to Batavia, he continued his mercantile pursuits until 1821. According to the Gazetteer and Biographical

Record of Genesee County, published in 1890, "his intimate relations with the Holland Land Company enabled him to take advantage of the purchase of land at low prices. He thus became the owner of large tracts of real estate which, in years, were greatly enhanced in value by the settlement of the country."

Two sons were born to the Brisbanes, Albert, born August 22, 1809; and George, born March 15, 1812. George followed in the footsteps of his father. His horizon was bounded by his personal economic problems, family interests, and the social life of Batavia.

Albert Brisbane was born in his parents' big home close to Tonawanda Creek, almost within hearing distance of the roar of Niagara Falls. When he was but three years old, America once more took up arms against the British. During 1813 and 1814, a good deal of fighting occurred not far from the Brisbane farm. Buffalo, a small town about thirty-five miles away, was burned by the British. James Brisbane served as a commissary for the American forces and left his wife to manage his affairs during his absence. Once, when the American forces had retreated to Batavia, with the British and their Indian allies reported close behind, Mary Brisbane showed her mettle by undertaking to supply the American troops with greatly needed provisions.

"Taking Old Chestnut, one of our best and fleetest horses, with the escort of a few soldiers, she scoured the country, making raids generally where she suspected supplies might be concealed. Whatever she found she took, giving the owner certificates in exchange, but forcing them to deliver. It was by these measures," says Albert Brisbane in his biography, "that a body of troops were preserved at our place, and the advance of the enemy retarded until other forces came up and caused their retreat to the Canadian side. All of that history seems a long way off now.....I remember a little fellow scarcely five years old, stealing up to the bedside of General Scott, when he lay wounded in our house, and his ordering me out of the room."

Young Albert loved the out-of-doors as much as he dreaded the long hours spent on the wooden bench at school, "pondering over subjects in which I took no interest and which I but poorly understood." The dull dry treatment given him both by teacher and text worried the youngster. "I remember pondering over the rules of Murray's Immortal Grammar, where I learned that a verb was a word which signified, 'to be, to do, or to suffer.' In my young imagination I wondered what possible relation there could be between I eat, I sleep and 'to be, to do, and to suffer'; and my efforts to disentangle the meaning of Mr. Murray's complex metaphysical explanations were crowned with total non-success."

But if young Albert didn't respond well to his teachers and school books, he more than made up for it by his interest in history and science as taught him by his mother. She talked to him of the stars, the planets, and the wonders of the cosmos as well as of the marvelous works wrought by the Chaldeans, Assyrians, Babylonians, and Egyptians until, "my infant mind was peopled with the heroes of antiquity.....It was thus that I began my synthetic education."

When Albert was fifteen he began to ask himself for the first time: "What is the work of man on this earth? Whatever it is, that I should do. It is not right for the individual to work for himself; he must keep on the great track which humanity is following."

His practical minded father, to whom he raised these questions, assured him that by diligent study great opportunities would open to him. He might even become governor of the state! The young idealist was not impressed. What he wanted to know was what the human race had to do, and then to coöperate with it in its work. To this, his father had no answer, but he agreed to give his son the kind of education he wanted. Albert was taken to New York City, which he found to be merely a systematized and improved Batavia. He applied himself to his studies until after his eighteenth birthday, but somehow the question of man's social destiny continued to be a problem to which he was drawn as by some irresistible force.

Europe, he said to himself, with its great thinkers, must have the answer. He *must* go to Europe. And so with his father's blessings and financing to back him up, Albert Brisbane sailed for Havre in May, 1828, to seek the answer to the question which was then puzzling him as it was many young Americans.

Though young Brisbane didn't know it, he was part of that intellectual ferment which was sweeping across the eastern seaboard—a ferment that was going to bequeath to the young Republic a group of truly great names: Emerson, Thoreau, Ripley, Channing, Greeley, Dana, and many others. And back of these marched a host of lesser men and women consecrating their lives to humanity. A great American dream was in the making—not a dream of a sordid acquisitiveness, but a dream of America taking the lead in building a citizenry of finer intellectual, moral, and religious qualities.

The period which Vernon C. Parrington calls "the romantic revolution" in American history was beginning. The eighteen year old boy from Batavia who was journeying to the old world to find the answer to the question: "What is the destiny of man and what can I do to accelerate it?" was to be both a creature of that romantic revolution and one of its potent shapers.

Nor was it an accident that the young humanitarian went first to France, for French revolutionary theory of that period gave the spark to America. Says Parrington:

"Its devious progress through the country can be traced fairly accurately. Landing first in Virginia in the early 1770's, it met with a hospitable reception from the generous planter society and spread widely there the fashion of Physiocratic Agrarianism. Traveling thence westword into the Inland Empire it domesticated itself in frontier log cabins under the guise of an assertive individualism, to issue later as the coon-skin democracy of the Jacksonian revolution. Eventually reaching New England, the last haven and refuge of eighteenth century realism, it disarmed Yankee antagonism by assuming the dress of Unitarianism and preached the doctrine of human perfectibility with such conviction as to arouse the conscience of New England to an extraordinary enthusiasm for reforming man and society. And finally coming to New York, it inoculated the mind of the emerging proletariat with its doctrines of the rights of man, with Fourieristic and other utopias, and turmoiled contemporary politics with equalitarian Locofoco programs. No other philosophy assumed so many and such attractive devices, or wrought such changes in American ideals, as this French romanticism with its generous humanitarian impulse. The ground was ready for the seed it was to sow, and if in the judgment of a hostile philosophy, the crop turned out to be tares, increasing thousands believed it to be excellent wheat, to the growing of which America was to be dedicated henceforth."

That long arid period extending from the surrender of Cornwallis at Yorktown to the close of the War of 1812 was at an end. A new and unbounded faith in the United States was apparent on all fronts. Massachusetts, in which, according to Emerson, "there was not a book, a speech, a conversation or a thought" from 1790 to 1820 suddenly leapt into the very forefront of the new awakening.

Utopia was just around the corner, though, to be sure, the Utopia of the Puritan mill owner did not exactly coincide with that of the prosperous cotton planter of Carolina, nor with that of the pioneer in the Ohio-Mississippi watershed. To the rising textile magnate Utopia was a highly efficient, well organized capitalist industrialism. To the planter it was the dream of a great agricultural state, built along the lines of ancient Greek Democracy—a Utopia whose roots were sunk deep into and drew their nourishment from chattle slavery. To the westerners, Utopia was "nourished on the idealism of the Declaration of Independence" but was interpreted to mean "the natural right of every free citizen to satisfy his acquisitive instincts by exploiting the natural resources in the measure of his shrewdness."

Europe was a revelation to the young truth-seeker from up-state New York. French cooking and the "independent dignity" of the working people intrigued him—especially the cooking. His explorations in diet were not profound, but he nevertheless often raised the question (to be answered of course by later day food faddists) that "future generations may be interested in showing how much of the moral turpitude of this enlightened age is traceable to the abuses of the stomach."

With the energy so characteristic of the Brisbanes, Albert plunged deeply into the study of French manners, history, literature and philosophy. Soon he was attending the lectures of Cousin, Guizot, and Villemain—the great men of that day. But it was to Victor Cousin that he gave most time and attention, for Cousin, then at the height of his fame, was to French philosophy what Hegel was to German. Brisbane was awestruck, but only for a time. Before the year had ended, he was beginning to doubt. Great truths which he had been seeking, and which, of course, Cousin felt he was promulgating, did not seem to be forthcoming. The French philosopher, who called his system "Nineteenth Century Eclecticism," had gone back through all previous systems of philosophies to dig out the nuggets of pure truth in each. Then he had synthesized or fused these many nuggets into *his* system—the final word on philosophy.

Young Brisbane said to himself, regretfully, "Is this the wisdom of French philosophy,—this Joseph's coat of all philosophical colors and shapes? . . . Philosophy, in fact, is yet in its infancy, and the speculations thus far being mainly errors, such a selection must necessarily be worse than valueless."

But there was a chance that Cousin had not interpreted the great philosophers correctly. Hegel, for example, the master mind of Germany who had unfolded the absolute logic of the universe. Why not go to him to snatch up some of his words of wisdom? On to Berlin.

Albert did arrive at one fundamental conclusion in France, however, though he didn't get it from any of his teachers. One night, while eating some ice cream between acts at the opera, the question popped into his head: "Who pays for this ice cream?"

"Well, I do."

"But where do you get the money to pay for it?"

"My father sends it to me."

"And where does he get it?"

"From the farmers of Genesee County."

"Does my father work to produce this?"

"No. He owns land and other properties from which he receives an income. That income comes out of the labor of the farmers and the working class."

"It is they, then, who are in reality paying for this ice cream."

"Do I give an equivalent?"

"No."

"Then I get their labor without equivalent; i.e. for nothing." The injustice of all this stirred the boy profoundly. How could this be? Why need this be? Surely such was not the preordained destiny of man! Someone surely had the answer, and he, Albert Brisbane, was going to find it.

The stage coach trip to Berlin gave the young American a chance to see the changing countryside and meet a different type of people. He took to the Germans at once, finding a "refreshing honesty" among them. They were "still innocent of the modern art of scheming and lying to impose upon strangers."

He stopped at Frankfort, home of the Rothschilds, with its ghetto—a queer combination of modernity and medievalism. And at Weimar, he saw Goethe, then an old man. "Though age had dimmed the eye and rendered the voice tremulous, the firm head was still well poised, and the finely cut features preserved traces of past beauty."

Fortune smiled on Brisbane in Berlin, for he was soon admitted to the homes of its leading intellectuals. There he met Hegel, then a man of sixty, at the height of his intellectual powers and with an academic influence never before known in German history. "His was the final word of human wisdom."

There were many able men in Berlin, but all of them

bowed before Hegel. Professor Michelet told Brisbane, "Hegel's logic is the history of God before the creation of the universe," while another remarked to him, "Schelling wrote on the last leaf of the mental evolution of mankind, but Hegel turned the leaf and on the last page completed the solution which Schelling attempted to give."

The entire fall and winter was spent by Brisbane studying under Hegel and discussing with his disciples the various points of his doctrine.

The procedure at the university was as follows: The students at the sound of a gong would rush pell-mell into the large hall where Hegel was to lecture.

"Presently Hegel walked in, in a business-like manner, and without salutation or preliminary of any sort took his place at the desk, opened a roll of manuscript, and began to read. His eyes were constantly fixed on the manuscript, while his head moved slowly from side to side of the page. His delivery was uniform and monotonous—his whole manner expressing a simple desire to present the subject matter without the slightest vanity of mannerism or any attempt at elocution. When the moment came to close the lecture, again indicated by the sound of the gong, it mattered not if it came in the midst of a phrase, all was stopped and snapped off with mechanical abruptness. The lecturer arose, and in the same unconcerned manner passed out of the hall."

Brisbane also found time to study anatomy and worked long hours in the dissecting rooms. It was there he arrived at the conclusion "if there is mechanical wisdom in the construction of the human body, there must exist a corresponding principle in the universe, as well as the power of applying that principle."

While pursuing his medical work Brisbane was absorbed in the study of the common cold. His theory was that the oxygen of the air contained a certain amount of electricity. This air was taken up by the red corpuscles of the blood, which act as a magnet by virtue of the iron which they contain. This was the one great source of the vital force in man. Colds, by causing the relaxation of their muscular sheaths, deranged the absorbing function of blood vessels. This theory led him to the conclusion that the vitality and flexibility of character which distinguish the American race were due to our vast forests, which produced more oxygen than was to be found in the barren over-cut regions of Europe—an important factor in determining the difference between the American people and their European ancestors.

His manner of solving the problem of getting up in the morning was typically Brisbanian. The young student informed his German house frau that when she had brought him his coffee in the morning, she should take away his bed clothes and carry them out of the room. She had never had such a request before, but being told that he would leave unless she complied, "the stern little woman, driven to the dire alternative, reluctantly acquiesced; and scrupulously exact in the performance of her duty, off flew the bed clothes every morning with an alacrity oft-times regretable; but having forced the contract, I had not the courage to back out, and regularity in early rising at least, was thus secured."

Even Hegel failed to satisfy the young truth seeker. Hegel's effort to evolve the universe and its laws from the recesses of his own brain was insufficient. The Hegelians looked upon contemporary European civilization as the highest of all social orders. This did not impress the truth seeker. He felt that a much greater advance could be made. He was not convinced that the divine purpose had reached its ultimate conclusion in contemporary civilization. Brisbane was left in darkness and despair. He grew melancholy and was seized with a sentiment of indignation at the creator of this puny being—man. He developed a distrust of man's mental capacity. Finally, deciding that he had seen enough of Christian civilization, he made a trip to Turkey.

Though the beauties of Constantinople and the Golden Horn fascinated him, Brisbane was distinctly discouraged by the new social world of the Near East. Political despotism had checked enterprise. There was very little individual freedom. Those few branches of manufacture which were carried on were poorly arranged. There was no real spirit of competition. Constantinople seemed a city of industrial stagnation and inertia.

"The neglected streets of the city swarmed with filthy half starved, diseased dogs which the Turkish religion forbade killing. On one occasion I stumbled over a body, and on looking back saw a man with his head cut off and lying between his legs. I found that executed criminals were often exposed in the street this way, particularly if they were infidels."

Such was Constantinople of 1830, the capital of a politically lifeless and industrially dying nation—a nation vegetating in ignorance and apathy, where the degradation of women had reached profound depths.

Brisbane felt he had found part of the answer to man's social status in the condition of woman. Among the savages she was a mere drudge, a useful domestic animal. In Turkey she was a piece of property owned and held by man for sensual purposes. Even in contemporary civilized society, she was a part of man's ambition, a being regarded with admiration, "but none the less dependent, without real equality and liberty of action." In the face of his great pessimism,

Brisbane arrived at two conclusions; first, that a primary condition for social progress depended upon the educational development and moral elevation of woman. "There is no grandeur for man but in the elevation of woman. When he drags her down and crushes her, he crushes and brutalizes himself; for it seems an incontrovertible law that he who would become a tyrant becomes himself a slave." His second conclusion was that mere changes in forms of government did not affect the fundamental constitution of society. A republic differed little from a monarchy; a monarchy but little from the land of a despot or feudal lord.

The answer to Albert Brisbane's quest had not yet been found, but he was rapidly establishing a solid background for it.

He returned once more to Europe by way of Greece, a Greece that had just been laid desolate by the Turks. Athens had been so completely destroyed that only a few houses were standing. "The very fleas had abandoned the place in disgust, finding no longer either nourishment or warmth." Denuded, desolate Greece with its absence of roads, its arid waste and its meager, poverty-stricken population led him to reflect: "It is not the moneyed capital of a nation that constitutes its wealth; it is the roads, the bridges, the wagons and plows; the herds and flocks and working animals. It is all the means of human labor, all the facilities of rendering the industrial activity of man fruitful. There is more wealth in the single county of Genesee in my native state than in all Greece."

That year two important events took place in Europe: the first railroad from Liverpool to Manchester was opened; and in July, the French Revolution of 1830, which for a second time dethroned the Bourbons.

Brisbane visited Malta, Sicily, and the mainland of Italy,

where he witnessed the coronation of Pope Gregory XVI. Then to Switzerland and, at last, back to Paris after a two years' absence.

Radical groups were once more flourishing in the capital. The Saint Simonists were particularly numerous and Brisbane was thrown into close contact with them from the start.

Count Henri de Saint Simon was the scion of a family belonging to the higher nobility of France. He had fought under LaFayette in the American war for independence, but played no active part in the French Revolution. His ideas developed during the first few years of the nineteenth century, were taken over by his followers and shaped into a system of utopian socialism. Saint Simon believed that the chief task of society was to promote the production of wealth and, as a necessary sequence, manufacturers, technicians, farmers, artisans, bankers and merchants formed the most important factor in society, far more important than the nobility or the clergy. Their talents should undertake the administration of the country. The claim to property should be based on the growth of wealth and the freedom of industry. His disciples and collaborators elaborated his scheme into a system of utopian socialism. They argued for an associated state—an association of active workers where everyone would occupy a position according to his capabilities and be paid according to his deeds. The privileges of birth should be completely abolished. The sole right to property was to depend upon the capacity to produce it.

Brisbane was prepared to accept the fundamental principles of the Saint Simonists, but the religious principles they preached seemed to him artificial, and the principles of authority which they argued were repugnant to him. It was at these Saint Simonist gatherings that he met the celebrated German Jewish poet, Heine. They became good friends and attended many meetings together. Heine's manner was silent and reserved. "I never witnessed in him a spontaneous outburst of any kind and in conversation he often gave evidence of repressed thought," Brisbane wrote, "It would seem as if he was eternally at work tearing to pieces every subject presented to him, and dissecting every idea that crossed his mind."

Because of his arguments with the Saint Simonists, Brisbane left for England. London was a disappointment to him. "I felt I had fallen upon a spiritual iceberg. Every man seemed drawn into his own individual shell, striving and struggling for a living or for wealth; burly in appearance, strong physically, and with a coldness and self-absorption quite beyond anything I had yet seen."

From London he went to Liverpool and then to Ireland. In Ireland he found a degree of misery surpassing any he could have conceived. The young American loved the Irish and admired their intellectual quickness and flexibility. He believed them to be a race naturally endowed with a superior mental ability. But the condition they were in he blamed upon the English aristocratic absentee owners as well as the industrial power of England which had paralyzed the manufactures of Ireland.

"Finally, I saw that the almost unquestioned sway of the Catholic Church, in its jealousy of modern thought and innovation, had stunted the spiritual development of the people. By dictating all the conditions of education it had kept the nation in a state of primitive ignorance."

Brisbane believed that had Ireland become Protestant at the same time that England did, Irish talent and genius would have dominated the more phlegmatic Englishman. She would have been "the leader instead of the oppressed."

Then followed a visit to Scotland. Its people were "Irishmen sobered down into Englishmen and Englishmen stimulated up into Irishmen."

In Holland he was impressed by the want of enterprise and innovation in the spirit of the people. They had become inured to a torpifying routine which led him to the conclusion that the military spirit plays a great part in the progress of nations. Modern commercial society, he felt, gives one but little to arouse the heroic and collective sentiment. Wars, on the other hand, despite their destruction, do something to man. He is wrested "from his commonplace ground of existence, subject to discipline, initiated into the art and practice of a wider scene of action, subject to the play of the higher sentiments—honor, heroism, patriotism—and returns to his native village far more of a man than when he left."

Once again, Brisbane returned to Berlin. He felt the need for a fundamental social reconstruction of society but all theories so far studied had been repugnant to him

Then came a milestone in his philosophical development A friend, Lechevalier, sent him a package containing two large volumes entitled, *L'Association Domestique-Agricole, par Charles Fourier*. The title displeased him. In ill humor he cast the books aside without reading them. Several days passed before he looked at them again. Glancing carelessly through the first volume, he ran across this phrase printed in large type: "ATTRACTIVE INDUSTRY." Brisbane read on, fascinated.

"I sprang to my feet, threw down the book, and began pacing the floor in a tumult of emotion. I was carried away into a world of new conceptions."

Here was a fundamentally new idea—"the idea of *dignifying* and rendering *attractive* the manual labors of mankind; labors hitherto regarded as a Divine punishment inflicted on man. To introduce attraction into this sphere of commonplace, degrading toil—the dreary lot of the masses—which seemed to overwhelm man with its prosaic, benumbing, deadening influence; to elevate such labors, and invest them with dignity were indeed a mighty revolution!

The first general result which presented itself to my mind was universal employment in productive industry, and the creation of all the means necessary to the prosecution of those scientific and higher intellectual pursuits now limited to the few. I saw a healthy rich humanity organizing everywhere its universities—its sources of mental development. In my enthusiasm I saw a million universities scattered over the globe, and the means of solving the great problems of human destiny."

Who was Charles Fourier? What was his influence on the social thought of the period?

Born in 1772 and originally a merchant and shop assistant, Charles Fourier saw the rapid disintegration of economic life during the last quarter of the eighteenth century. The fierce competition of the period had caused the downfall of thousands of small enterprises.

In 1808 there was published at Leipzig his work, "Quatre Mouvements," which expounded his fundamental ideas.

He believed: 1, That human motives and passions are on the whole good. If given proper scope they would lead to happiness. This can be accomplished through appropriate social institutions. 2, that commerce is the *base soul* of civilization. Commerce is the thing which corrupts human nature, rendering it morally and materially pernicious. It must and can be replaced by an associated and cooperative mode of economy of life. 3, marriage is hypocrisy and means slavery for womankind. It must be replaced by free love. 4, civilization, though full of evils, nevertheless is preparing the forces needed to raise mankind to the stage of association and harmony where human motives will find scope for their free play and will create wealth and peace.

No one can accuse Fourier of being modest. He regarded his discovery as more important than "all the scientific labors since the emergence of the human race." He chided the philosophers: "I, who am ignorant of the whole mechanism of thought, and have read neither Locke nor Condillac, have I not enough ideas to discover the whole system of general movement, of which you have only discovered a quarter, that is, the material part? And this, moreover, after 2,500 years of scientific effort. Present and future generations will have me alone to thank for inaugurating their immense happiness. As possessor of the book of definitions, I disperse the political and moral-philosophical thought and build on the ruins of precarious science the theory of universal harmony."

Fourier maintained there were three centers of attraction around which gravitated all human passions. First the sensual (or the five senses). Second, the intellectual passions (such as family feeling, love, reverence and friendship). Third, the refined passions (love of change or novelty, of organization, emulation, etc.). These twelve passions are "like twelve needles, which drive the soul towards the three crucibles or goals of attraction."

The most important group is the third, whose aim is social and general unity. According to Fourier's mathematics, a combination of the twelve passions would yield about eight hundred different characters so that "all perfection would be potential in an assembly of eight hundred people." For example, if the population of France, numbering 36,000,000, be divided by 800, we should find among them 45,000 individuals capable of equaling a Homer, a Demosthenes, a Moliere, etc."

The stages through which mankind had already passed were: 1, state of nature; 2, savagery; 3, patriarchy; 4, barbarism; 5, civilization. That which will follow civilization is called by Fourier Guaranteeism, a transitional stage leading to socialism or, as Fourier calls it, Sociantism, where mankind would live in complete happiness and harmony, dwelling in Phalansteries and working cooperatively in groups of 1600 or more. These Phalansteries were to be free associations of capitalists, workers, and talented officials. The product of labor was to be divided as follows:

Labor	5/12
Capital	4/12
Talent	3/12

Truly remarkable achievements would arise from this new social order: there would be free love, ample education of children at the cost of the group, not less than seven meals a day, and a round of drama, opera, music, and all of the joyous things of life, thus making it possible for men to attain an average age of 144 years and a height of seven feet.

In the face of such prodigious achievement, is it to be wondered at that Fourier felt the works of the great philosophers from Plato to Voltaire would vanish into oblivion while his would remain the cornerstone of a new world? Politically, Fourier was indifferent. He hated both the French revolution and the Jews, even as he revered the great Napoleon.

This self-appointed Messiah was always seeking some great, rich, good man who would finance his project. He once announced publicly that he would be at home every day at a certain hour to await any philanthropist who felt inclined to give him a million francs or more for the development of a colony based upon his principles. And for more than twelve years thereafter he was at home every day punctually at noon waiting for the generous stranger who never arrived.

Fourier's imaginings, as has been already indicated, were both strange and crude. In his theory of universal unity, he declared, for example, that once the world had adopted his plan of associations, it would enter upon a millennium of 70,000 glorious years, "when the lions would become the servants of man, draw men's carriages in a single day from one end of France to another; when whales would pull their vessels across the water; and when seawater would taste like delicious beverage. Then following this, would come an age of decline and the fourth and final era of dotage before the world died out."

Fourier believed in peace. He was opposed to all violence and in his opinion one honest experiment in communal living according to the principles which he had laid down, would be sufficient evidence to convince the entire world of the correctness of his views. He also believed that the millenium would be attained within the short space of a decade, so why the need for violent revolution? In fact, that good time—that golden age—seemed to Fourier and his followers so close at hand that they decided not to put their money into real estate since a Fourieristic advent would cause it to lose value.

Albert Brisbane at once became a most enthusiastic propagandist for his newly-found mentor. To the drawing rooms of intellectual Berlin he went with a message of the French messiah. But unfortunately, the men and women to whom he spoke did not seem to develop the enthusiasm he had shown. Their mental obtuseness made Brisbane and his small circle the more militant in their determination to push forward the principles of Fourier. His activities as a propagandist soon turned the eyes of the Berlin police upon him and he was under constant supervision until he left for France, which he did in May, 1832. He was impatient to meet the great Fourier, the man who had given him his first glimpse into the destinies of humanity.

Princes and potentates, philosophers and scientists, had passed before the gaze of young Brisbane. But none of them impressed him as did this French messiah, then a man of sixty. To Brisbane there was a striking resemblance between the face of Fourier and a portrait he had seen of Dante while in Italy. He was broad shouldered, though of medium height. It was the head which attracted the attention of everyone, being almost spherical. The chin was firm and strong. The brow was large and slightly retreating. The large mouth curved downward, "the lion mouth." The nose was aquiline. Fourier had "a large grey eye, the pupil of which was so small that it seemed a mere pin point." The great master was seriousness itself. Although Brisbane was closely associated with him for more than three years, he says he never saw him smile. "I saw him among his disciples; I saw him at dinner parties; I saw him at the society's celebrations, but never did I see that concentrated expression of the face change."

When Brisbane asked Fourier why he had not given solutions to some higher question of a cosmic order, the philosopher answered, "*Les civilisés* have their faith in the mud; they are not capable of understanding these higher doctrines."

Fourier, not content with developing a theory for man's social perfectibility, had also evolved a series of theories with reference to the universe. He was no materialist. He believed in the immortality of the soul, which, he thought, had gone through a long series of evolutions to arrive even at its present state of development. But it would continue—going from planet to planet in ascending scale and performing in each the functions which belonged to it. The sun, a magnificent solid body surrounded by an atmosphere of light, was inhabited by the souls which had undergone the complete evolution from lowest to highest stage, where they were promoted to the rank of "Citizen of the Universe" with the "privilege of passing from sun to sun and visiting the infinite variety of worlds which the telescope reveals to us."

Brisbane was more than impressed. He was bewildered by the sublime privilege of participating in this amazing life of the universe and having it described to him by such a great man. He remarked in later years, "I hardly took the trouble to keep from under the feet of the horses; it seemed to me of little consequence should I be run over, so absorbed was I in my desire to get to those grander spheres."

A wealthy Englishman, Arthur Young, who had been converted to Fourierism, gave the society some 400,000 francs. A daily paper was started at once, "La Democratie Pacifique," which continued functioning until 1852, when it was suppressed by the second Bonaparte.

For nearly two years Brisbane remained at the feet of his master and carried on actively the work with other Fourieristic disciples. In the spring of 1834, Albert returned to America full of enthusiasm and ideas for reforming society. His health had been shattered, owing "in a degree, I think, to the atmosphere of Europe, less oxygenized than that which I had been accustomed to in my native land."

For four years Brisbane fought his way back to health and vitality. He became interested in the currency problem which was engaging the Democratic Party during the late 1830's and wrote a pamphlet on the subject. Currency based upon gold and silver, he felt, was an artificial and false currency. What was needed was a currency that would fairly represent the products of industry and the labors of man. This should be created by the government in such a way as to prevent monopolies by the bankers and usurers. It is quite obvious that many years later, Albert's son, Arthur, used his father's monetary ideas as his own.

Regretfully, Albert Brisbane confessed that his first attempt at pamphleteering was a complete failure. One of his friends remarked to him that there were not five men in Buffalo who had comprehended what he wrote. Albert concluded; "This illustrates how difficult it is to get people to understand an idea outside of the beaten track of popular opinion."

2

AMERICA'S FIRST SOCIALIST

At the age of thirty, Arthur Brisbane's father was unknown except to a small circle of personal acquaintances.

At thirty-two, he was an important political figure in American life to whom the advanced thinkers of the day were looking with eagerness. His newly published book, *The Social Destiny of Man*, was being read in the drawing rooms of Boston, the brick flats of New York, and the wooden shacks of a small town named Chicago.

The thirties were to the nineteenth century what the inflated twenties were to the present century. Industry and commerce boomed as never before. The success of the Erie Canal, completed in 1825, brought on a plethora of other canal schemes. Soon speculation in that newest mode of transportation, railroads, was equally enthusiastic. The year 1836 alone saw two hundred such companies organized. The tremendous movement westward of native and foreign born populations was soon paralleled by an equally unprecedented movement eastward of corn, wheat, hogs, beef, and cotton flowing in a steady stream to the eastern seaboard, and then to the British Isles and western Europe.

Land speculation mushroomed into a fevered policy. During the three years, 1834-35-36, the amount of land bought from the Federal Government alone amounted to nearly half of the total amount purchased since the beginning of the Republic. Within the span of a decade, the land from eastern Ohio to the Mississippi River became a vast assortment of real estate enterprises. Cities and towns were laid out in the forests or on the open prairie and advertised as great future centers of trade and industry. "Scorning cheap clocks, wooden nutmegs, and apple parers, the Yankee, stepping from the almost ridiculous to the decidedly sublime, went out West, and traded in the progress of the country," according to an English observer. But the fever reached back to the eastern seaboard, where clerks, laborers, farmers, and storekeepers were soon speculating their all on western lands and cities.

Banks and bank credits multiplied. At the time of the crash in May, 1837, there were 700 banks with a total capitalization of $300,000,000. Credit buying and selling reached a new high. Meanwhile, European business men, caught in this fever themselves, proceeded to export to the United States great quantities of goods so that we soon had a very decidedly unfavorable trade balance. But these goods had to be paid for in specie and, as the coin was withdrawn to Europe, the credit bubble, which had already been inflated to the point of bursting, exploded. The crash came in the spring of 1837. Nearly all banks in the United States were compelled to suspend specie payments. Some of the larger ones began to resume payments in the spring or the summer of 1838. Those optimists of the period who hadn't gone down in the first deluge were convinced that the golden days had begun anew. But the crisis was by no means over, for in October and November of 1839 a second suspension followed, participated in by almost every bank in the country except the larger ones in New York State.

The intellectual ferment of the previous decade was given a leftward jolt as a result of the two long years of panic. Leaders of religious unrest likewise turned their eyes away from heaven to the conditions here on earth. Farmers and small shopkeepers began to doubt the advisability of get-rich-quick schemes of speculation. The wage earner lost a good deal of interest in the early trade unions. Even his newly acquired right to vote hadn't helped him much. The confusion of the time seemed a challenge to common sense. America possessed in abundance all of the resources needed for a common well being. America had promised that to one and all. That generous right which it had seemed to hold out for the great mass of the people, had been snatched away overnight. Unregulated competition and speculation had brought disaster to everyone. People cursed the new fangled devices and methods: railroads, factories, canals, installment selling. Says John R. Commons: "The remedy they sought was in a return to an idealized colonial system of economics dominated by agriculture and domestic industry."

By 1840, the soil had been prepared for the propagation of schemes which promised the reorganization of society. That year, Brisbane presented his American version of Fourier's method of Association to the American people.

1

Albert Brisbane had already enlisted a number of earnest and active adherents during the year 1839. He, himself, besides writing commentaries and illustrations of Fourier's work suitable to American conditions, also lectured in some of the larger cities,—New York, Philadelphia, Boston. A room was rented near the center of Manhattan's business life, on Broadway near Canal street, where lectures and discussions took place.

When Brisbane's manuscript was nearly completed he asked Park Benjamin, an experienced practical journalist, to look it over and indicate such material as he thought might be out of tone with the general views of the public. Discussing the probable effects of the book on the public, with Brisbane, one day, Benjamin exclaimed:

"There is Horace Greeley, just damn fool enough to believe such nonsense."

"Who is Greeley?" I asked.

"Oh, he's a young man upstairs editing *The New Yorker*."

"I took my book under my arm and off I went after Greeley. As I entered his room, I said, "Is this Mr. Greeley?' "

"Yes."

"I have a book here I would like you to read."

"I don't know that I can now," he replied. "I am very busy."

"I wish you would," I urged. "If you will, I'll leave it."

"Well," he said, "I'm going to Boston tonight and I'll take it along. Perhaps I'll find time."

Greeley took the book with him and read it. When he came back, he was an enthusiastic believer in Industrial Association.

The Social Destiny of Man opens with: "We assert, and will prove, that Labor which is now *monotonous, repugnant,* and *degrading,* can be *ennobled, elevated,* and made honorable;—or in other words that Industry Can Be Rendered Attractive.

"Let this great and productive reform be once effected and three quarters of the evils, which oppress mankind will be done away with as if by a magic influence."

A little later, it says: "The secret instinct of the individual is truer than the reasonings of science. The destiny of man is to be happy on this earth, but not in our subversive society, characterized by indigence and discord."

The ideas of Fourier were expounded and modified to suit American thought and outlook. At one point, to clinch his argument, Brisbane exclaims: "God, as supreme economist, must have preferred Association, the source of all economy, and reserved for its organization some means, the discovery of which was the task of genius.

"If Association be the *wish of the Divinity* . . . it is self-evident that (the bases of barbarism and civilized society—O. C.) are an abyss of error, the antipodes of the views of God, from which man can only escape by the invention and the organization of Association and Combined Industry."

It is doubtful if, even with such fertile soil, Brisbane would have succeeded had he not obtained as his journalistic mouthpiece a man like Horace Greeley, the young New Hampshire radical.

Greeley was no Bostonian intellectual. He came of plain people; possessed much common sense and practical intelligence; and was able to apply it. He was no innovator of social panaceas, but his eyes were open to the wrongs and injustices around him. He always tried to square theories with realities and was prepared to adopt whatever social machinery might be necessary to make the government, national or local, function better.

The intense sufferings of the panic 1837-39 had opened his eyes as nothing else could have done. He saw people who had died of cold and others who, through long exposure and privation, had contracted fatal diseases. He saw masses of beggars on the street—masses who asked only the right for a job. Never before had New York seen such suffering as during the winter of 1837-38. Horace Greeley heard and saw it all. His newly established paper, *The New*

York Tribune, soon became a potent force, not only in the city, but also among the mass of the farmers in the north and west where its influence was positively amazing.

Greeley believed that agriculture and manufacturing complement each other; that they must be drawn close together for the benefit of the nation as a whole. The appeal of Attractive Industry was as great to him at it had been to Brisbane a few years previous. Little wonder, then, that he opened his columns to the Fourierists. The first notice about Brisbane and his Fourieristic ideas appeared in the *Tribune*, October 21, 1841. The *Tribune*, then only six months old, was already building a large circulation.

In the spring of 1842, the readers of that paper saw a column on the front page headed ASSOCIATION: OR, PRINCIPLES OF A TRUE ORGANIZATION OF SOCIETY.

"This column has been purchased by the advocates of Association, in order to lay their principles before the public. Its editorship is entirely distinct from that of the Tribune."

In this column, appearing first twice a week, but after August, 1842, three times a week, and still later, every day, Brisbane set forth in glowing terms the advantages of "Attractive Industry," "Compound Economics," "Democracy of Association," and the "Equilibrium of the Passions." The arrangement entered into was mutually beneficial. To Brisbane it gave a large daily audience for the propagation of his theories; to the *Tribune* it gave an additional circle of readers among persons interested in social problems, as well as much needed financial aid. Albert Brisbane paid one hundred and fifty dollars a week for the column.

The biographer of Greeley, James Parton, writing in 1869, said with respect to these articles: "At first they seemed to have attracted little attention, and less opposition.

They were regarded in the light of articles to be skipped, and by most of the city readers of the *Tribune*, I presume, they were skipped with the utmost regularity, and quite as a matter of course. Occasionally, however, the subject was alluded to editorially, and every such allusion was of a nature to be read. Gradually Fourierism became one of the topics of the time. Gradually certain editors discovered that Fourierism was unChristian. Gradually the cry of 'Mad Dog' arose. Meanwhile the articles of Mr. Brisbane were having their effect upon the people."

The fervor of the proselyte was in Brisbane's bones. But he did not confine his writings to mere theoretical dissertations. Practical problems were dealt with as much as any others. Also, he developed the use of bold-face type, italics, and capitals in his column—devices appropriated long afterward and improved upon by his son, Arthur. Nor did he try to reach merely one segment of the population. A contemporary declared: "The rich were enticed; the poor were encouraged; the laboring classes were aroused; objections were answered; prejudices were annihilated; scoffing papers were silenced; the religious foundations of Fourierism were triumphantly exhibited."

Soon other important persons joined the cause: Parke Godwin, associate editor of *The Evening Post* and son-in-law of its editor-in-chief, William Cullen Bryant; George Ripley, founder of Brook Farm, a profound scholar and able leader of men; Charles A. Dana, then a young man and secretary of the Brook Farm, later to become a member of Horace Greeley's staff and eventually, editor and publisher of *The New York Sun*. Others were Nathaniel Hawthorne, Ralph Waldo Emerson, Theodore Parker, James Russell Lowell, Margaret Fuller, T. W. Higginson, Henry James and John S. Dwight.

Greeley himself, through the columns of The *Tribune*, entered into a discussion on the merits of Fourierism with Henry J. Raymond in the *New York Courier* and *Enquirer*. The debate was conducted with ability and spirit on each side. It was later published as a pamphlet and gained widespread distribution.

Brisbane, himself, now finding a warm reception for his ideas among people of intelligence, took over the editorship of a small daily called *The Chronicle*. Twice weekly, he wrote articles for a radical democratic paper, *The Plebeian*. He controlled a monthly magazine, *The Democrat*, for which he wrote, and he contributed as well to *The Dial*, published by Emerson and his friends. Soon editors of the other papers were engaged in long and bitter controversies on the merits of Brisbane's and Fourier's ideas, thus giving an even wider audience to the plan of reform and its leaders.

"We aroused the attention of the South," remarks Brisbane, "by proposing a plan of commercial emancipation from the North, and the organization of a direct trade between the Southern cities and Europe—especially for their cotton. We also excited a good deal of interest among certain railroad companies, whose roads had been stopped by the hard times, by suggesting a scheme which we claimed would enable them to obtain the means necessary to carry through their project; we attacked the banking system; we showed up the fraud, the over reaching, the lying and cheating, the adulterations and the monopolies of commerce. But our criticism on religion were cautious: I held that it was not worth while to excite religious antipathy to the idea of an industrial free form. The great point to be gained was the organization of society on a true practical basis. I saw that when once the material operations and relations of men were properly organized, opinions would modify themselves by the influence of a new life and a higher education."

The enthusiastic reception given Brisbane's ideas meant that sooner or later the conservative press would begin attacking him. This took place sooner than he anticipated. Preachers and public officials joined in the attack on the theory of Association. It was treated as atheistic, immoral, and tending to break up the family. The same charges were soon leveled against Brisbane himself. He was also accused of fomenting class war. "No colors were too black in which to paint my character. For a while I endeavored to defend myself, but the attacks were so varied, the blows seemed to come from so many quarters at once, that I soon felt the impossibility of meeting them and gave it up."

By May, 1843, the big rush of Young America to the Fourierist experiments began. The lunatic fringe and the visionaries who early attached themselves to Brisbane were augmented by wage earners in New York, Philadelphia, and other cities. Then came a group of leading intellectuals. The advance guard of Puritan ministry likewise joined in the procession. And finally, even the farmers began flocking to the movement.

Upstate New York, the home of Albert Brisbane and his parents, developed an amazing fervor for Fourierism. A convert, T. C. Leland, writing from Rochester in April, 1844, described the mass turnout for the Socialist Convention at Batavia:

"Nearly every town and hamlet of Genesee County was represented. Many of these men and women came on foot, over muddy roads from five to twelve miles, to participate in the gathering. Indeed, all western New York is in a deep, a shaking agitation on this subject . . . I have no hesitation in saying that 26,000 persons, west of the longitude of Rochester, in this state, is a low estimate of those who are now ready and willing, nay anxious, to take their places in Associative Unity."

Meanwhile, Brisbane had become a polished platform speaker. The tremendous crowds which turned out in his own county to hear him, in 1843-44, greeted him as they would a returned hero. This response of the hard-headed farmers delighted Brisbane, who reported that they were "beginning to see the truth and greatness of a system of dignified and attractive industry, and the advantages of Association, such as its economy, its superior means of education, the guarantee it offers against . . . spoliations by those intermediate classes who now live by their labor."

Fourier had early foreseen the danger of hasty experiments in the development of Phalanxes. A membership of about 1600, and a capital of about 1,000,000 francs he felt would be needed for each one to succeed. Brisbane modified his master's proposals. He argued that the easiest plan for starting an Association would be to induce 400 people to unite, each to take $1,000 worth of stock. One quarter of the product of the Association would be turned over to the stockholders, or they could receive a fixed interest of 8%, which would amount to eighty dollars annually. The Association, in turn, would guarantee to each person a place to live, and board. Brisbane argued that the cost per annum for rent would be $37.50. The Association would, of course, raise all its own fruit, grain, vegetables, cattle, and would economize in fuel, cooking and everything else. In this way, it could furnish good board at $60 a year. "Thus a person who invested one thousand dollars would be certain of a comfortable home and board for his interest, if he lived economically, and would have whatever he might produce by his labor in addition. He would live, besides, in an elegant edifice surrounded by beautiful fields and gardens."

The popular enthusiasm for Associationism soon grew beyond the control of its leaders. Security, peace, and happiness seemed so easy to realize that broad masses joined in the clamor for establishing Fourieristic colonies.

People everywhere planned the organization of Phalanxes. They did not wait to assemble four hundred people, nor did they try to get the necessary capital proposed by Brisbane. New York, New Jersey, Michigan, Wisconsin, Indiana, Massachusetts, Iowa, and Illinois joined in establishing these cooperative organizations. Of a total of fifty-four, some lasted only a few months; one continued to function, after a fashion, for eighteen years; only three attained actual significance and seemed to justify the expectation of permanent success: the North American Phalanx in New Jersey, The Brook Farm Phalanx in Massachusetts, and the Ceresto, or Wisconsin Phalanx in Wisconsin.

With the possible exception of these three, the history of Fourierist Phalanxes was one monotonous record of failure. Horace Greeley, who had ardently supported the schemes, finally confessed that in most cases the men who undertook the experiments were "destitute alike of capacity, public confidence, energy, and means."

John Humphrey Noyes, founder of the Oneida Colony, writing in 1870, placed the blame directly on Albert Brisbane, "for spending all his energy in drumming and recruiting, while, to insure success, he should have given at least half his time to drilling the soldiers and leading them in actual battle. One example of Fourierism carried through to splendid realization would have done infinitely more for the cause in the long run, than all his translations and publications. As Fourier's fault was devotion to theory, Brisbane's fault was devotion to propagandism."

But the blame cannot be laid solely at the door of Brisbane.

Those who flocked to the meetings were united in their desire to obtain all of the ideal conditions pictured to them. They gave but little thought to many of the difficulties such an undertaking would present. The hastily constructed Phalanxes possessed neither adequate capital, adequate numbers, nor adequate spiritual preparation. The principles of Association seemed so plain and so easy that they were organized without careful thought. Brisbane confessed that he had been entirely unprepared for such a mass enthusiasm: "I had contemplated years of patient, careful propagation," he said, "before the means of a single Association could be obtained."

The record of the Fourierist Phalanxes of the year 1840 has been duplicated over and over again. Nearly every state in the Union has seen one or more attempts to develop little ideal colonies. Without exception they have failed. The few which still remain today drag on through a monotonous existence, more because of the tenacity of their members than because of any success obtained.

Morris Hillquit, writing at the turn of the century, gave the best analysis of the break-down of the Phalanxes:

"The experimenters, as a rule, had to satisfy themselves with a small parcel of barren land in the wilderness, and that one heavily mortgaged. The distance from the city, and the scantiness of their means, relegated the settlers to agricultural pursuits exclusively, although very few of them were trained farmers. One or more miserable log huts took the place of the gorgeous social 'Palace'; and the 'Attractive Industry' dwindled down to a pathetic and wearisome struggle of unskilled and awkward hands against the obstinate wiles of a sterile and unyielding soil. The struggle, as a rule, lasted until the first installment on the mortgage became due; and as the mortgagee was never satisfied with the three-twelfths of the profit allotted to capital by Fourier, the domain was almost invariably foreclosed."

Though all other Phalanxes have been forgotten, one of them, Brook Farm, has left an indelible imprint on the American mind. Founded in the spring of 1841, by George Ripley, a young Unitarian minister from Boston, as a practical application of the principles and theories advocated by the Transcendentalists, it did not become a Phalanx until 1844. The sermon-proof and gospel-glutted generation to which the young idealist of Boston and its vicinity belonged realized that the defense of Calvinism built up since the days of Jonathan Edwards was no longer a living faith. Clinging stubbornly to its theological creeds, it refused to recognize the changes which had taken place in both English and Continental theology. Its ministers, according to Parrington, annually turned over the exhausted soil and reaped an ever scantier harvest. Sunday after Sunday they would repeat the same argument and then retire to their studies, where each would engage in "spinning cob-web systems between the worm-eaten rafters, quite oblivious to the common sense world without his walls."

The Brook Farm Institute for Agriculture and Education obtained a small farm in West Roxbury, about nine miles from Boston. It proposed to substitute a system of brotherly cooperation for one of selfish competition. This, by a method of attractive, efficient, and productive industry, was to guarantee to each, "the means of physical support and of spiritual progress, and thus to impart a greater freedom, simplicity, truthfulness, refinement, and moral dignity to our mode of life." There was to be free education and medical attendance, a uniform rate of compensation for all labor. Employment was to be provided each member according to his ability or taste, and the property of the community was to be held in common, no one possessing more shares than the other. Beginning with twenty members, within less than three years' time the farm had seventy.

The members of the community were of more than average ability. Though financial success was very moderate, they managed to cover their poverty with an attractive veil of poetry and to infuse charm and romance into their most prosaic everyday occupations. William Ellery Channing, the great Unitarian, was one of the Transcendentalists. Nathanial Hawthorne, the author, Ralph Waldo Emerson, and Henry D. Thoreau, critics and essayist, John S. Dwight, Margaret Fuller, Elizabeth P. Peabody were among those associated with the enterprise from its origin. A young man of twenty-three, Charles Anderson Dana, by name, became the recording secretary of the community.

Young Dana, who later became a close friend of Albert Brisbane's and who got a job on Horace Greeley's *Tribune* through Brisbane's influence, came of straight Yankee stock. He had been born in New Hampshire, 1819. In the face of his father's serious advice to "ponder well the ways of life lest they lead down to the very gates of hell," he entered Harvard university. The religious flux of the period stirred him as profoundly as it did many another. Writing to a friend from Harvard, he said, "I feel now an inclination to orthodoxy and am trying to believe the real doctrine of the Trinity. Whether I shall settle down in Episcopacy, Swedenborgianism, or Goethean indifference to all Religion, I know not. My only prayer is, 'God help me.' "

Together with Osborne Macdaniel, Brisbane established another magazine, *The Phalanx,* in October, 1843. It was replaced by *The Harbinger*, published at Brook Farm beginning in 1845. This magazine continued its existence for four years. To list its contributors is to call the roll of every important figure in the American literary firmament at that time. Brisbane himself was a frequent contributor, but George Ripley with his 315 articles and Charles A. Dana, with 248, led the roll.

The winter of 1843-44 saw numerous local conventions of Fourierist Societies and on April 4, 1844, there assembled in New York the first and only national convention of Associationists. Letters of encouragement from all over the country were received and many resolutions were adopted dealing with the ways and means of organizing Associations. A permanent confederation of Associations was established. It was likewise decided to engage in international cooperation. Albert Brisbane was appointed to confer with the European Fourierists on the best mode of undertaking this work.

Brook Farm became a Phalanx at the time of the Convention. George Ripley was chosen president of the Convention, with Horace Greeley, Albert Brisbane, Parke Godwin and Charles A. Dana as vice-presidents. The movement had reached its high point. None there could realize that within a decade, the many Fourierist Colonies of the country would be merely a memory.

Despite the charges of atheism, the Fourierist movement had a very strong religious background and following. The plans of both Fourier and Brisbane appealed to people of faith. This was the "heaven on earth" which God had promised. In their enthusiasm they sprinkled their speeches and their tracts about Association with Biblical phrases to prove the Divine character of the movement they had joined. Emerson somewhat sadly shook his head at the strange gathering. "Mad men, mad women, men with beards, Dunkers, Muggletonians, Come-outers, Groaners, Agrarians, Seventh Day Baptists, Quakers, Abolitionists, Calvinists,

Unitarians, and Philosophers—all came successively to the top, and seized their moment, if not their hour wherein to chide, or pray, or preach, or protest."

There was a heavy influx of Swedenborgians into the Fourier movement. In turn, many of the Fourierists became actively interested in the spiritualist sect. Robert Dale Owen, son of Robert Owen, the great British Utopian, turned spiritualist. Brisbane, himself, was for a time, a constant attendant at those mysterious meetings held by the Swedenborgians.

The Brook Farm Phalanx came to an end in the spring of 1846. Enthusiasm was already dying down. A disastrous fire in their central frame structure brought it to a rapid close.

The North American Phalanx, developed at Westbank, New Jersey, in 1843, is the only other one worthy of consideration. About ninety actual settlers participated in it. They built a three story mansion, a grist mill, and developed a seventy-acre orchard. The work was hard; the income, small. But, as at Brook Farm, the social life was very pleasant. The experiment endured for twelve years. Like Brook Farm, the North American Phalanx was dissolved after a disastrous fire.

These many failures did not dampen Brisbane's spirit. He had an ample income, thanks to his father's judicious investments in real estate. This he used unsparingly for the cause in which he believed. But at the close of the forties new problems and issues were confronting the American people. Greeley, Dana, Emerson and others realized this and set their course accordingly. Not so Brisbane. The tenacity of his Scotch forebears was in his bones. He was bound to remain with his cause.

A few years of economic recovery had made people forget the miseries of the panic of the years, 1837-39. Gold had been found in California. Europe was shaken by upheavals. A new movement called "Communism," at whose head stood two young Germans, Karl Marx and Frederick Engels, was winning the support of its discontented. Here, in the United States, the issue was chattel slavery. The probability of the conflict between North and South was growing more acute and overshadowing all other issues.

Early in 1844, Brisbane returned to Europe a second time. His object was three-fold: first, to study the numerous manuscripts left by Fourier, who had died in 1837; second, to study music; third, to learn something about the science of embryology.

It was Brisbane's belief that the whole universe was a grand expression of certain laws of cosmic harmony. An organic harmony underlay all planetary distribution. If he could only arrive at a clear comprehension of how the mind marshals sounds and how it distributes, coordinates, arranges, combines and systematizes them, then perhaps he could apply this information to the field of social science as well.

Embryology was important since humanity was still an infant in its social life. A study of the physical development of the individual should reveal to him some of its inner laws which might be applied to society.

By the close of the year Brisbane had steeped himself in the voluminous writings of his master. He had spent six months studying music and he had applied himself as well to embryology. He returned to his home in December, more certain than ever that the ideas of Fourier and himself were fundamentally the salvation of mankind. Momentary failures could no longer daunt him. He would carry on. To him "the human mind acting in unity with the Cosmic Mind creates in its sphere as the Cosmic Mind creates throughout the Universe; and the manner in which man distributes sound to produce musical harmony does not differ from the manner in which the Mind of the Universe distributes worlds to produce planetary harmony."

He likewise perceived that "embryonic evolution of man was but a repetition of the organic evolution in nature from the radiate upward. When nature had completed her grand fugue from the first organic animal cells to the creation of the human brain, the individual man took up this cosmic fugue and conceived it in the individual embryonic evolution of each factor in the race."

Instead of setting out to rebuild the American Phalanxes, or to develop propaganda for the Fourier system, Brisbane turned aside from practical action altogether. The phase of propaganda was over for the time being. He needed to study the whole thing through once more, so he retired to his father's home in Batavia to check and recheck upon his master's theory, upon the theory of musical harmony, the science of embryology, and to review the history of mankind from the ancient Egyptians through to his own day. By the summer of 1846, Brisbane thought it was time to sum up what he knew. But the more he tried to disentangle Fourier's speculations, the greater was his perplexity.

"If ever a man deserved to be hanged for intellectual rashness and violence," said Brisbane to himself, "it is Fourier!" There seemed to be so many speculations in which Fourier offered no proof. "I felt that for myself I stood on the shore of the vast unknown; that I must cut loose from my intellectual path and start out anew. Again I stood face to face with an unknown immensity; the same as when on the shores of Greece, I first saw the possibility of a new order of society."

He retreated to the Alleghany Mountains, there to think out these great problems. Alas, his long period of soul-seeking brought no answer. All that came was a series of new problems.

When the third French revolution broke out in 1848, followed in rapid succession by revolutions in Germany and Austria, Albert Brisbane hastened to Europe to see the effect of these actions on the public mind. He reached the French capital on June 23, and saw much of the violence that took place. Poverty and destitution among the working people had finally produced the revolt. Albert soon found himself in a part of the city held by insurgents. "In this strange place, surrounded by a half-starved populace. I felt that I might easily be disposed of and no questions asked; so in preparing for bed, I placed my purse and my watch on a table in the middle of the room, saying to myself, 'that is all they can want of me!' In the morning my guide presented himself at my chamber door. 'It is time to leave,' he said, and, taking up his gun as we started off, added, 'A man may as well die by lead as by starvation! I've only had a loaf of bread for myself and my family for two days.'"

In the midst of the panic that then reigned, Brisbane went to meetings of workingmen, of the Fourier group and other reformists. Using his letters of introduction, he also attended many of the salon gatherings. Among the workers he found a seriousness and an earnestness bred of desperation. The speculations and theorizings of the vague intellectuals bothered him. As for the salons of the bourgeoisie, he found them oppressive with their pretension, frivolity and vanity. He recalled in later years how he would leave drawing rooms of his rich acquaintances with a feeling of relief to join a gathering of workingmen, where he found real passion, with serious questions discussed seriously.

"On the one hand," says Brisbane, "were the middle and upper classes, occupied with their frivolous dreams and plans for personal aggrandizement; on the other hand, were the laboring classes occupied with questions which were real and fundemental, because they concerned the elevation of an oppressed people."

The reverberations of the Paris insurrection spread north, east, and west. Albert Brisbane in his desire to understand these social upheavals followed in their wake. At Cologne he met Karl Marx, then a young man of thirty, just rising into prominence. The American Fourierist saw in Marx "a hatred of the power of capital, with its spoliations, its selfishness, and its subjection of the laboring classes.....His expression was that of great energy, and behind his self contained reserve of manner was visible the fire and passion of a resolute soul.....He saw the fundamental falseness of our whole economic system.....presenting it clearly to the minds of advanced thinkers, and out of it has grown the great movement now deeply agitating the progressive thought of Europe. The indications are that he is destined before long to revolutionize the whole economy of our civilization. It will introduce an entirely new order of society based on what we may call socialist equality: the proprietary equality of humanity and equality of industrial rights and privileges.....

"I remember that young man uttering his first words of protest against our economic system. I reflect how little it was imagined then that his theories one day would agitate the world and become an important lever in the overthrow of time-honored institutions. How little did the contemporaries of St. Paul imagine the influence which that simple mind would produce on the future of the world! Who could have supposed at that time that he was of more importance than the Roman Senate or the reigning emperor—more even than all the emperors of all Christendom to follow? In modern times Karl Marx may have been as important in his way as was St. Paul in his."

Brisbane went to Frankfort, where he met Froebel, the founder of the kindergarten system. He visited Berlin and saw the Prussian Parliament in session. He arrived in Vienna two days after the return of the Austrian army, which had been driven out by the revolting populace. The revolutionary movement was completely suppressed. Its leaders had fled or hidden themselves. The city appeared like one just conquered by an invading foe. Italy was likewise shaken by political agitation at the moment. Pope Pius IX had fled from Rome just two days before Brisbane arrived. In France, the revolt was serious, popular and impassioned; it swept in against those institutions which gave to the upper classes their domination of the social world. "The French masses were deeply imbued with a sentiment of *progressive destruction, the underlying characteristic of all the popular movements of our age.*"

The German movement was likewise earnest and profound. "But there was a certain kindness and goodness, inherent in the Germanic soul, which tempered those feelings and took from the revolutionary movements of Germany its violent character—preserving the people from those cruel excesses which took place in Paris in the days of June."

Of the Italian revolution, and the spirit prevailing among its leaders, Brisbane wrote, "there was a mild type of revolutionism; a kind of *dilettanteism* in reform, exciting the imagination but not reaching down into the sterner passions; furthermore, it was limited almost exclusively to the educated classes; the people had no understanding of political questions and remained outside of the political agitation."

Albert Brisbane had no love for the Catholic church. Stage coaches still functioned instead of railroads in the papal dominion, for Gregory XVI, in his "divine wisdom," had stated that railroads were the invention of the devil. Pope Pius the Ninth, who had possessed mild liberal tendencies prior to the revolt, returned to the Vatican, "thoroughly cured of his liberal tendencies; and during the long reign which followed he maintained a firm fossilized conservatism." The mental and material poverty of Italy Albert Brisbane blamed on the church and the feudalistic landed system there existing.

Once again Brisbane retraced his steps to France and found it in the hands of reactionaries. He attended many small secret gatherings of the revolutionists. Frequently he made visits to the prison Mazas, where Pierre Joseph Proudhon, the leading anarchist revolutionary of the day, was incarcerated. Proudhon, at that time, was editor of *La Voix du Peuple*, a paper with 200,000 circulation. He used it as a propaganda vehicle to convince both the upper classes and the masses that the root of all social ills lays primarily in the monopoly of land. He coined the phrase, "property is robbery." The form of society which he desired was one without government, without property, without inequality. As a first step toward the accomplishment of this, he proposed the establishment of a great national bank which would issue paper money to all in exchange for goods and services deposited with it. There would be no interest. This bank, with its new type of currency, would soon pave the way to an equalitarian society. To Brisbane, Proudhon, "combined great clearness of insight and intellectual power with firmness of character. He was a man who feared nothing, and who was endowed with immense moral energy."

The existing government kept a close watch on all suspected of revolutionary ideas. Among them was the American, Brisbane. On the twenty-fourth of February, 1849, the first anniversary of the revolution, mass gatherings took place all over Paris. Brisbane attended one of these at the Salle Martel. Unexpectedly, he was called upon to say a few words to the assemblage. He felt that the speeches already made were too violent, so he made "intentionally, a most conservative speech; telling the people in substance that unless they instructed themselves in the principles of social science, the revolution would be a failure. I expected to be hissed rather than applauded; but after I had spoken a little while, I observed in the audience a general air of interest.....I made some general remarks on the great part which France had played in the history of the world, and her devotion to principles.....I left the stage amid tremendous applause, waving hats and handkerchiefs, while La Grange, one of the leaders of the popular movement, he who, it was said, had started the revolution of the year before by firing the first pistol shot in front of the residence of Guizot, the Prime Minister, clasped me in his arms with great enthusiasm."

Brisbane's speech was broadcast through the radical as well as conservative press of France. Two weeks later he was summoned to appear at the office of the Prefecture de Police and learned to his amazement that he had to leave the country within twenty-four hours. No stranger had a right to make such a speech in France. Despite his protestations, the expulsion order stood. Brisbane went into hiding for a few days, but finally left for Brussels.

Four years later he returned to France and was witness of the coup d'etat of Napoleon II, December 2, 1852. The conservative republic gave way to the Third Empire. The fact that a great city of two million people could be conquered in a single day, and the rights of the people trampled under foot, with so little opposition, shook Albert's faith, momentarily, in the capacity of man for self government.

The officials who had been wary about permitting the radical American to return to France once more summoned him to appear before them. He was informed that his record had been closely watched for years, and it was a bad one.

Once again, Albert journeyed homeward.

Meanwhile, James Brisbane had passed away. George and Albert had to straighten out affairs between themselves. It was a one sided task. Albert devoted himself mainly to rereading the works of the great political economists of the time; checking their statements with his own. He arrived at the conclusion that they "are really the blind servants of perdition; they are without either the philanthropy or the clearsightedness necessary to raise them above the common places of habits and custom." As to socialism, this new system of political economy to which he now gave time and attention, it was in his opinion "the beginning of a new phase of social evolution—a revolution in the field of the practical interests of society."

3

THE SON OF A REFORMER

If the pressure of personal business problems and the never ceasing criticism of his friends and family failed to force Albert Brisbane to establish stability in his personal life, his marriage to Sarah White and the birth of his five children compelled him to terminate his travels and content himself with permanent residence in the United States.

It was in 1853 that Albert, at the age of forty-four, came back to this country with his bride. She was a woman of unusual ability. The Brisbanes divided their time between upstate New York, New York City, and Fanwood, New Jersey. Sarah Brisbane bore her husband five children in rapid succession: Alice, Hugo, Albert, Arthur and Fowell.

To be the wife of a man whose mind was constantly groping and delving into the problems of the cosmos was most difficult. Though Albert was by nature kind and considerate, and deeply loved his family, he at no time sacrificed his all-consuming social dream for them. If Albert had been more impressed with his own self-importance, if intrusions on the manner of living to which he had accustomed himself tended to destroy his philosophic endeavors, if he had felt the need of an immediate environment conforming to his intellectual fancies, he might well have developed a definite resentment toward his wife and family. But Albert was not egotistical, nor was he tempermental or rigid in his reactions to immediate personal problems. Conscious concern with the petty affairs of domesticity simply did not exist for him. Albert Brisbane was a dreamer and one of the aspects of the philosopher's personality which protected him from that which might possibly result in intellectual suffocation was his great concern with humanity's ultimate goal. The problems of mankind were so great and so constant that Albert lost complete sight of the perplexities of individual man. So completely had he submerged himself in the quest for truth that his channels of escape were thoroughly adequate. In the face of the most trying private situations he could execute a hasty retreat.

If it be true that the social dreamer is, in reality, an escapist who utilizes his dreams to free himself from that which is unpleasant in his surroundings, then it may well be said that though he fails to realize the dream itself, the very concept of it removes him far enough from the unpleasantries of the world in which he lives to make his problems vague and remote.

Thus it was that without the slightest realization on the part of her husband, the young mother of Albert Brisbane's five children suffered a tragic and brief married life. Economic problems were always present. It was not because she did not have an adequate source of income, that Mrs. Brisbane worried about the family finances. Where the income came from and when she could expect it were matters most difficult to determine. Albert so completely lacked a money sense that often he would go down to New York City to renew contacts with his former followers and be totally unaware that his business interests demanded his immediate attention. His wife, in utter helplessness, would consult Albert's brother, George, who for years had been forced to assume the responsibility of Albert's holdings. Once in sheer desperation, George wired Albert: "Forget your damned socialism and come back and tend to your own business." Albert usually was unperturbed by such messages. They served only to remind him that his brother George was, unfortunately, very limited in his outlook on life.

Nor could Mrs. Brisbane entrust her husband with the care of her children for even the briefest moment. Once, thoroughly submerged in philosophic speculations, Albert boarded a street car. In a vague way he glanced at the people about him. At brief intervals he was attracted by a pretty little girl sitting on the lap of her nurse at the far end of the car. Though in a meditative mood, his eyes occasionally shifted, almost instinctively, back to the child. When he reached his destination, Albert noticed that the little girl and her nurse also alighted. Then, to his amazement, he realized that the attractive child was his own daughter.

The birth of her youngest son, Fowell, left Mrs. Brisbane in ill health. Though she was never very strong physically, she did not complain of her weakened condition. So unconcerned was Albert that he failed to notice any change in her. As she watched her baby grow, Mrs. Brisbane felt her own strength fade. In the year 1867, when Fowell was only a year old, Sarah Brisbane was seized with an attack of pneumonia which swiftly carried her to her death.

Albert was grief stricken and shocked at the sudden death. Only a few days before he lost her, Albert was unaware of the critical nature of his wife's illness. While other members of the family came at once to care for the children and arrange the funeral, Albert withdrew from the chaos and tried to realize what had happened.

Alice Brisbane, the eldest child, who was then ten years old, felt the loss of her mother most keenly. She brought her rocking chair to her mother's funeral and placed it beside the open grave where she sat for hours, rocking and weeping and pleading that she be permitted to stay there forever. Hugo, who was then four years old, understood what had happened. The other two children (Albert, the third child, had died shortly after birth), Arthur, age two; and Fowell, the baby, were too young to comprehend the tragedy.

For the first time Albert realized that in some imperceptible manner his children were important to him. He agreed to part with the two eldest, but determined to keep the two younger ones himself. Alice and Hugo were sent to live with an aunt in Ohio, where they remained for many years. The father would journey to see them from time to time and would intersperse these visits with long philosophical letters to the children which they but half understood. When Albert Brisbane made the decision to keep his younger children it was without the faintest conception of the care, attention, and responsibility involved in raising them. To him, having them was a romantic notion. That they might suffer from his innocent neglect never occurred to him.

An exhausted Confederacy was making its last desperate stand in December, 1864, the month that saw the birth of Arthur Brisbane. Like his father before him, Arthur was born on the land of the Holland Purchase. But it was in the City of Buffalo instead of nearby Batavia, and the date was December twelfth.

The State of New York was far from the scene of conflict. Though the war spirit ran high, crops had been good, prices high, and the demand enormous. Despite the casualties caused by the war, the population grew rapidly. Commerce, trade, and industry boomed and the farmers who had heeded the call of Albert Brisbane and his Fourierist Utopia twenty years earlier were now among the most ardent land speculators.

Albert Brisbane, then fifty-five years of age, was one of the few who had not yielded to the war hysteria; nor had he sought to enhance his fortune on the strength of inflated land values. In this respect he was far different from the father of another youngster born a year and a half earlier in San Francisco, California. There big, gruff, jovial George Hearst, the father of William Randolph Hearst, though avowedly a supporter of the Confederate cause, had utilized the partisan feelings of the period to encourage Northerners and Southerners alike to sell out their mines or claims to him at ridiculously low prices so they could engage in the battle. George Hearst had never worried about the social destiny of man, nor had he tried to develop a blueprint of a better social order. He had gloried in the struggle for gold and once that gold had been obtained, he had used it to get still more. The paths of the two youngsters, the millionaire's son from the golden west, and the social reformer's son from upstate New York, were to cross before the century had concluded. They were to become the yardsticks of journalistic achievement, and were to be labeled indelibly as the greatest publisher and greatest editor of yellow journalism.

Arthur's early childhood years were marred by the absence of his mother and by the lack of permanent association with a woman who could take her place. The youngsters were placed under the care of nurses or neighboring mothers intermittently. But too often they had to depend on their father, who, stunned by the loss of his wife, was helpless.

For a long time Albert had the children sleep in the same bed with him. Though he tried to remember when to feed them, when to change their clothes, and when to wash their faces, such matter of fact things were very frequently forgotten. The children were permitted to rummage around the house or out of doors as they wished. Albert, himself, never a very tidy man, failed to notice in his home the accumulation of dirt and rubbish which was dragged in from the streets and alleys by the little ones. When they cried, he would give them money to buy food or candy at the nearby grocery store. Their purchases were seldom supervised.

Many times, when the family lived in Brooklyn, the father would go into New York City, remaining there all day and far into the night while the two boys were left at home to look after each other.

Fowell and Arthur could not understand their father; neither could he understand them. At times he would take them upon his knee and tell them of the beauties of a well-ordered universe based upon scientific and mathematical principles. He would try to repeat to them the stories he had heard as he sat at the feet of his mother. He forgot that his own mother told the stories in a simple manner understandable to a small child. Albert felt the need to undertake lengthy explanations of the whys and wherefores of the actions of the people of antiquity. These discourses upon the Intuitive Internal or the External Rational factors in the make-up of Alexander the Great, or Caesar, or Archimedes, didn't help in the telling of the story.

Mesmerism and spiritualism now became the object of Albert's investigation. As a result of this study, he came to the belief that there are two distinct states in the physical man: a dual system of nervous action involving the "*exter-*

nal rational" and the "*internal intuitional.*" He attempted to pass the information on to his young sons in order that they might understand the creation of a Beethoven, a Michael Angelo, a Shakespeare, as well as the scientific achievements of a Newton, a Watt, or a Cuvier. From Spiritualism, Brisbane went on to a study of psychology and from psychology to astronomy. The sun was a vast organic body, he assumed. As such, it must show the same characteristics of metabolism and catabolism as did all other organisms. "What was the nature of the food the sun consumed?" asked the gaping youngsters. Brisbane had a reply.

"It is furnished in part by comets, in part by the electricity of the planets, as well as the myriad little meteoric bodies which surround it. The cosmic vapors also serve as nourishment to the sun. In short, there is an immense amount of cosmic matter circulating in our solar system which the sun must draw in and assimulate to itself. I would even go so far as to suggest that it may be at the poles that this cosmic matter is taken up and by some process which we do not yet divine, is elaborated and thrown off at the equator."

The pink of the carnation and the luscious red of the strawberry were due, he explained, to vaporized iron transmitted through electric currents from the sun to our globe.

In 1876, Albert Brisbane married Redelia Bates, the daughter of a respectable New England family. Though thirty years younger than Albert, the second Mrs. Brisbane cherished her husband's ideals and ideas and cheerfully accepted the task of raising his children. Albert took his young wife to his home in Fanwood. She found it in a most disorderly condition. "I remember the singular impression his little Fanwood home made upon me when he first took me there," wrote Mrs. Brisbane. "Conducting me to a small room piled pell mell almost to the ceiling with books, manuscripts, old letters, journals, and what not, in the most chaotic confusion, he said pleasantly: 'Mon amie, with all my worldly goods I thee endow!'

"By the carelessness of servants, who during his absence had overturned a lamp while playing cards, the residence proper had burned down, and all the household goods had been thrown out precipitately. This was the most precious part of the wreck."

From the study, they went into the living room to talk, but scarcely had they settled themselves in the somewhat shabby chairs when Mrs. Brisbane noticed two children coming down the road in an old wood wagon. "They were most raggedly dressed and their hair stuck out through holes in their caps. Never had I seen such pitiful sights as these two youngsters. To my amazement they came to the house and entered the room. I was sitting in a chair near the fireplace. Albert walked over to the boys, took each of them by the hand, led them forward to me, and said, 'These are my boys. I give them to you.' The youngsters looked at me somewhat credulously. They sat down in front of the fire place looking so weak, so forlorn, so ill at ease. Little Fowell, then about seven, kept looking at me for a long time. Finally he got up, came towards me, opened his arms, and clambered up on my lap burying his head in my bosom. Arthur looked on in silence."

Mrs. Bates, Redelia's mother, was an efficient and practical woman. She came to live with the Brisbanes and in a short time, the chaos in the Fanwood home was brought to an end. The little boys, who had been playing with "questionable companions", were sent to school regularly. They had their meals on time, were made to wear the new clothes purchased for them, and were given their first lessons in order and discipline.

The new Mrs. Brisbane determined that the boys should receive a good education. The schools which they then attended were inadequate. Their stepmother felt that they should have the same opportunity their father had to learn foreign languages, customs, and institutions. Albert agreed to this. The idea was excellent. Months passed while Mrs. Brisbane waited for Albert to arrange the European trip.

Home life at this time, according to Mrs. Brisbane, was most harmonious. To be with Albert and in his presence was peace itself. He was very fond of the children, but the one thing he could not tolerate was ceaseless laughter and chatter at the dinner table. He therefore arranged for the children to eat with Mrs. Bates while he and Redelia supped by themselves. After dinner, he would go up stairs and spend at least an hour with the children before their bedtime.

It took Mrs. Brisbane some time to comprehend fully the extent of her husband's procrastinations about practical matters. But once she did understand, she acted herself. "I finally made up my mind to take the children across by myself. I packed our bags and off we went to France. Mr. Brisbane made haste to follow."*

Arthur Brisbane was taken to Europe when he was thirteen years old and returned to America shortly before his nineteenth birthday. Prior to his departure from this country, Arthur attended school in Brooklyn and also in New Jersey. At Fanwood, his teacher was a young man of eighteen by the name of Dunning—a man who later achieved world-wide fame as a professor of political science at Columbia University.

* Redelia Bates Brisbane, as these words are written, is living in Los Angeles. Ninety-four years of age, Mrs. Brisbane still retains a remarkable memory and is a woman of amazing vitality. In an interview with the author, she described to him Arthur Brisbane's youth.

When Fowell and Arthur were taken to France by their stepmother, they attended school in Paris at the *Ecole Alsacienne*. There they studied languages, literature and history. Both of the boys learned French with amazing rapidity, but Arthur was the more able of the two. The children also attended school at Ivry and at Asnieres, and when they returned to Paris they went to the *Ecole Keller*. When Arthur and Fowell had a good command of the French language, and some training in history and literature, Mrs. Brisbane moved them on to Germany, where they studied at Stuttgart. For a while the children lived with a professor and attended the Rauscher School in the daytime. They had ample spending money. They met famous people, learned new languages, new customs, and new habits, and became quite Europeanized.

Arthur was a fine physical specimen, unusually handsome. His high forehead and keen blue eyes were arresting. The nose, like his father's, was aquiline. In his youth, the mouth was soft, small, and effeminate. As he grew to manhood, the gentle face lost its tenderness. The keenness of the eyes and the expression of the intellectual remained, but the mouth hardened and the chin became more aggressive.

The boy loved sports and the outdoors. Early in life he became an excellent horseman. In group activities Arthur led and the other boys followed. He never missed an opportunity to dominate. Fowell was seldom allowed to forget that his older brother was more capable than himself. Of all the Brisbane children, Mrs. Brisbane believed Hugo to have been the most exceptional, but Hugo's early death left Arthur in a superior position.

In addition to being physically handsome and an alert student, Arthur was gifted with an unusual degree of social adaptability. He felt at home anywhere. During his youth he developed a suave manner, genial and witty. Arthur had been encouraged by his father to take flight into the realm of imagination—to play with all possible ideas. He enjoyed his history; he grew especially fond of French literature; he developed a love for the French people. His father's discourses on spiritualism led him to a study of comparative religion, and the long conversations of father and son on the problems of science and the character of the cosmos became a fertile source of fact and fable which Arthur constantly drew upon in later years.

The one thing which the boy did not care for was writing.

When Arthur came back from Europe, he was a striking young man, sophisticated beyond his eighteen years. He felt his student days were over. There was much in life that he must learn from some other sources than books. A love of clothes, a slightly artificial manner, a tendency toward ostentation, and an extraordinary awareness of the opposite sex, characterized his adolescence. Most of his energies were now directed at the attainment of worldly pleasures. Arthur lacked the mental curiosity and zealous idealism of his father. The life of a dilettante seemed at the moment well worth emulating.

Albert Brisbane was somewhat disturbed by his son's attitude. He decided to take him on a trip to Kansas City, where the father had to supervise some real estate he owned. No sooner had Albert and his son arrived in the middle western town than Arthur made the acquaintance of some vivacious young girls and proceeded to spend his nights attending parties at which the burden of respectability was taken none too seriously. The young man caused his father a good deal of trouble. When Albert finally realized the situation was out of hand, he wrote his wife. She advised Albert to send Arthur home.

Arthur Brisbane obtained his first position on the *New York Sun* through his father, according to a widely circulated story. According to Redelia Bates Brisbane, she spoke to Dana while her husband was in Kansas City and Dana promised the young man work. He was given a job at the salary of fifteen dollars per week.

"He knew nothing about newspapers," Mrs. Brisbane says. "He was unable to write news stories, but an office boy on the *Sun* showed him how. Arthur was sent out to cover small social gatherings, strawberry festivals and dances."

The story has also been generally accepted that Arthur Brisbane remained steadily with the *Sun*; that he was promoted steadily and finally sent abroad to take over the foreign correspondent's job in London. According to his stepmother, Albert Brisbane became worried at the energy and time Arthur was devoting to his newspaper work and had him quit his job to go abroad with the family. They went to Paris and then to London. Arthur had a gay time, but the virus of journalism had gotten into his blood. He wrote to Dana about his experiences. Dana finally suggested that since he was abroad, he might as well take over the job as London correspondent, then a poorly paid position.

The previous correspondent, said Mrs. Brisbane, "had been ineffective. Londoners generally paid no attention to a correspondent from an American paper such as the *Sun*. Arthur decided to change all this. He rented a most expensive suite of rooms at the Victoria Hotel in London. He dressed as did the gentlemen of fashion, sent out fine announcements that the Albert and Arthur Brisbane News Service was opened, and rigorously observed all of the finer points of the grand manner which upper class London affected during the heyday of Victorianism."

Arthur was soon a very popular person. Not only had he no difficulty in winning the admiration of a host of feminine friends; he also succeeded in winning his way into the homes of many leading politicians.

When a position as night editor of the *Sun* was open, Arthur applied for the job and won it. Then he returned to America. He was to return to Europe only a short time later when Joseph Pulitzer, of the *World*, hired him and spent the better part of a year traveling on the Continent with Arthur as a guide. Together they visited Nice, Cannes, and the French Riveria. While Arthur supplied his publisher with genial companionship, Mr. Pulitzer trained the young reporter in the finer points of journalism.

Albert Brisbane lived long enough to discover that his son's life would not be devoted to his own social theories. When young Brisbane returned to New York and renewed his activity in newspaper work, a young reporter who was interested in Socialism eagerly approached Arthur on the subject. In a tone which did not disguise his disgust, the cynical son of one of the first American Socialists said: "I was brought up on that stuff!"

The idealism which Arthur heard preached at home didn't jibe with the realities of life outside. The heroes of the day in Europe and in America were not the social thinkers of Albert Brisbane's youth. They were business men who achieved power and prestige through the acquisition of money. Europe, the social setting of Arthur's youth, had settled down to the Victorian Era. Revolutions and social unrest lay in the past; their reverberations were smothered by conventionality and stability. The rising middle class dominated society in its economic exploitations, its political parliamentarianism, and its optimistic cultural view.

Britain had climaxed her imperialistic endeavors with the

conquest of India, the acquisition of Egypt, and the building of the Suez Canal. Germany too, at this time, was laying the basis for her great international role. Under the iron heel of Bismarck, she was geographically consolidated, and was rapidly becoming a militarist power. While Arthur studied in Germany, Bismarck was handing down reforms to the German people. Reforms, always from above and never from the people themselves, were placed before the German masses in quiet and orderly manner; and with them intense patriotism was propagated among the newly united peoples.

In France the fragmentary remains of a powerful revolutionary movement were finally crushed in the defeat of the Paris Commune in 1871. The Franco-Prussian War also aided in dissolving the remaining elements of discontent. Intense nationalism and the establishment of the French Republic followed in its wake. For the first time in more than a century, not a solitary social thinker of importance appeared on the French scene.

And in the United States, the idealistic humanitarianism of the thirties and forties was smitten down in the onrush of hard boiled money-grubbers who launched an era of cynicism and ostentation shortly after the Civil War.

The soldier-hero, General Grant, took office as President in 1869 and ushered in that hustling period of the 1870's, when the dominant dream of America was get rich. Paradoxical as it may seem, the development of mass industries was bringing about the most complete flowering of modern individualism. These new Americans were primitive souls, ruthless, capable, single-minded men; rogues and rascals often, but never feeble, never hindered by petty scruples, never given to puling or whining—the raw materials of a race of buccaneers. "Pirate and priest," says Parrington,

The man in the derby is Arthur Brisbane in his youth, when he served as European correspondent for the New York Sun.

"issued from a common source and played their parts with the same picturesqueness." The standard of the lowly Nazarene and the black flag with the skull and cross bones were kept in the same locker to be flown as the wind dictated.

In his father's drawing room young Arthur heard denunciations hurled at the rulers of Wall Street, men like Jim Fisk who jovially proclaimed, "I worship in the synagogue of the libertines." There were Jay Gould and Jay Cooke who gambled with stacked cards; the picturesque Commodore Vanderbilt and a tribe of other swindlers and railroad wreckers, rascals one and all. But to the man in the street, these were heroes to be cheered for their audacity. Those who grumbled at their ways were told, "you'd do the same thing if you only had the chance."

Political corruption, too, had attained new heights. The "Washington Ring" plundered the Capitol itself. There was a huge "Canal ring" in New York State; a "whiskey ring" with its headquarters in St. Louis; and charges of corruption in the Credit Mobilier Case ascended to the speaker of the House of Representatives, the Vice-President of the United States, and the Secretary of the Treasury. Boss Tweed controlled Tammany in New York. The aim and end of politics became the capture of office. With the capture once achieved, it became possible to buy and sell legislators, judges, and executives; to loot the public treasury with impunity until a more successful political gang succeeded in gaining the right to this plunder. The keys to salvation were in the hands of men like revivalist Moody, psalm-singing Sankey, and T. DeWitt Talmage; these were ably seconded by such professional keepers of the public morals as Anthony Comstock. Epitomizing the whole show was Barnum, "a vulgar, greasy genius, pure brass without any gift," growing rich in the profession of humbug.

Arthur Brisbane could chose between devoting his life to his father's philosophy, accepting with it the social ostracism and personal economic instability which it entailed; or he could set as his goal the standards of success of the new era—the acquisition of money, power, and personal prestige. The younger Brisbane was a true product of his age. He chose the latter.

While Albert Brisbane devoted the last days of his life to analyzing his experiences, closeting himself for long sessions of discourse with Henry George, the single-taxer, and Edward Bellamy, the socialist, and aiding them in hammering out their own conception of what the new social order should be and how it should be attained, Arthur was busy establishing himself in the field of journalism.

Despite young Arthur's ambition, it was many years before he was referred to as anybody but the son of Albert Brisbane. This annoyed him. He did not like the thought of having a father superior to himself. Albert was unassuming; Arthur, dominating and aggressive. His stepmother once said to him: "If that is all you want (personal esteem), then you are not very big after all."*

Arthur's early life and the neglect he suffered at the hands of his father must have contributed something to Arthur's attitude. In his acquisitiveness he was much like his grandfather James and his Uncle George. Perhaps the manner in which his father had thrown away his fortune in what seemed to Arthur useless and visionary schemes, aided him in arriving at this point of view. The ostracism which his father suffered in polite society was not for the son who craved popular applause.

One could never picture young Arthur acting as his

* Mrs. Brisbane asserts that Arthur never read the biography of his father. "He was too proud to read it."

father had done when a famous European scholar had told him at great length of all his achievements. When the noted man concluded, Albert said, "and you, sir, are meeting the most unimportant person in the world."

In his declining years, Albert Brisbane devoted some time to puttering with various inventions. He invented a new form of steamship; a compressed wood pavement; an oven designed to cook in a vacuum, thus dispensing with yeast and other artificial means of raising bread and pastries. None of them ever yielded financial returns. To the very end of his life Albert demonstrated his distain for popular approval. A few days before his death he wrote to Arthur, then on the *Sun*, expressing the belief that he would not recover. "I want you to remember, when I am dead, to let nothing be said of me. Heed me in this, Arthur! Do not speak of me in your paper, nor let any other do so, if you can prevent it."

The world passed by Albert Brisbane. He remained an aged and aging social reformer in the period of America's guilded age. His compatriots in the period of America's Romantic Revolution had died long years before. He remained alone and almost forgotten by America—that new aggressive, uncouth, corrupt America that followed in the wake of the Civil War.

But Albert Brisbane never lost confidence in the schemes for reforming mankind and society. To the day of his death he was a social reformer applying himself to the sciences in an endeavor to find the answer which he had been seeking all his life: "What is the social destiny of man?"

Arthur Brisbane, on the other hand, cared little for such speculations. He was now engaged in the serious work of building his journalistic career—a career which was to bring him a kind of fame his father had never known.

4

FLEDGLING JOURNALIST

THE WELL dressed and well educated playboy, Arthur Brisbane, had given no serious thought to his future profession. His father hoped he would follow in his footsteps, but refused to press the point when Arthur evinced a total lack of interest. The study of books and manuscripts belonged to older men like his father who had no desire to face the facts of life. Arthur had been fed on a heavy diet of philosophy, economics, and sociology. As far back as he could remember, these were the subjects of constant conversation among his father, his stepmother, and their circle of friends both in America and abroad. From his teachers in the French and German schools he had received a large dose of literature and history. The thoughts and efforts of men long dead were usually recorded in a dull, leaden style. The life of a scholar was obviously not for Arthur.

On one occasion father and son discussed the problem at length. What about a musical career? Or that of an architect? Both were dignified, ennobling. Arthur thought not. A career as a banker, broker, or business man was out of the question—he might as well be a horse thief if he were to make his fortune out of the legalized exploitation of others. That would never do for the son of Albert Brisbane.

"What about journalism?" asked the son.

"A good idea, Arthur. The power of the pen is infinitely greater than that of the sword or the money-changer's gold. Were Horace Greeley still alive, I'd certainly suggest you work with him. He was the greatest and finest character ever known. I could give you a letter of introduction to Mr. Dana of the *Sun*. He was a close friend of mine and he worked with me in trying to educate the American people to the necessity of social reorganization. I fear that in recent years, Mr. Dana has forgotten most of what he believed in at that time. However, he is a good man and his paper is powerful. And there is Mr. Jones of the *New York Times*. I've known him for years. He comes from upstate and your grandfather, James, gave him permission to put a newsstand inside the Albany station. It was, I believe, one of the first newsstands ever put in a station in this country.....Have you any preference?"

"No, father, but I'll think the matter over."

Arthur did think it over, but he preferred to make no immediate decision. He felt sure he could write. He knew that his knowledge of French and German would aid him. He had already met many great men through his father. The names and works of philosophers, scientists, and economists were familiar to him. He had a good mind and was aware of it. He was ambitious. The *New York Times* was a good paper, but its influence didn't compare with that of the *Sun*. Charles Anderson Dana was the outstanding editor of the day. Therefore, if work he must, he preferred to get his training on the *Sun*.

It was at Albert Brisbane's request that Charles Dana was given his first real chance in New York as a reporter on Horace Greeley's *Tribune*. Within a few years, he was the leading spirit of that paper. But as the times changed, Dana's idealism soured. The ardent Utopian socialist of the forties and fifties became a materialist. He decided to play the game in the fashion of the day. With his abilities he was a success from the start. When he took over the ownership of the

New York Sun not even the empty shell of his earlier idealism remained. His editorial policy was one of stark individualism harnessed to his own prejudices and private interests. His paper became the accepted organ of the wealthy and the respectable. A brilliant writer and an able executive, he made his paper a power in New York. Every proposal for progressive legislation met an ardent and able opponent in Mr. Dana. He feared "class government" and wrote feelingly about it whenever legislation to help the poor was proposed. On the other hand, every measure calculated to give new land to private railroad companies, to grant franchises to speculators, and to prevent governmental interference in the doings of the rich and powerful, he hailed as beneficial and necessary legislation. He attacked greed and corruption in public office with all the moral indignation of his youth. Even as his right hand wrote those flaming words, his left hand was arranging deals with another group of political spoilsmen about to take office.

His former friends and associates despised him and refused to talk to him. Even Albert Brisbane, the soul of kind heartedness, shook his head sadly at the thought of his old associate. Dana became a jingo who called for further annexation of territory. He wanted Haiti, Cuba, Mexico, and even Canada annexed to the United States. A constant chip-on-the-shoulder attitude in foreign affairs was now his policy. His cynicism knew no bounds. "The last forty years of his life," according to Parrington, "were spent undoing the work of his earlier years."

This was the man and this was his outlook at the time young Arthur Brisbane entered upon his journalistic career. Dana knew the patter of Fourier Philosophy and Socialism as well as Albert Brisbane. But while Albert Brisbane was a financial failure and a social outcast, Dana was a power and a social leader in the new guilded age. That the cynicism and crass materialism of Dana had an important effect on all of his subordinates, and especially upon his latest acquisition, young Brisbane, soon became obvious.

In later years Arthur Brisbane said it was his father's poverty which compelled him to go to work. This was not true. His earlier escapades abroad augmented by those in Kansas City caused his father no end of mental unrest. His father and stepmother sought to solve the problem by sending him to work.

Arthur was, so to speak, catapulted into his future profession.

The blue eyed boy who walked into the office of the *New York Sun*, December 12, 1883, to embark on his career as a journalist was nineteen years old. Dana read the letter and sent the boy to see Chester F. Lord, the managing editor; Lord sent him to the city editor, John Bogart, with instructions to put him on the payroll.

The first few months were difficult ones for Arthur. No one seemed to give him instructions; he didn't know what to do. His early writings seemed forced and pedantic. The other reporters with their sloppy speech, their cheap talk about sex and gambling and their constant trips to the nearby saloons left an unfortunate impression on the young man. They, in turn, thought he was a prude and a dandy. His curly hair, his soft blue eyes and effeminate mouth didn't help matters for him with this hard boiled crew.

"He was a puzzle," says Frank M. O'Brien, "to his superiors, his colleagues, and perhaps to himself."

"He sat around," said one of the reporters, "like a fellow who didn't understand what it was all about."

Those first few months, while they did not seem to accomplish anything, were a period of genuine apprenticeship for young Brisbane. He began to understand the art of reportorial observation, to familiarize himself with the make-up of a modern newspaper. Above all, he began to study people—the people in the streets, in the shops, but especially the men about him.

Thirty-five years later, when Brisbane was testifying before a Senate investigating committee, he declared: "I went from Paris to New York, and became a reporter on the *Sun*, under Charles A. Dana, at nineteen, and saw the young men on the newspapers drinking whiskey, and a great deal of drunkenness. In those days the newspaper men drank a great deal more than they do now, and drunkenness was much more common." He told how, as a boy at school, he had learned to drink wine. "No boy in the school ever drank a glass of pure water." The drink given to the boys, he admitted, was very weak claret. One part claret and four parts water.

Although Arthur, like his father, was an active opponent of whiskey, he admitted on the stand at Washington that it was perhaps to whiskey that he owed his first success in newspaperdom. His first real chance to write a story of any interest, so he said, was "when I was sent to get the names of prominent people at a fight at which John L. Sullivan participated, and some of the experienced newspaper men were drunk, and that gave me my first opportunity to write a good story. So that I owed that to whiskey. Perhaps I am the only man who can say that he owes anything to whiskey."

Arthur applied himself diligently to learning the trade he had selected. He familiarized himself with the town and its personalities. Having mastered this background, "he came out of his trance like a shot from a gun and seemed to know everything about everything." He shot up the journalistic ladder with amazing speed.

"At that time I was full of ambitions," he recalled, "and deeply resented that the Constitution of the United States fixed the minimum age of the President at forty-five. I felt I had too long to wait."

Brisbane's earliest newspaper writings were unsigned and therefore difficult to trace. Charles Edward Russell, himself a newspaper man for many years and co-worker with Brisbane both under Pulitzer and Hearst, maintains that the first big story written by Brisbane was one dealing with the blowing up of a rocky ledge at Hellgate which had long been an obstruction to East River navigation. General John Newton of the United States Engineers planned and executed the destruction of this ledge. Hundreds of deep chambers were drilled into the ledge which were filled with dynamite—then a new type of explosive. New York and the whole eastern seaboard was greatly excited about this operation. Newspapers seized upon the excitement to carry many stories debating the possibility of such a vast piece of dynamiting. The big moment of the explosion which blew three hundred thousand cubic yards of reef into fragments, was described in the *Sun* by Brisbane as follows:

"A tremendous volume of water rose to a height of one hundred fifty or two hundred feet, masses of white foam shining in the sunlight, resembling the appearance of a fantastic iceberg lifted bodily upon a solid basin of dark, frozen water. For five or six seconds it bubbled aloft, and then sank back into the river, where a yellow sulphurous glow prevailed for a minute, after which the river resumed its wonted course."

Dana had not been impressed with young Brisbane up to this time. He thought "that young man imagines he can write like Dickens." But now Brisbane was becoming acclimated to the newspaper shop and newspapermen. He was by no means a "good fellow," but in his peculiar way he began to make friends. He was an athlete of no small ability, and one of his favorite diversions in those early newspaper days was to race several reporters to the restaurant where they dined. When he won, as he usually did, he glowed with triumph.

Kind hearted Albert Brisbane began to worry about Arthur, who, by this time, could think or talk of nothing but newspapers and newspaper work. Eighteen months of such work, thought Albert, sufficed. He asked Arthur to leave his position with Dana to join the family on a trip to the Continent. This Arthur did. For seven or eight months he renewed his acquaintance with Paris, Rome, Berlin, the Riviera, and London. A reporter by now, he couldn't help sending newsy letters with good local color to his former employer. Dana was impressed. He had never been successful in getting good European correspondents for the *Sun*. When young Brisbane wrote to Dana from London, suggesting he be put back on the payroll, Dana agreed forthwith.

T. P. O'Connor, the aggressive Irishman who later achieved fame as a member of Parliament, was Brisbane's immediate predecessor as correspondent for the *Sun*. But T. P. was busy with politics, even at that time, and his articles from London dealt too intimately with that aspect of British life to make good copy for the *Sun*. Young Brisbane, on the other hand, knew all the patter of continental politics and was in no way involved in them. His apprenticeship on the *Sun* in New York gave him an understanding of American newspaper needs.

When the gruesome murders by Jack-the-Ripper took

place in London, it was Brisbane who pictured them in their most horrible details for the readers of the *Sun*. They thrilled and shivered at the word pictures drawn of this dastardly fiend who ripped open the bodies of his unsuspecting female victims.

Brisbane went into the heart of Whitechapel, most notorious slum in the world. There he saw misery and drunkenness unequaled even in New York's lower east side or on the Bowery. Again he sent his word pictures to the paper. They created a sensation and were as effective in their day as were Jack London's stories about the "people of the abyss" dealing with the same region twenty years later.

In the course of his duties as correspondent, Brisbane often went to the House of Commons, where he witnessed the debates on the problems of the British Empire. He saw and met Gladstone, then nearly eighty years of age. He became an intimate friend of Gladstone's son, "and sat at the feet of the old religionist, learning from him all the tricks of moral and political hypocrisy."

Brisbane went to Paris for interviews and news reports. He also went to St. Peter's in Rome, where he met and interviewed Pope Leo, then nearly ninety years of age. "I read his poem advocating the use of red wines very moderately."

But it was as a reporter of the famous John L. Sullivan-Charlie Mitchell fight at Chantilly, France, on March 10, 1888, that he gained general recognition as a competent newspaperman. It was Brisbane's human interest angle which caused Park Row to acclaim him an excellent sports writer. In his story he represented Mitchell as being inspired by his seconds to fight the good fight on behalf of the "dear little kids at home." It made a tear-jerking story even if Mitchell did suffer defeat at the hands of the great Sullivan:

"Baldock, the tough second, was an interested spectator.

He was forbidden by Mitchell to practice the tricks of his trade by trying to gouge Sullivan's eyes out, and he could not have done it anyhow as Sullivan was never prostrate on the ground. He therefore had to find other ways of relieving his feelings.....At one time he besought Mitchell to think of his children: 'Think of the kids, Charlie. The dear little kids a callin' for you at home and a countin' on you for bread. Think of what their feelings will be if you don't knock the ear off him and knock it off him again.' "

Dana realized that he had a "find" in Brisbane, so when his star correspondent applied for the position of editor for the *Evening Sun*, Dana gave it to him. Arthur could hardly believe his eyes when he read the cablegram giving him the position. He was tired of Europe. Besides, the new position would command a higher salary.

When Brisbane, shortly after his return, told Dana how glad he was to be back, his publisher remarked: "You will soon get over the desire to live in New York after your experience in London."

The twenty-three-year-old editor was wined and dined at Dana's home on Madison Avenue with the editorial staff. It made a great impression on him. Years later, Brisbane recalled that Dana "was much pleased when toward the end of the dinner, at which various wines were provided, he produced a certain bottle and said to me: 'Brisbane, you have been in Paris, you ought to know what that wine is. What is it?'

"I told him immediately that it was Chateau Yquem, and excellent, which it was.

"The fact that I recognized this wine, and the fact that I was able to tell him the meaning of various French slang expressions pleased him more than any newspaper ability that I might have."

The *Sun* at that time had the largest evening circulation in New York. The paper was run on what might be called a literary basis. On its staff there were such outstanding writers of the day as Charles E. Tyler, Richard Harding Davis, Frank Wilson, afterward editor of the *Police Gazette*, who wrote many brilliant stories according to Brisbane. Davis began his Van Bibber stories then, "based on a story by Manchecourt, which I translated for him from *La Vie Parisienne*."

The success of the youthful editor made a great impression along Newspaper Row. One man in particular kept a close watch on Arthur Brisbane and determined to bring him to his own staff at the earliest possible moment. This was Joseph Pulitzer, publisher of the *New York World*.

The rise to fame and fortune of the German-Hungarian immigrant, Joseph Pulitzer, was the talk of the day. A few months before Arthur Brisbane was born the young foreigner had arrived in New York. A few days later he enlisted in the Union Army. Within a year he was mustered out and returned to New York with the sum of thirteen dollars in his pocket. He made his way west to St. Louis, where he became active in the *Deutsche-Gesellschaft*, and became a member of Carl Schurz's *Westliche Post*, the leading German daily of the town.

Less than six years after he had landed in the New World Pulitzer was a member of the Missouri State Legislature on the Republican ticket. He was one of the outstanding radicals of the region. On December 9, 1878, he purchased at auction the St. Louis *Dispatch*, for $2,500, A few days later, the *Post*, another local sheet, merged with the *Dispatch*. The new paper was a success from its inception. Within four years, Pulitzer had made enough money to go to New

York and buy the *World*, for $346,000. This he did on May 10, 1883, just a few months before Arthur Brisbane entered upon his newspaper career. "The tall young adventurer from the west," says his biographer, Don Seitz, "his language still laden with the accent of his foreign tongue, radiating excitement and infusing energy, came like a tornado. Soon all was in confusion. The old fashioned staff viewed his coming with tremulous dismay."

In announcing the new creed of the *World*, Joseph Pulitzer declared that the paper would be "different in men, measures and methods—different in purpose, policy and principle—different in sympathies and convictions—different in head and heart." He added: "There is room in this great and growing city for a journal that is not only cheap but bright, not only bright but large, not only large but truly democratic—dedicated to the cause of the people rather than that of the purse potentates—devoted more to the news of the New than the Old World, that will expose all fraud and sham, fight all public evils and abuses—that will serve and battle for the people with earnest sincerity."

Pulitzer at once attacked the local aristocracy, "ready to sell their daughters for barren titles to worthless foreign paupers."

The *World* proclaimed the beginning of a new aristocracy,—the aristocracy of labor. Its new program favored taxing inheritances, luxuries, large incomes and monopolies. It demanded a reform in the civil service and the punishment of corrupt office-holders as well as vote-buying.

Within three weeks the paper had made a fifty percent gain in circulation. Pulitzer raided other papers for the best journalistic talent available. To meet the competition of this new comer from the west, the other papers cut their prices. They even advertised in the *World*. But to no avail. Its circulation grew, while that of its most dangerous rival, the *Sun*, shrank from 137,000 to 85,000. When the *World* passed 100,000 circulation, "100 guns were fired in City Hall Park and every employee received a tall silk hat."

Ballard Smith was taken away from the *New York Herald* and made managing editor. William H. Merrill was lured from the *Boston Herald* to become chief writer for the *World*, where he remained for many years. Bill Nye, the humorist, was added as a special writer and Ward McAllister, famed dictator of fashions in the homes of New York's four hundred, edited the society news. S. S. Carvalho, a close friend of Brisbane's and one of the most talented members of the *Morning Sun's* staff, was brought over as editor of the *World*.

In 1887, the *Evening World* appeared—a one-cent paper. Fortune continued to smile upon the German-Hungarian immigrant. Soon he was erecting the greatest newspaper building of the day. The building was completed shortly after Arthur Brisbane joined Mr. Pulitzer's staff in 1890.

The publisher's zeal for social reform together with his amazing success as a money-maker and journalist all appealed to young Brisbane. There seemed to be only one subject upon which they didn't see eye to eye; that was the question of drink. Arthur had lost no opportunity to moralize against the dangers of strong drinks in his numerous articles for the *Sun*. As he confessed years later, "when I came back to this country, whenever I wrote for the newspapers, I wrote in favor of light wine and beer, and against whiskey. I do not believe there is anyone who has written more strongly in favor of temperance and against whiskey and drunkenness than I have, or who has done more to arouse the feeling against whiskey in this country."

Pulitzer did not look upon Demon Rum as the outstanding menace to humanity. In fact, on one occasion when the entire editorial force of the *World* seemed to need an invigoration, he discussed the question with his business manager and suggested that the reason for the let-down was due to the fact that no one on the staff got drunk. "Brad (Bradford Merrill, then editorial manager), never gets drunk; Burton (city editor) lives in Flatbush—he never gets drunk; Van Hamm (managing editor) lives out in New Jersey, he never gets drunk; Lyman (managing night editor) he's always sober. You live in Brooklyn and never get drunk. When I was there, someone always got drunk and we made a great paper. Take the next train back to the city. Find a man who gets drunk, and hire him at once."

For seven years Brisbane remained with Pulitzer serving him in various roles; as companion, reporter, feature writer, and finally, as editor of the Sunday *World*.

Brisbane spent a great deal of time with his publisher. Pulitzer's failing eyesight made it impossible for him to read or even to play chess, the game he loved so dearly. Arthur sought to allay the tedium of his days by reviving Mr. Pulitzer's interest in the seductive game of draw poker. "All went well," according to Don Seitz, "until Arthur's winnings at a sitting ran up to $500. Mr. Pulitzer paid up but discontinued the diversion."

During this period when Brisbane was being developed under the master's eye, they made a stay at Newport. Both Pulitzer and Brisbane were good horsemen and prepared for an early morning ride. The road was barred by toll gates, so Brisbane was told to get some money. He procured a two dollar bill from the private secretary's funds, and stood outside awaiting J. P. The morning was misty and he came out to the street grumbling about the darkness. Brisbane was twisting the bill into an imitation of a lamp lighter.

William Randolph Hearst and Arthur Brisbane at a party on the Lord of Saint Simeon's famous estate in California.

"Fog, fog, nothing but fog," growled the great man, "How can I see to ride, I'd like to know, in such a mist as this?—Brisbane, give me that money."

Together with Charles Edward Russell and other press representatives, Brisbane was admitted to see the first electrocution in the state of New York at Sing Sing Prison. This was in February or March of 1891, according to Mr. Russell. The Aldrich T. Gerry Act had made it a crime for any newspaper to publish more than eight lines about a public execution, but the act had just been repealed. This gave the press its first chance to report an execution in all its gruesome details. "I kept looking over at Arthur," said Russell, "and noticed that as the convicted man was being strapped into his seat, Arthur's usually ruddy face turned a greenish white. He was visibly shaking. He remained through the electrocution, but he became so sick that he couldn't stay for the official autopsy."

"We were a couple of radicals in those days," said Russell, "and after the paper had gone to press, we would sit and talk for hours and hours on sociological matters. Brisbane at that time was at least as radical as I was. I heard him say on many occasions that he was more than willing to sacrifice himself for the cause of the common people. In fact, he declared himself willing to go to jail for them. Of course he wanted his job and he was desirous of making as much money as possible. But, nevertheless, there was still some of the idealism of his father left in him. Arthur radiated optimism and believed that basic social reforms would soon be established." Russell was of the opinion that Brisbane possessed no real fundamental knowledge of economics or of socialism, though he wrote and spoke glibly about them at all times.

Henry George, the single taxer, was then at the height

of his power. Brisbane met him frequently at his father's home. The Californian reformer and the old Fourierist were close friends. In later years, Arthur confessed to intimates that it was Henry George's analysis of the way in which property values rise because of increased populations that led him to speculate in real estate to such a large degree. "What I know about real estate and real estate values, I learned from the teachings of Henry George, though he was opposed to these things and I am in favor of them."

Another young man was at this time making his personality felt in New York. He was the newly appointed head of the New York Police Force, Theodore Roosevelt—an ambitious, energetic, and colorful fellow. Here was a character for Brisbane to feature, and he did. His opening lines about the new police commissioner began: "Sing, heavenly muse, the sad dejection of our poor policemen!

"We have a real Police Commissioner. His name is Theodore Roosevelt. His teeth are big and white, his eyes small and piercing, his voice rasping. He makes our policemen feel as the little froggies did when the stork came to rule them. His heart is full of reform, and a policeman in full uniform, with helmet, revolver, and night club, is no more to him than a plain, everyday human being....."

During the summer of 1892, a bloody strike occurred at Homestead, Pennsylvania. The use of Pinkertons as well as the Coal and Iron Police (private agents hired by the steel and coal companies) opened a new chapter in the relations of labor and capital. Most of the metropolitan papers took the side of the corporation. The *World* supported the striking men and Brisbane wrote many articles on their behalf. The "respectable" element condemned Pulitzer and his paper for this action.

Two years later, when another great labor conflagration

broke out—this time in Chicago—between the American Railway Unions and the Pullman Car Corporation, Colonel Charles H. Jones, who was then editor of the *World*, thought it timely to support the strikers and did so. The United States Court denounced the action of the strikers and issued an injunction against them, and Federal military forces were sent in to the strike area. Jones wrote a vigorous editorial entitled, "Government by Injunction" in which he denounced the action of the courts and unreservedly supported the position of Eugene V. Debs, the leader of the striking railway men. This was too much for the other responsible men on the *World*. Carvalho, Brisbane and others notified Pulitzer and Pulitzer put his foot down. From that time on Jones was permitted to write no more editorials. The *World* was prepared to continue its fight for social reforms, but it was not going to become involved in labor disputes.

To Pulitzer must go the credit for preventing a possible war between the United States and Britain in 1895, growing out of the dispute with reference to the boundaries of Venezuela. Jingoism was running high. Editors, preachers, and public officials were beating their breasts and demanding an armed showdown with Britain. Pulitzer threw all of his weight against these tendencies, and Brisbane, ever faithful, became an anti-jingoist once Pulitzer had given the cue.

Pulitzer fought the Wall Street crowd, too. He forced the United States Treasury to make direct bond sales to the public. In this way he saved the Government millions of dollars. The issue of $100,000,000 was over-subscribed six times by the public. Mr. Pulitzer personally offered to buy a million dollars' worth of the bonds at whatever price was demanded. He got them at $114. Within a few days it was obvious that at least fifty thousand dollars profit would be made on them. This troubled Mr. Pulitzer, since he did not wish to make a profit. He sought ways of ridding himself of this unearned increment. His biographer tells how a council was called of all the wise heads in the office to advise him.

"All sorts of queer suggestions were put forth, including one from Arthur Brisbane that the unfortunate incubus should be given to West Point Military Academy, which of course could receive no gifts. Finally, after two hours of wearisome debate, the business manager remarked, speaking for the first time, 'Why not keep it?' This advice was duly presented to the agitated gentlemen at Lakewood—and accepted!"

It was approximately at this time that Brisbane was first introduced to the writings of Shakespeare. He was well versed in French, German, and Continental literature, but woefully ignorant of English and American, according to his friend, Charles Edward Russell.

"I don't know what prevented Brisbane from reading Shakespeare, though at that time he had a definite anti-British bias," said Russell. "I, myself, was a Shakespeare enthusiast. Finally, after much discussion, I prevailed upon him to read A. W. Schlegel's book of lectures on Shakespeare.

The young editor had long desired to see his name in print at the head of a special editorial column. The column conducted by his father in the *New York Tribune* nearly half a century earlier intrigued him; and it had been effective. There was no doubt about that. His own style of writing was a decided improvement over his father's involved and heavy sentences. He had learned much from both Dana and Pulitzer. From Dana, himself, came the idea of constant iteration and reiteration of the basic ideas he wanted to put over; from one of Dana's editorial writers and book reviewers, Willard O. Bartlett, he had learned how to use simple words, short sentences, and even shorter paragraphs. This last was, of course, in direct violation of the long, involved sentence structure of the "good" writers of the period. But it brought readers! Readers meant a following! A following meant success! And success meant more money!

From Pulitzer he learned how to judge social movements, when to support them, and when to withdraw from them; in other words, how to combine the fire of the agitator with the tact of a politician.

The idea of a column set boldly on page one, column one, haunted Brisbane. He wanted to comment on the happenings of the day in short, pithy paragraphs. Nor did he wish to be tied down by the prevailing editorial policy. He wanted to say whatever he felt like saying, whether it coincided with the *World's* policy or not. Above all, he wanted *his name* to appear on the masthead of the column. The anonymity of the editorial "we" displeased him. Brisbane wished to speak out in the first person singular.

Time and time again, Brisbane asked permission from Pulitzer to sign an editorial column either on the morning or the evening *World*. But Pulitzer was adament. No one but himself would determine the policy of the paper. There could be no two editorial policies. Each time he refused Brisbane's request, saying: "You may do features or news stories; you may travel to any part of the globe on assignments. But these newspapers belong to me and so long as I live, no one will express an independent editorial opinion in my newspapers."

Pulitzer spent more and more of his time aboard his yacht

traveling to the far corners of the world. On one of these occasions, according to John K. Winkler, young Brisbane decided to test his pet idea. He was in complete charge of the *Evening World* and he thought: "I know my idea is a good one. If I can do one or two of these columns and get away with them, Mr. Pulitzer may let me keep on." So he wrote one column, a second, a dozen. They were placed each day on page one in column one of the *Evening World*. Weeks went by. Brisbane was beginning to congratulate himself. Then came a furious cable from a European port: 'Stop that column at once. I don't want the *Evening World* to have an editorial policy. If you want good editorials, rewrite those in the *Morning World*.' "

Brisbane obeyed, but he was very much disgruntled. What saved the day for him was the entry into New York Journalism of another crusader from the west—Mr. William Randolph Hearst.

Willie Hearst took over his father's political organ, the *San Francisco Examiner*, on the same day that George Hearst assumed the senatorial toga on behalf of the State of California in the nation's capital. Willie Hearst had studied the spectacular rise of Joseph Pulitzer and determined to follow in his footsteps. Hearst had unbounded energy, imagination, and a desire to do the unusual and the spectacular. Above all, he had an unlimited bank account at his disposal. His outstanding success on the Pacific Coast soon made him the newspaper sensation of the day.

Long before he ventured to try his hand at New York journalism, Hearst had obtained permission to use the *World's* special news service. He established offices on the eleventh floor of the Pulitzer Building and paneled its walls and fitted it with furniture made of California redwood.

Albert Pulitzer, brother of Joseph, had founded the *Morning Journal* in New York a few years previously. It was a sheet featuring back stairs gossip and the more sensational doings of New York aristocracy. Soon it had built a circulation of 100,000. Albert Pulitzer wisely sold it to John R. McLean for a million dollars. McLean, who owned the *Cincinnati Enquirer*, tried to make of the *Journal* a respectable, middle western type of paper. The sensational features were dropped and the price was raised to three cents per copy. Disaster followed. Circulation fell to 20,000. By September Mr. McLean was ready to sell at almost any price. Hearst got the *Journal*, together with a small German edition, *Das Morgen Journal*, thrown in, for $180,000.

The new owner at once reduced the price of the *Journal* to a penny, thus becoming a competitor of relatively weak papers. He brought to New York the best of his San Francisco staff, and began at once to copy both the size and format of the *World*. From the start, he imitated it both in technique and content. Within three months Hearst had spent an additional half million dollars on the paper, and restored it to the circulation it had under Albert Pulitzer.

Soon secret negotiations were being carried on in the *Examiner* office of Mr. Pulitzer's building to take away from him the entire staff of the Sunday *World* under Morrill Goddard. They were offered terms so much better than those given them by Pulitzer that one day late in January, 1896, they moved out en masse to join the *Journal* staff. Pulitzer was both surprised and enraged. His Sunday *World* was a money-maker, with its large type and profuse illustrations. But Goddard's specialties were crime, underwear, and pseudo-science. The curdling details of a murder were related by him with great gusto. Given the slightest clue he could build up all the neurotic elements in a sex story. So far as science was concerned, he could devise theatrical presentations better than any other editor. Instructions on how to handle a Sunday supplement page ran about as follows: "Suppose it's Halley's comet. First you have a half page of decorations showing the comet with historical pictures of previous appearances thrown in. If you can work a pretty girl into the picture, so much the better. If not, get some good nightmare idea, like the inhabitants of Mars watching it pass. Then you want a quarter of a page of big type sentences. Then four inches of story, written off the bat. Then a picture of Professor Halley down here and another of Professor Lowell up there, and a two column boxed brief containing a scientific opinion, which nobody will understand, to give it class."

Brisbane had been fascinated by Goddard's inventiveness. Pulitzer, too, had recognized his abilities, but he tried to keep the sensational within some bounds of journalistic respectability.

Carvalho and Pulitzer held a council of war. Their staff must be induced to return. They were offered much better conditions than those promised by Hearst. They returned—but for a mere twenty-four hours, since Hearst, not to be outdone, resumed his check-book argument once more. For a second time the staff disappeared in direction of the Journal office, never to return. In desperation Pulitzer offered the job of Sunday editor to Brisbane, who immediately accepted. "Mr. Pulitzer asked me to take charge of the Sunday *World* and 'hire anybody in New York you want to.' In ten weeks our readers were increasing at an average of 11,000 each Sunday. Pulitzer's delight was intense."

The battle was on. The *Examiner* had to give up its office in the Pulitzer building. Brisbane with carte blanche to go ahead threw more crime and sex and pseudo-science into the Sunday paper than Goddard had ever dreamed about. The art staff concocted the most weird and bizarre illustrations know to date. Bold face type, italics and exclamation marks were scattered freely throughout each page. The era of yellow journalism had begun.

Remarking about this period many years later, Brisbane chuckled: "Circulation came so easily, he (Pulitzer), as sometimes happens with owners, had an attack of 'respectability.' Both the Sunday *World* and the Sunday *American* were excluded from certain clubs. I had no objection to this, since it compelled club members to buy the paper individually.

"Mr. Pulitzer did not like it, and decided to overcome objections of clubhouse committees by displaying such intense respectability as would impress them. He sent me this message: 'Please have on the front page of the magazine in next Sunday's *World* the fine portrait of General O. O. Howard, head of the army, done by Mortimer, and an interview with Howard.' Mortimer made fine portraits in pen and ink. General O. O. Howard would have talked fine platitudes. The following Monday I sent Mr. Pulitzer this telegram: 'Sorry we did not have that O. O. Howard picture and interview. Instead, on the front page, I had a wonderful picture of Kate Swan in the electric chair and circulation is up 15,000.' Mr. Pulitzer telegraphed back: 'You know perfectly well I am blind, and must rely on you. Congratulations.' "

But no matter how rapidly the circulation of the *World* grew, that of the *Journal* grew even more rapidly. It published huge advertisements in all of the regular papers and in trade organs. Bill boards were erected on every vacant lot. Sandwich men paraded the streets spreading the legend of the *Journal's* merits. And the Hearst staff was told to go the limit in their fight for supremacy. They did. Hearst himself, it is estimated, spent within a few months' time, nearly two million dollars in this campaign.

Goddard went the limit: "Using streamer headlines and splashing pen and ink drawings all over the page, he now went in for crime and underwear on a scale to which even New York was wholly unaccustomed. He sent Alan Dale, the dramatic critic, a minor acquisition from the *World*, to interview Anna Held, the French commedienne, and the carefully staged meeting was reported under the title: MLLE. ANNA HELD RECEIVES ALAN DALE, ATTIRED IN A NITIE. Under Goddard's inspiration, Dale's dramatic criticism became largely a comparative study of shoulders, bosoms and legs. To introduce a saving romanticism in the midst of the salacity, Winifred Bonfils wrote articles under such heads as WHY YOUNG GIRLS KILL THEMSELVES OR STRANGE THINGS WOMEN DO FOR LOVE. And the whole enterprise was sanctified by Goddard's frequent use of Biblical references—the origin of the Hearst custom of running Bible texts at the top of the editorial page—while the paper ran riot with pseudo-science, 'just to give it class.'"

Pulitzer, in desperation, did the same thing Bennett had done to fight the *World's* competition years earlier. He reduced the price of his paper one cent on Monday, February 10, 1896. The *World* circulation momentarily leapt upward, increasing 88,000 in a single day! It was believed that it would reach the million mark. With this move, Pulitzer thought he would wreck the *New York Herald* and stop Hearst's *Journal*. Alas, nothing of the kind happened. The smaller papers were crushed, but Hearst gained. Pulitzer increased his advertising rates. As a result his big advertisers reduced their copy. The increased circulation merely put a severe dent in the profits of the paper. Years later, in one of his musing moments, Pulitzer remarked: "When I came to New York, Mr. Bennett reduced the price of his paper and raised his advertising rates—all to my advantage. When Mr. Hearst came to New York, I did the same. I wonder why—in view of my experience?"

Fortune favored the young Californian in more ways than one. That year, 1896, was an election year. The Democrats, much to their own amazement, nominated the Nebraska firebrand, William Jennings Bryan. The Metropolitan papers almost without exception, including Mr. Pulitzer's *World*, threw their support to McKinley, the Republican. Hearst alone campaigned for Bryan and won additional tens of thousands of readers from the poor and discontented. Brisbane had been for Bryan and kept urging Pulitzer that it would be a good tactics to support Bryan, especially from the point of view of newspaper circulation. Pulitzer refused to heed his proposal.

Not content with those whom he had already taken from Pulitzer, Hearst continued his raids. Carvalho went over—a serious loss to Pulitzer. In August, 1897, Charles Edward Russell joined the migration. "Brisbane objected strenuously to this action on my part. I had been with Hearst but a short time when Brisbane took me out to his home at Hempstead, Long Island, and had an all-night session with me.

" 'Charlie, don't be a fool,' said Brisbane.

" 'What makes you think I'm a fool? Hearst is giving me more than Pulitzer did.'

" 'It's not the question of money alone,' said Arthur. 'You've got to take a long view on this matter. Both of us are young. We've gone far but we can't afford to spoil our future.'

"Thus we argued hour after hour. Brisbane was eloquent and logical and had me almost convinced that I had made a mistake. At one point he tried to clinch the argument by stating: 'Such an unknown upstart as Hearst can never succeed here in New York. Why, just look at the difference in the heads of Pulitzer and Hearst. Jo Pulitzer has a head as long as that of a horse. Compare it with Hearst's! Then you'll realize how obvious it is that Pulitzer will lick Hearst in short order. Quit your job as soon as possible and return to your position with us. Remaining for any length of time with that California millionaire is plainly a case of journalistic suicide.'

"I agreed to give the matter serious consideration but said I couldn't quit just then. By the end of the year it would be possible. Imagine my amazement when, less than six weeks later, Brisbane himself came over to work for the man whom he had declared a journalistic upstart and who would surely fail in his fight with the great Pulitzer."

5

HEARSTMAN

GEOGRAPHICALLY THE *World* and the *Journal* were close together. In almost every other respect they were miles apart. The short trip which Brisbane took when he left the Pulitzer building for the last time to go to work for Hearst (the *Journal* was then located in the *Tribune* Building) was of momentous importance to him as well as to Hearst. The Brisbane of the *Sun* and the *World* would soon be forgotten. The name of Arthur Brisbane, whose editorials were to become household property for two generations of Americans, was to be linked irrevocably with that of William Randolph Hearst.

The millionaire publisher and the young editor complemented each other perfectly. They saw eye to eye on most problems. Hearst's father had taught him that you can buy almost anyone. Young Hearst had the money with which to do the buying. Brisbane, on the other hand, was willing to be bought. Mr. Hearst's fingertip control on the Brisbane editorial and newspaper outlook was complete and efficient. In a second, he could reverse himself on any issue and write with equal fervor for either side, or take a fence-straddling position if that was desired.

Many stories have been told about the reason Brisbane left Pulitzer. Mrs. Fremont Older, the authorized Hearst biographer, says it was due to a spasm of economy on the part of Pulitzer, who reduced Brisbane's salary. According to her version, Pulitzer said: "It oughtn't to cost very much to get socialist editorials written." To which Brisbane replied: "It would cost a good deal to get them well written by a man who believes in them." Brisbane at the time was getting $15,000 a year.

John Winkler, on the other hand, says that Brisbane was disgruntled because Pulitzer would not let him publish his signed front page editorials. The transfer to Hearst's dominions was quite accidental. Brisbane had sauntered into the Café Martin, where he ran into Hearst. They chatted together for a while when Mr. Hearst said: "Mr. Brisbane, I wish you were with us. If you will come over, you may name your own salary. Suppose we talk it over tomorrow." Brisbane agreed and met Hearst at the latter's bachelor apartment in the Hoffman House, where the arrangements were worked out.

In an interview with Mr. F. T. Stockbridge, editor of the *American Press*, in April, 1931, Brisbane himself tells this story: "I did not see Mr. Hearst when I went to work for him. I don't think he cared to see me. I had been rather disagreeable in various ways, hiring away men like Davenport and Alfred Henry Lewis, then saying to them: 'Go back and get more money, I don't need you, the *Journal* does.' Whether Mr. Hearst knew about that and was annoyed, I didn't know."

According to Will Irwin, it was Brisbane who approached Hearst for the job. He offered to take charge of the *Evening Journal* for $100 a week plus a dollar a week increase for every thousand a week he added to the circulation.

Finally, in an interview given to Henry F. Pringle, less than three weeks before his death, Brisbane remarked that he was discontented with his job on the *World*. He saw Charles M. Palmer, Hearst's legal representative, who offered him a job at eight thousand a year, which was sever thousand dollars less than he was then getting from Pulitzer. Brisbane had also cabled Bennett with reference to buying the *Evening Telegram,* which he had just scrapped. Bennett refused to sell. Instead he offered him a job at twelve thousand dollars. Hearst was obviously the coming man, so Brisbane threw away his job with Pulitzer and his chance to work for Bennett, and took the job on the *Journal.*

"I'm leaving to join Mr. Hearst," he muttered to the World's cashier, Frank McCabe, as he drew his last pay check from Pulitzer, adding, "I'm not appreciated here."

Arthur Brisbane's agreement with Pulitzer provided he could draw in advance up to ten thousand dollars of his salary. He owed, so he claimed, eight thousand at the time he quit his job. He would work for Hearst if he could get in advance the salary for one year. This was agreed to. Shortly thereafter, an arrangement was made whereby he received a bonus for increased circulation of one thousand dollars per ten thousand increase in net paid circulation.

"At the time I took the job," remarked Brisbane, "I thought Hearst didn't know much about the newspaper business. I was wrong."

Brisbane wanted to function on an evening paper. But the *Evening World* was not doing so well. Hearst declared, "I'm not an evening paper man. I think I'll scrap that little sheet." To this, Brisbane replied "I *am* an evening paper man. I've been building up the *Evening World* and I started the *Evening Sun.*" Hearst consented. "All right, go ahead."

Several weeks elapsed before Brisbane saw Hearst again. Meanwhile, he received messages from his new employer urging him to be in his office by six o'clock in the evening. To these, Brisbane shot back word: "I'm here from 4:30 A. M. to 4:30 P. M. Then I go home to write more editorials and plan the work for the following day."

It had been customary for reporters on evening papers to come to work about nine o'clock. Brisbane changed that. Not only did he himself report at 4:30 in the morning, but his staff had to come at the same time. He scooped all other papers on important news items. The *Evening Journal* was on the street hours before the other afternoon papers. This innovation by Brisbane multiplied circulation. Soon other papers were compelled to follow. Ultimately this method became so chaotic that evening papers were on the street at six in the morning, while morning papers were out at six in the evening. Not until 1935 was an agreement reached between the morning and evening papers of New York regulating their hours of sales.

Brisbane told his secretary, Mr. Flynn, when he took charge of the *Evening Journal*, that he believed he could make it pass the *Evening World* in circulation within seven years. At the time this was said, the *Evening World* had 325,000 circulation; the *Evening Journal*, 40,000. Brisbane vowed he'd drink nothing stronger than tea and milk until the circulations were identical.

Within seven weeks, the job had been accomplished, to the amazement of the editor, publisher, and Newspaper Row. The following spring, the *Evening Journal* attained a net paid circulation of 1,300,000—the highest in its entire history. Mr. Brisbane's bonus arrangement stepped up his income to almost fabulous heights. "My salary remained at eight thousand dollars, but I remember that I made a commission of nine thousand dollars in January, 1898; large commissions in other months, and finally, in one month, I think it was June, I made twenty-three thousand dollars—all within six months of my taking charge of the paper. I called off the commission arrangement and Mr. Hearst increased my salary. But I forget whether he made it twenty-six thousand dollars or fifty thousand dollars. It was fifty thousand dollars, I recollect, inside of the first year, which was considered a good salary in those days." No other salaried newspaperman's income approached it.

In view of the fact that Hearst spent more than three million dollars during the first three years of his ownership of the Journal, it is difficult to comprehend the following statement by Brisbane:

"The interesting thing about the *Journal's* success under the management of Mathews and myself, with S. S. Carvalho as publisher, was the demonstration that newspapers don't get circulation from spending money. Expenses were cut ruthlessly because we felt it was necessary. I wrote the editorials, which I had never done before, in order to save the expense of an editorial writer. I decided to write them, as it took only fifteen minutes a day, after I had tried in vain to get Vincent W. Byars, a brilliant man, from St. Louis, to come and do that work."

No one who visited the *Evening Journal's* offices in the early fall of 1896, would have surmised that that paper would soon become the world's greatest in circulation. It was a squalid shop occupying the second floor of the Tribune Building. The room was filled with old desks and typewriters. Young men in shirt sleeves dashed about in a nervous scurry. At one end of the room was an elevated platform protected by a wire netting. There sat the editor-in-chief, Arthur Brisbane, pecking at his old fashioned invisible action Remington typewriter, mapping out his campaigns for the day or the week and summoning subordinates for the work to be done. According to one of his reporters of those days, "Brisbane was the czar of the paper. Next to him was Carvalho, the publisher—a satanic appearing gentleman who walked with a limp and raised Russian wolf hounds. It was a contemptible, scurrilous, lying sheet. Brisbane aimed for the tenement house trade by raising hell about the oppressed. He startled the town on one occasion with 'Poor Old Moses. He didn't have an icebox!' The piece was an attack on food dealers who endangered health by improper refrigeration. At other times he carried sensational stories about the coal miners. Fake stories were run. Imaginary mothers in the coal fields described their pangs of starvation. Trains were run to relieve victims of floods. Petitions were circulated—the *Journal* was always strong on petitions. Nor must we forget the 'womanhood in distress' stunt. Many an astonished prostitute got out of jail because of this policy. The whole idea culminated in the Hearstian campaigns for outraged womanhood on the eve of the Spanish-American War."

Dorothy Dix, whose advice to the lovelorn has lured many thousand readers to the Hearst press, has described that early office as she recalled it, "with bare floor, its unpainted board walls, its comfortless desks above which an avalanche of old papers always threatened destruction, and its litter of books in three or four languages. It made an incongruous background for the man who sat in the midst of the confusion—handsome and young and with still something of his gardenia and silk-hat days when he was the pet of London society and the boy wonder of the newspaper world about him."

Brisbane worked like a man possessed, determined to succeed. If circulation were to be gained in large quantities, it must come from the large immigrant population—the Irish, the Germans, the Poles, the Jews, the Italians. Many of them were semi-literate. They did the hard work of the city and had neither time nor inclination to read lengthy, ponderous articles written in stylistically correct English. The obvious thing to do was to use the most simple words, the most simple sentences, the most simple paragraphs; large type, italics, capital letters, and above all, pictures—lots of pictures for those who did little reading. The whirlwind editor developed what is called "the double-truck picture", which covers two pages. He used this for the first time to print a picture of a baby buffalo, in life size. The smash head on his news stories soon used up the largest type available in the Journal's printing office. Brisbane gleefully announced that he needed still larger type. So he had wooden type made, seven inches high. Even Hearst was amazed at what his new editor did with the *Journal*. But since the paper grew in circulation and influence, he was ready to permit Brisbane to do whatever he wished.

Brisbane delighted in the fact that janitors and elevator men and other plain people read and enjoyed and wrangled over his articles. On the streets, in the parks, and in the street cars, he watched the people to see whether or not his articles and editorials were read by them. When they were, he was pleased; when not, he felt they were a failure. Being a practical man, he used to try out his editorials on his German housekeeper and later he always kept her in mind when writing: "If I think she would miss the point of a sentence, I write it over again in clearer form with fewer big words."

To the reporters he constantly preached the virtue of simplicity. "There's no need ever to use a word of more than three syllables in a newspaper. Remember that a newspaper is mostly read by very busy people, or by very tired people, or by very uneducated people none of whom are going to hunt up a dictionary to find out what you mean.

"And never forget that if you don't hit a newspaper reader between the eyes with your first sentence, there is no need of writing a second one."

Just before Brisbane joined the payroll, Hearst purchased a special color press able to print from four to sixteen pages in color. This mechanical device, together with the first-string writers already obtained by Hearst, enable the Sunday *Journal* to blossom forth with an enlarged comic supplement. "Eight pages of irridescent, polychromous effulgence that makes the rainbow look like a lead pipe." The Sunday *World* was called a weak, wish-washy four page comic suffering from a "desolate waste of black". The *American Magazine*, a sixteen page addition to the Sunday *Journal*, soon appeared—forerunner of the later *American Weekly*.

"While others talk, the *Journal* acts" became the new slogan of the Hearst-Brisbane combination. They denounced predatory wealth and began legal proceedings against corporations allegedly dipping into public funds. They obtained an injunction to prevent the Brooklyn Aldermen from granting a franchise to a gas company. In December 1897, the *Journal* could proudly announce that the gas franchise grab in Brooklyn, the death terminal of the Brooklyn Bridge, the dilatory work on Fifth Avenue, the $10,000,000 light monopoly in New York had been stopped by its energetic action.

The staff of the *Journal* now comprised more feature writers and reporters than had ever before been assembled on any American newspaper. Hearst had been lavish with his father's money in luring them away from other publishers. There were Richard Harding Davis, Alfred Henry Lewis, Edward W. Townsend, and Rudolph Block contributing to the magazine section. Others included such well known novelists as Edgar Saltus, Julian Hawthorne, Mark Twain, Bob Davis, later editor of Munsey's Magazine, as well as James L. Ford, A. C. Wheeler, Henry W. Fischer,

Julius Chambers, and W. J. Henderson with Sam Chamberlain directing field operations.

Hearst had a special "wrecking crew" as well as a "murder squad" to solve crimes in advance of police action. The report of a big news story about to break would cause a mass exodus from the *Journal* office, from editor to office boy. Bicycles, carriages, hansom cabs or whatever contraption was available would be seized upon as Sam Chamberlain's boys rushed into action. The hunt for news is well described by Ferdinand Lundberg, who writes: "Outriders on cycles rang warnings, the horses' hoofs struck sparks from the cobblestones. After Hearst came to Park Row, the locality attracted the most reckless of the city's cabmen, and these were inspired under the influence of heavy tips, to procure former fire and cavalry horses. Some bystanders always fell in with the dramatic spirit of these representatives of 'New Journalism', as Hearst called his farrago—messenger boys, delivery wagon drivers, and stray dogs would follow pell-mell after the Hearst legions. Hearst himself would often come leaping, long-legged, wild-eyed, intent, out of the Tribune Building, and hop either into his French road burner or a handy gig, to be whisked like a field marshal to the scene of battle."

New York City's election of 1897 promised a display of fireworks. The Republican state boss, Thomas C. Platt, had extended the mayor's term of office to four years and looked forward with certainty to a loyal Republican's capturing the office. His candidate was General Benjamin F. Tracy of Brooklyn. The Tammany group nominated Robert A. Van Wyck. Independents rallied behind Seth Low, then president of Columbia College, who had served two terms as Mayor of Brooklyn. The radicals, progressives and single-taxers united upon Henry George. Pulitzer backed Low, but it was generally believed that Hearst and Brisbane would throw their support behind Henry George, for they boosted him and praised him during the early days of the campaign. But at the last moment, a secret deal was negotiated with Tammany. Brisbane turned upon George, denouncing him in his editorials as a fanatic, and called upon the good citizens of New York to rally behind Van Wyck. Van Wyck was elected, which at once gave to the Hearst-Brisbane combination an inside track on municipal politics, municipal advertising, and municipal graft.

The part played by Hearst and Brisbane in fomenting the Spanish-American War has been dealt with in numerous articles and by every biographer of Hearst. At least one of these biographers in a long drawn out process of questionable logic supplemented by circumstantial evidence arrived at the conclusion that Hearst was responsible for blowing up the United States Battleship Maine. Such a statement, according to Charles Edward Russell, who was city editor of the Journal at the time of the sinking of the Maine, is "preposterous and beneath the dignity of serious authorship." But that Hearst and Brisbane used the Cuban insurrection to stir up hatred against Spain is well known. It boosted the Journal circulation to an all-time high and raised (or lowered) yellow journalism to a new level.

The desire for American expansion into the West Indies and south of the Rio Grande was no new thing. It had been advocated by influential groups since the early 1840's. When troubles between the Cubans and their Spanish oppressors started anew in 1893-94, Hearst's *San Francisco Examiner* at once advocated American intervention as the only natural solution. When he transferred his activities from the Golden Gate to New York City, he merely continued the same policy in the *Journal* in a more sensational manner. For New York was a scant two days' journey from the war torn islands, and the Cuban insurgents had established in New York a headquarters from which their whispering campaign against the Spanish Government was developing momentum. American big business generally was not especially interested in Cuban affairs. But to an enterprising newspaper publisher trying to gain the widest possible circulation, and who, at the same time, had the typical schoolboy conception of war as a romantic enterprise, this was a heaven-sent bit of news. The campaign on behalf of the poor downtrodden Cubans had been well developed by the *Journal* long before Arthur Brisbane joined its staff. President Cleveland didn't want a war, nor did McKinley after he entered the White House.

The continuous buildup of atrocity stories, supplemented by sensational photographs, some real, mostly faked, in the columns of the *Journal*, built an increasing resentment against Spain on the part of hundreds of thousands of American citizens. It was through the columns of the Journal that the American public learned that "the daily practice of the Spanish jailers is to take several prisoners from the fort and shoot them"; that Spanish troops had a habit of "beating Cuban prisoners to death;" that they specialized in attacks upon unarmed peasants, women and children. The commanding General of the Spanish forces was dubbed "Butcher Weyler." Circulation boomed. Within a year after Hearst took over the ownership of the *Journal*, its circulation had increased from 77,239 to 430,410.

Pulitzer, sensing belatedly the circulation to be built upon the Spanish atrocities in Cuba, followed Hearst's lead. He sent his most able correspondents, Sylvester Scovel and William Shaw Bowen, to cover that field. Hearst, too, placed his best reporters and artists on the job. There was Richard

Harding Davis and the artist, Frederick Remington, as well as Senator-elect Fernando DeSoto Money, as special Journal commissioner. James Creelman covered the events at the Spanish Court in Madrid.

When Remington protested to Hearst that he could not draw scenes the paper wanted because they were non-existent, his boss cabled the order: "You make the pictures, I'll make the war." Remington obeyed.

Davis had reported that a girl suspected of carrying secret messages through the lines to the insurgents had been examined by women searchers. Remington drew a picture showing a half naked Cuban girl being stripped by lustful Spanish officers. The *Journal* changed the text of the Davis report to conform to the sensational drawing. The girl indignantly denied the whole story, which Pulitzer printed gleefully as indicative of the reliability of the *Journal's* news. But the damage had already been done. Public opinion was aroused; it wanted atrocity stories.

Arthur Brisbane had written hundreds of headlines about Spanish atrocities in Cuba while still on the staff of the *World*. His own advice in the editorials written a few years earlier on the Venezuelan crisis was conveniently forgotten. The smashing headlines, the lurid pictures, the front page stories which he now helped to concoct, were soon having their effect upon him. Arthur Brisbane began to believe his own stories—to accept as facts the illustrations made by his artists at his direction. Working with Hearst he became as ardent a jingo as Hearst himself. He could and did whole heartedly throw himself into the campaign against Spain.

Soon McKinley himself was charged with "the betrayal of Cuba."

In August, 1897, the daughter of a prominent Cuban insurgent, Evangelina Cisneros, was removed to the Havana prison from the penal settlement on the Isle of Pines. It was a grand story made to order for the *Journal*. Seniorita Cisneros and her tortures at the hands of the Spaniards became the talk of the country. She was pictured, "as ignorant of the world, as cloistered as a nun—delicate, refined, sensitive, and unused to hardship." The tales of how she was compelled to scrub floors and sleep on bare boards with outcast negresses until, shattered in health, she was threatened with an early death, were repeated again and again in all the bold face type that the *Journal's* composing rooms could produce. The editorial indignation of the *Journal* knew no bounds. "Can America stand idly by?" challenged the *Journal*. "The unspeakable crass fate to which Weyler has doomed an innocent girl whose only crime is that she has defended her honor against a beast in uniform, has sent a shudder of horror through the American people."

Brisbane joined the staff in time to aid in enlisting "the noblest representatives of American womanhood" in a campaign to stop the execution of the sentence upon this innocent girl. Julia Ward Howe, a grand-niece of George Washington, the wives of Senator Mark Hanna and Secretary Sherman, as well as the widows of Ulysses S. Grant and Jefferson Davis joined in cablegrams to the Queen Regent of Spain and the Pope at Rome. The war spirit swept over America; and the frantic efforts of Pulitzer's reporters to check the story and expose it for the large measure of fraud it contained, could do little to stop the emotional onrush.

On October seventh, Evangelina escaped from prison. She had been, strangely enough, rescued by a *Journal* reporter and was soon on her way to America, where the *Journal* arranged a monster reception for her in Madison Square Gardens. Young Brisbane dashed madly from desk to desk issuing orders, inventing new sensational methods of handling the news, and writing flamboyant editorials. It was a happy time in his life.

The Spanish minister, Dupuy de Lome, had written a letter of Jose Canalejas, the unofficial Spanish agent in Cuba, in which he referred to McKinley's annual message to Congress as showing "once more what McKinley is: weak and catering to the rabble and, besides, a low politician who desires to leave a door open to himself and to stand well with the jingos of his party." An insurgent sympathizer had obtained a copy and the *Journal* obtained the exclusive facsimile rights. Brisbane played it to the limit. In his usual scare-head manner he wanted to know what McKinley was going to do about it? He charged that the Spanish minister had committed the "greatest offense of which a diplomatic officer can be accused." The *Journal* clamored for the immediate recall of de Lome, and when word got out that he was going to return to Spain, the exaltation of the *Journal* was expressed in verse:

> Dupuy de Lome, Dupuy de Lome, what's this I hear of you!
> Have you been throwing mud again, is what they're saying true?
> Get out, I say, get out before I start to fight.
> Just pack a few possessions and take a boat for home
> I would not like my boot to use, but,—oh—get out, de Lome.

Brisbane polished off the insult to deLome by one last story which he planned personally.

For some time the rumor that de Lome's wife had been more than friendly with Senator Hale had been common gossip. Senator Hale had refused to be browbeaten by the demands of the *Journal* and the *World*. As soon as deLome and his wife had boarded the boat, Arthur Brisbane wrote the Journal's headline and had it set up in the largest type available. And as deLome and his wife sailed out of New York Harbor an hour later, the Journal was on the streets with the banner head:

THE QUESTION OF THE HOUR—WILL HALE SAIL?

The sinking of the Maine meant bigger headlines and more audacious editorials from both Brisbane and Hearst. The country was now fully aroused. It was merely a question of days before the war would be declared. There was little sleep for Brisbane during the fevered days following the Maine disaster. Orders were issued every few minutes. Headlines were run in black and red, and the circulation crossed the million mark for the first time in American history.

Brisbane wrote the smash headlines when the news about the Maine reached his office. THE WAR SHIP MAINE WAS SPLIT IN TWO BY AN ENEMY SECRET INFERNAL MACHINE. Reiterating the charge the next day, The *Journal* shrieked: *The Maine was destroyed by treachery*. Then followed day by day smash heads such as these:

RECRUITING ALREADY BEGUN; TROOPS IMPATIENT TO MARCH

CITIZENS DEMAND CONGRESS SHALL TAKE ACTION

CITIZEN SOLDIERS EVERYWHERE AROUSED BY THE WAR SPIRIT

THE UNION ABLAZE WITH PATRIOTISM

EVERY STATE READY TO SPRING TO ARMS AT A MOMENT'S NOTICE

McKinley's failure to act at once brought down scathing abuse upon him. His advisor, Mark Hanna, was caricatured in the guise of the goddess of liberty. His robe was plastered with dollar signs and he held a ticker tape ribbon in his hand. Another cartoon represented Uncle Sam sweeping from a ship's deck a lot of rubbish labeled, "McKinley," "Wall Street," "Woodford," "The Twaddle," "Fake Ultimatum," "Peace with Dishonor," "Cowardly Foreign Policy," and "Peace at any Price." Soon the *Journal* came out bespangled with little American flags. This was Hearst's own idea, to be repeated later but without great effectiveness during the World War.

Pulitzer could not keep up with the inventions and fakes staged by Brisbane in the *Journal*. Indignantly, he exclaimed that the *Journal* war news was "written by fools for fools."

When ex-President Cleveland was asked to serve on a committee arranged by Hearst to provide a memorial to the victims of the Maine disaster he wrote: "I decline to allow my sorrow for those who died on the Maine to be perverted to an advertising scheme for the *New York Journal*." Theodore Roosevelt, then Assistant Secretary of the Navy, was charged with endorsing the work of the *Journal*. This he denied. "I never have given a certificate of character to the *Journal*."

The cupidity of the American business man was not forgotten by the *Journal*. It announced that shrewd American speculators were traveling up and down the Island taking up options and making outright purchases at prices so low as to promise an enormous return in the future. "The exploitation of Cuba by American capital is a certainty."

Godkin, editor of the *New York Post*, was the only New York publisher who had kept his head. But the *Post's* circulation was small and Godkin's influence necessarily limited. He denounced the methods used by both the *World* and the *Journal* to promote their circulation schemes at the expense of the people. "A yellow journal office," he remarked editorially, "is probably the nearest approach, in atmosphere, to Hell existing in any Christian state. A better place to prepare a young man for eternal damnation than a yellow journal office does not exist."

War was declared. The yellow journals, with Hearst and Brisbane in the lead, rushed tugs, and yachts loaded down with reporters, artists, and cameramen to the probable scene of battle long before the troops arrived. Hearst himself journeyed down to Cuba. Brisbane remained to concoct a new type of headline, the opening line of which, in huge type, gave one idea and the second line, in very small type, a very different one. Typical was the head:

BIG BATTLE

IS EXPECTED

Walter Millis has described how the war correspondents flocked into every camp and naval station and loaded the wires with detailed accounts of every move that was made or contemplated. "Any feeble opposition put up by the browbeaten authorities on the score of secrecy was imperiously brushed aside. After all, if it was not the newspaper's war, whose war was it? When the Navy fitted out a vessel as a hospital ship, she was immediately stormed by whole battalions of reporters, who calculated that, as she would have to hurry from the scene of battle to land the wounded, she would be the first to reach the telegraph wires. . . . . A triumphant journalism was definitely in command!"

In short order the Spaniards were beaten on land and on sea. Tales of heroism, real and imaginary, filled the Hearst press. Brisbane, as editor in chief of the *New York Journal*, had become, in the short span of three years, the most potent figure in the "New Journalism" of America. Whatever fears he may have entertained when he left the service of Pulitzer had long been forgotten. Brisbane was now a Hearstman in body and soul—and he gloried in the thought.

6

A REFORM EDITOR AND HIS RADICAL BOSS

CANNON BOOMED, sirens shrieked, church bells tolled and there was rejoicing. A new century had been born. It was time to take stock of one's self, to forgive old grievances, forget old debts and resolve to do bigger and better things in a bigger and better way.

Few Americans could view the new century with the equinimity of Arthur Brisbane. He had just passed the half-way mark of man's proverbial three score and ten years. He was in the best of health. A man slightly over five feet ten inches in height, and weighing about one hundred and seventy pounds, he looked the part of a college athlete. His shoulders were broad, his hips narrow, and there was a great depth to the high-arched chest. His arms, long and thick, tapered down to small but powerful hands. His legs were muscular but thin, and he walked with the springy, alert step of a professional boxer. The curly hair of his youth had straightened out. The top of the head was massive and symmetrical over his shrewd blue eyes. The small mouth was no longer effeminate. The lower jaw had squared out and was well thrust forward. He dressed well but not flashily. He boxed, he wrestled, and above all, he was an excellent horseman—a skill for which he was known far and wide. He ate well, but sparingly, abhorred tobacco in all its forms, and took wine with each meal.

Seventeen years earlier, upon his return to America, young Brisbane had spoken English with difficulty. He couldn't write it at all. Now he was a great editor—certainly the most notorious editor in America. His name was a household word with millions who avidly read and repeated whatever he had to say, whether he wrote about men or monkeys, star dust or sportsmanship, advertising or adversity, science or superstition.

He had money, plenty of money to do with as he wished. He could buy land, houses, speculate in stocks or bonds or give to his less fortunate friends and relatives. He was a bundle of energy, writing, editing, making speeches, and traveling. He had helped to make a war and now that the war was ended he was prepared to turn his editorial guns upon a foe closer to home. The great crusade for the underdog was about to begin.

Together with his boss, Brisbane was about to launch a campaign against the trusts, against predatory wealth, against unfaithful public servants. A great national political campaign was approaching. McKinley must be ousted. Bryan, now almost the political puppet of Hearst and Brisbane, must replace him in the White House. Brisbane and Hearst—these two young men were determined to dominate the American political scene, to pull the strings and make the puppets jump, even as they had controlled New York journalism. Arthur Brisbane had tasted power. As the twentieth century dawned, he thought, with one of Voltaire's characters, that "this is the best of all possible worlds."

The Republican party pressed for the continuation of "the white man's burden." Bryan made the issue of imperialism one of the main points of his speeches. He denounced the war against Spain and the seizure of the Spanish colonies. Neither Hearst nor Brisbane found any difficulty in joining this campaign, though only a year before they had shouted for the annexation of the Philippine Islands. Now it was

McKinley and Hanna and the corrupt Republican leadership who were trying to override and overrule the unfortunate people of the West Indies and the Philippines by military force. The *Journal* wanted peace—peace with everyone. That is, almost everyone. The Republicans, Wall Street, the corrupt politicians, and McKinley—with such there could be no peace.

The attack on McKinley grew more vicious each day. It was his "fat white hands" according to the *Journal* which had tossed to the starving Americans the answer from out the White House window: "A trust can do no wrong." Arthur Brisbane grew more and more denunciatory. Delving into the past he came forward one day with a proposal that the readers of the *Journal* think over the advantages of political assassination! This was a new line for American journalism. And for this bold act, the *Journal* was soon to pay heavily.

"Napoleon gradually developed into a pretty strong man and nobody bothered him." editorialized Brisbane. "If Marat had been living when Napoleon returned from Italy and he retained populistic pull, it is quite likely that he would have got hold of Napoleon and cut his head off. He had a passion for cutting off the heads of those who made themselves conspicuous. His murder might have changed the world's history.

"Was not the history of the world changed when the father of Alexander the Great, Philip, was murdered in the midst of festivals and rejoicing? Let unmurdered he might have reigned until long past the day that Alexander the Great died and went under the ground.

"Philip's ambition was really modest. He simply wanted to rule Greece.

"Compared to his son, Alexander, he was like the humble

president of the Stove Trust compared to John D. Rockefeller. If Alexander had died before his father, who would have known how to thrash and coax the Greeks into line? Who would have conquered Persia and provided such fine historic reading?

"If Cromwell had not decided to remove the head of Charles I from his lace collar, would England be what she is today—a really free nation and a genuine republic?

"Did not the murder of Lincoln, uniting in sympathy and regret all good people in the North and South, hasten the era of American good feeling and perhaps prevent the renewal of fighting between brothers?

"The murder of Caesar certainly changed the history of Europe, besides preventing that great man from ultimately displaying vanity as great as his ability.

"When wise old sayings, such as that of Disraeli about assassination are taken up, it is worth while, instead of swallowing them whole, to analyze them. WE INVITE OUR READERS TO THINK OVER THIS QUESTION. The time devoted to it will not be wasted. Any kind of harmless exercise is good for the brain as any kind of harmless exercise is good for the muscles."

Continuing the discussion for "harmless exercise of the brain" the *Journal* said, after McKinley's second victory: "If bad men cannot be got rid of except by killing, then the killing must be done."

The assassination of Governor Goebel of Kentucky in 1901 gave Ambrose Bierce a chance to do a political verse for the *Journal* in line with this new political policy.

> The bullet that pierced Goebel's breast
> Cannot be found in all the West;
> Good reason, it is speeding here
> To stretch McKinley on his bier.

On September 6, 1901, President McKinley was shot by Leon Czolgosz at the Pan-American Exposition in Buffalo. The other papers, anxious to stop Hearst-Brisbane and the *Journal*, recalled the editorials about political assassinations. They mentioned too that the assassin had had a copy of a Hearst paper in his pocket when the deed was committed.

The result momentarily was disastrous for the *Journal*, its publisher and editor. Circulation fell. The publication was banned from schools and clubs and respectable homes. The clergy denounced the *Journal* and Hearst was hung in effigy and charged with being the foulest person in American life.

One of those lightning-like shifts was made in the *Journal's* editorial policy. The dying president was referred to only in words of praise.

"The thoughts and hopes of every American mind are fixed upon the President battling courageously, patiently for life," Brisbane wrote. He was pictured as wanting to live not only for his beloved wife but so that he might devote his days and his strength "to the program of national duty and national prosperity which his latest speech outlined."

The Hearst cartoonists were told to do sob-sister jobs and when McKinley died, the Hearst press outdid all others in its lament for the "beloved leader" of the American people.

But the storm would not die. Circulation continued to fall. Hearst and Brisbane found themselves cut off from their former friends. Senator Henry Cabot Lodge said the *Journal* was "an efficient cause in breeding anarchists and murders."

New York's former Police Commissioner stepped into the shoes of the assassinated President. In his first message to Congress in December, 1901, he referred to his predecessor's assassination and in no uncertain terms fixed the blame where he thought it belonged.

The assassin had been inflamed by the teachings of professed anarchists, said Roosevelt, "and probably also by the reckless utterances of those who, on the stump and in the public press, appealed to the dark and evil spirits of malice and greed, envy and sullen hatred. The wind is sowed by the men who preach such doctrines, and they cannot escape their share of responsibility for the whirlwind that is reaped."

To bolster up his falling circulation as well as to prove he was no disciple of alien thought or institutions, Hearst changed the name of the *Morning Journal* to the *New York American.* It became the first of a long string of "Americans" owned by Mr. Hearst.

The *Chicago American* was launched by Hearst July 4, 1900, supposedly at the behest of William Jennings Bryan and his Democratic supporters who wanted a powerful popular paper in the midwestern metropolis. Arthur Brisbane was sent west to take charge of the new publication. The opening issue contained a long laudatory letter from Hearst to Bryan. And it was Bryan who flashed the message, "start the presses." The issuance of this paper on July Fourth was carefully timed. The Democratic party was holding its convention in St. Louis that day. Of the first edition printed in Chicago, tremendous quantities were shipped to St. Louis. The delegates and their friends were flooded with the latest of the Hearst publications. On July fifth Bryan was renominated for the Presidency.

Charles Edward Russell and Andy Lawrence were installed as Hearst lieutenants in Chicago in charge of the *American.* Brisbane returned to New York, there to devise new methods of sensational journalism and to write his editorials on science, literature, philosophy, how to raise babies, and a hundred other subjects.

It was an exciting time for Brisbane. He was as proud of having invented the screaming headlines in huge bold faced type as was Bell of inventing the telephone. Those foot-deep heads on his papers attracted immediate attention to the reader, no matter how many other papers were on the newsstand or under the newsboy's arm. Brisbane's device of placing the comic strips and editorials and the little moral sermons on the back page of the paper was likewise a scheme to make of his readers involuntary sandwich men advertising the wares of his master. "To read them," says George T. West, "you must turn the front page outward so the scare headlines strike all within reading distance smack in the face, thus letting them know that you too are a patron of the Hearst press."

The editorial page technique begun by Brisbane at the turn of the century has remained fundamentally the same ever since. The articles themselves could easily be transposed from the issues of 1900 to those of ten, twenty, or thirty years later without noticeable difference to the reader. The Sunday editorial page invariably carries a seven column illustration or series of illustrations whose purpose it is to point some moral. Fables are drawn upon with unceasing regularity. At one time, the readers are asked in a full page editorial WHAT ANIMAL CONTROLS YOUR SPIRIT? Another time, WHAT KIND OF BLINDERS DO YOU WEAR? The illustrations show a large horse with blinders, surrounded by smaller men wearing blinders labeled respectively, CONCEIT, IGNORANCE, SUPERSTITION, GREED, ENVY, and SELFISHNESS. The moral is obvious.

Science and prophecy join hands in an article written for the *Cosmopolitan* magazine of September, 1901, entitled THE

INCUBATOR BABIES AND NIAGARA FALLS. They were the two extremes which impressed Brisbane at the Buffalo Exposition. The one, the river, "represents material force, the mere force of gravity. The child's brain represents spiritual force, the force of organization and speculation." Naturally the incubator babies are the thing that really concern Arthur. "All kinds of living human dynamos lie in those little hot air boxes."

For the average mortal it is necessary to fingerprint or footprint new born babies to indicate their identity, but Arthur Brisbane differed from commonplace people. He saw profound differences even in these incubator babies, most of them prematurely born.

"One with a few spears of red hair and a very determined expression at feeding time is of pure Irish stock. If his emotions could be translated into coherent speech, he would undoubtedly express a desire to challenge any baby of his weight in Incubator Row.....Another.....is of German blood. In spite of his youth, he is distinctly philosophical. It is easy to imagine that he devotes hours of speculation to a nearby shed in the Exposition where scientists are experimenting with different breeds of cows, testing their good qualities with various kinds of food, and especially their availability for nourishing motherless infants....."

The perspicacity of bachelor Brisbane was amazing. Farther down the row were "three little creatures whose relationship is recognized at a glance. These are the Cohen triplets.....Possibly you would envy the man who would own the falls of Niagara.

"But you would envy much more wisely him who shall possess for his own the possibilities of development wrapped up in those little Cohen triplets.

"You would possess the possibility of wealth beyond the

dreams of avarice, as Dr. Johnson prophetically said when auctioning off the Bass Ale Brewery. And you would possess, also, possibilities of power, intellectual and artistic, beyond the dreams of human ambition."

The triplets didn't pan out so well. No one has heard of them since. It remained for the French-Canadian Dionne family with their quintuplets to accumulate that wealth which Arthur saw possible from the incubator triplets.

Not content with merely reading the thoughts of the incubator babies, Brisbane went on to give some good advice to mothers as well as to pass on information that will undoubtedly cause the raising of gynecologists' eyebrows.

"Mothers would do well to remember that the chief thing in caring for a baby is to keep its brain quiet." (Brisbane described how the little German baby was removed from the incubator at the end of six weeks and almost died.) "It suffered not merely through irregularities of temperature, but through brain fatigue.....a fact generally unknown to mothers and nurses."

Passing easily from the discussion of babes, Arthur would go on to a Sunday editorial entitled LONGEST AND MOST USELESS LIFE (illustrated by a tortoise). The fight against the trusts and predatory wealth was constantly dealt with. At another time the Sunday editorial (with an illustration of a man whose hands and feet were chained and who faced a huge monster head,) was called SOME GREAT MONSTER ALWAYS CONFRONTS US. The editorial indicated that primitive man fought beasts. Now he must fight the influence of the moneyed and the powerful. Arthur would tell how John D. Rockefeller taxed this country $50,000,000 a year. "But," he added, "he puts it back again in wages, schools, etc." "Money is powerful," he concluded. "It controls us to a great extent. It controls our happiness. Yet the money power of today is a feeble thing as compared to any of the great powers that have ruled man in the past..... (Brisbane was, after all, a perennial optimist in such matters)....."The great man's word was once law. His word is not law now; sometimes, but only when he can buy those that make the law. He has to go behind the people's backs and cheat them—he cannot defy them to their faces.....We should resolve to put an end to it, and we should hurry to carry out the resolve. But meanwhile we should not be frightened. We should not forget that the money boss can be disposed of just as soon as we make up our minds to act in concert."

Another of the many editorials along this vein was entitled, MANY TEMPLES HAVE RISEN AND FALLEN. The illustration showed lions labeled "the trusts," "money power," "corrupt law makers," roaming amid fallen temples. History was reviewed in typical Brisbanian style, but, with an optimistic insistence, Brisbane again concluded: "The picture here presented the world will never see. Justice, in the long run, conquers money and selfishness. The majority will rule the minority in the end."

Brisbane did not marry until he had reached his middle forties. In the meantime he had written literally thousands of paragraphs of advice on love and marriage. One of these, WHY IS MARRIED LIFE DULL?, he considered sufficiently important to be later incorporated in a book of his outstanding editorials.

"The conventional honeymoon," he wrote, "is often a dismal, foolish, instruction.

"The young couple set off by themselves, traveling in railroad trains, stopping at strange hotels, or, most idiotic of all, going on an ocean ship to become seasick.

"Young people that are just married—the young wife especially—ought to be at home, with the people they are accustomed to, and with ordinary amusements to keep them interested, and to keep them from thinking too much about each other and getting tired of each other."

The possession of another person through matrimony Brisbane compares with acquiring a huge mince pie.

"Surely," he says, "no sensible human being would go off for several weeks on a mince pie honeymoon with nothing on earth to fill in the time; yet that is exactly what people do when they get married, and there ought to be a modification of that foolishness."

The dullness of married life, Brisbane wrote, out of his lack of experience, "is chiefly due to men. Just about ninety-nine percent of it is *man's* fault. They become selfish and dull, thus making the home atmosphere dull. They are selfish and above all they lack imagination." There is a final word of advice to women, larded with compliments. "Women make one great mistake—it contributes to the dullness of married life and the failure of happiness. They are not *selfish enough*. They don't calculate enough. They ought to keep themselves to themselves more than they do. They ought to have control of the situation at the beginning of their married lives, and keep control until the end. They ought especially to keep their husbands occupied with some slight feeling of uncertainty."

There were many who read the editorials on marriage, love, and constancy with tongue in cheek. Some recalled the stories of Willie Hearst's escapades while at Harvard. In San Francisco the young millionaire's son and publisher had led a wild and almost dissolute life. He had brought back with him from Cambridge Tessie Powers "the college widow" and had installed her in a huge mansion at Sausalito. The wining, dining, and carousing at the Sausalito estate became notorious throughout the Golden Gate area. Young

Willie sowed his wild oats with abandon, causing consternation to his kind hearted mother and friends. Respectable San Francisco society repudiated him.

New York to Willie Hearst was not different from San Francisco. When not editing his paper, conducting sensational raids upon his competitors for their best men, or making deals with the local political leaders, he was to be found at the theatres and music halls, in the cafes and the restaurants accompanied by one or more actresses of the day.

Brisbane, himself a handsome young man full of life and energy, enjoyed feminine companionship as much as did his publisher. Furthermore he tried to ape and imitate Willie Hearst in more ways than one. Rumor had it that he was on distinctly friendly terms with many of the young ladies of the newspaper staff, among them Nellie Bly, the most famous of the women journalists of the nineties and early nineteen hundreds.

In a forthcoming biography of Nelly Bly, Miss Evelyn Burke tells of this friendship. Brisbane, in a letter to Miss Burke, has denied this implication with the statement: "I knew Nellie Bly, concerning whom you write, quite well for a number of years. She worked for me as a reporter, and I believe she was the best reporter, man or woman, with the possible exception of Dorothy Dix. I cannot give you any personal details concerning Nellie Bly, as I knew her only as a working newspaper woman. Her hair as I recollected, was brown; later, when I saw her on her return from Australia just before she died, it had turned grey."

Henry H. Klein, who wrote "Romances of the News" for the *Journal* at ten dollars each during the early days, declared in his biography: "I remember the Wilson sisters, actresses, coming to the office nightly with Mr. Hearst after eleven o'clock, and W. R. kneeling on the floor nightly, studying and changing the proposed makeup of the pages."

The fabulous salaries of those days must have gone only to the leading men. Klein, functioning in the triple capacity of night rewrite man, secretary to Rudolph Block (editor of the comic section), and music editor for the Sunday magazine section of the *American*, drew a total salary of nineteen dollars a week. He reports that Rudolph Dirks, the creator of the famous Katzenjammer Kids, received twenty-five dollars a week at that time; and George Creel used to submit cosmic squibs at a dollar an item. "I was the only person on the paper permitted to draw more than one salary at a time, by special permission of S. S. Carvalho, the publisher, but in spite of my apparent importance, I was fired by Charles Edward Russell, city editor, who was known as 'iron-faced Charlie.' "

Grove L. Johnson, the father of Senator Hiram Johnson of California, knew Willie Hearst and his San Francisco background very well. In a speech delivered in the House of Representatives, January 8, 1897, Grove Johnson created a sensation on the floor by the charges he made against the young San Francisco and New York publisher. "We knew him to be a debauchee, a dude in dress, and an Anglo-maniac in language in manners," said Johnson. "We knew him to be licentious in his tastes, regal in his dissipations, unfit to associate with pure women or decent men.... We knew he was debarred from society in San Francisco because of his delight in flaunting his wickedness, but we believed him honest, though tattooed with sin."

In his castigation of the young publisher, Johnson charged Hearst with having blackmailed the Southern Pacific Company into a contract whereby they were to pay him $30,000 to let them alone. But it seems the company did not pay the full amount so Hearst returned to his attack against the corporation, "but pleaded in extenuation that he did not keep his contract, but swindled them out of their money.....He showed himself to be the correct exponent by a scoundrel, as defined by Bill Tweed, namely, 'a man who wouldn't stay bought.' "

Arthur Brisbane's views of his boss did not coincide with those of Grove Johnson. To the readers of *Cosmopolitan*, Hearst, as seen through the eyes of Brisbane, was a model character. "He drinks nothing but water and milk, does not smoke and has absolutely no interest outside of his newspapers, except a mild interest in the collection of paintings and other works of art."

Hearst had become a power in spite of his great wealth. Hearst believed in public schools, in the public ownership of public franchises, in the public election of senators. It was his intention through his newspapers "to fight persistently the cause of genuine democracy.....not merely the democracy of a political party, but the real democracy upon which the government is founded." And last, but by no means least, Hearst was for America first and all the time.

The laudatory article by Brisbane marked the public opening of a campaign on behalf of Hearst for political power. He no longer wanted to be merely a power behind the throne. He wished to occupy the throne himself. To his leading editorial writer was given the job of putting Hearst over.

Because of his good work for Bryan, Hearst had been made president of the National Association of Democratic Clubs with their three million members. He now determined to use this position and the organization behind it as stepping stones to the White House. The whole Hearst newspaper organization was put into motion behind this idea. Max F. Ihmsen, Washington correspondent for the Hearst press, was installed as secretary of the National Association. Bryan, wearied by his two successive defeats, was sent abroad to do a series of feature articles for the Hearst Press which kept him out of the way while the Hearst-Brisbane combination developed their machine.

The road to follow was first of all to make a deal with Tammany for a seat in Congress; then, with the nation's capital as a sounding board, to prepare the way for capturing the Democratic nomination in 1904.

Charlie Murphy was then boss of Tammany Hall. To be sure the *Journal* in its columns and cartoons had let loose many a blast at Tammany and its corrupt leader. But both Hearst and Murphy had a broad enough view to be able to forget the charges made against each other in the interests of "party harmony."

Brisbane was dispatched to Murphy to patch things up. Thus began Arthur Brisbane's thirty-five years of service to his employer as political "stooge" and "fixer." Murphy was willing to talk business and agreed to accept Brisbane as a candidate for Congress in one of the solid Tammany districts. In return for this Hearst was to advance cash for the 1902 campaign. Once the deal had been made and Hearst knew he had Tammany committed, he announced that he, not Brisbane, would run. Brisbane, ever obedient to his master, retired from the scene.

Murphy was taken by surprise and could not get out from under. Hearst's leading men shook their heads and admitted in private it would be impossible for Hearst to go before the electors in the face of the campaign that had just been concluded. To be sure he had a great following among the foreign-born: Irish, German, Italians and Poles. The attacks upon his private character, as well as the charges leveled against him as a result of the McKinley assassination, could not easily be lived down. But the yes-men were mistaken.

Why did Hearst want a public office? Skeptics might question his statement of the time, but it sounded honest, realistic, and in line with the *Journal's* campaign for busting trusts and putting honest men into public office. "My early ambition was to do my part in newspapers, and I still propose to do a newspaper part. But when I saw Mayors, and Governors, and Presidents fail. I felt that I'd like to see if I couldn't be better. I felt I'd like to go into office, any office almost, to see if I couldn't do the things I wanted to see done."

The 1902 congressional campaign in New York City's eleventh district was unlike any preceding one. The Hearst machine went into action just as it had when it launched the *Journal*. Sandwich men marched the streets with advertising matter boosting the new enterprising candidate. Multicolored illustrated posters were pasted on every ash can, billboard, and telephone pole. A deluge of pamphlets, leaflets, and special newspaper articles flooded the entire district. Hearst reporters interviewed people in all walks of life and printed their comments, real or imaginary. Others were sent out to bring pressure to bear upon small business men, teachers, and citizens generally. Tammany Hall, itself adept at the job of putting over a candidate, gazed in startled admiration and awe at the job now being done.

When the night of November 4, 1902, rolled around, Hearst was elected to Congress by a safe margin. A victory celebration had already been planned long in advance. It, too, was of the "stupendous, colossal" kind. The big bust was to take place at Madison Square Garden. Tons of fireworks had been purchased for the occasion. The milling crowds who gathered to witness the affair became instead the participants of a tragedy. About ten o'clock that evening, the fireworks blew up. Explosion followed explosion in quick succession. When the ground was cleared, there were seventeen dead and many wounded. The banner heads to announce the festivities had to be discarded. New heads were written. An inconspicuous story under the headline "Twelve Killed By Fireworks Explosion," in which Mr. Hearst's connection with the affair was somehow unmentioned, was all that appeared. Lawsuit followed lawsuit. The Hearst legal organization fought them all. Some were settled out of court. The last case was concluded thirty-three years after the tragedy took place.

As editorial director of Hearst's pre-election campaign, Brisbane had struck a popular note, a championship of the average American citizen whom Hearst wished to represent. "I feel that Mr. Morgan can take care of himself," Hearst would say. The problem of the hour for the people of the country was the regulation of the new financial power in the hands of the trusts. Trust-owned and trust-controlled Senators must be eliminated through the direct election of senators. There must be a tariff revision to prevent them from selling their products cheaply abroad. The government must step in and obtain the ownership of certain public utilities, beginning with the railroads and telegraphs. The anthracite coal mines should also be included. Because of the "intolerable situation," adequate laws should also be passed to punish the trust owners and the officers who had committed criminal infractions of the law.

The points made a great appeal to the poor people of the district. It made first class reading in every newspaper in the country. Even the progressives and radicals began to look upon Brisbane's words with favor. They seized upon these issues and said: "Hearst is our friend; we must support him. This is the kind of a man we want in the White House." Tories and conservatives quoted the speeches and writings at length and said: "Such a man is a danger to society; watch out for him."

Both ways it made news. It flashed the name of Hearst and Brisbane and their program to millions of people who up to that time had not heard of them. Friend and foe alike were unconsciously united in greasing the skids for the time when Hearst was prepared to slide into the Democratic presidential nomination.

The charges of immorality against the forty year old congressman-elect subsided to a whisper when Hearst, a few weeks after taking his seat in Congress, married Millicent Wilson, April 28, 1903. Millicent was one half of a sister dance act then playing in "The Girl From Paris." Together with his secretary, George Pancoast, and his chief editorial writer and stooge, Brisbane, Hearst had been frequenting the theatre for months. There had been after-theatre parties in unending number. Staff members who had to participate in these as well as function on the paper, were glad when the marriage took place. Mr. and Mrs. Hearst sailed for Europe to celebrate their honeymoon. The following year, their first child, George was born. Hearst was now a family man, so Arthur Brisbane could run innumerable pictures of the happy father and mother with their child to prove the point. Stories were circulated of how friends calling upon the famous publisher would find him stretched out on a bed beside his infant son, holding a baby's bottle at which the child sucked vigorously. And when the baby cried, Mr. Hearst would kick up his heels delightedly crying, "Uxtry! Uxtry! Uxtry! Uxtry edition!"

Speaking before the Presbyterian Ministers' Association of New York in 1905, Brisbane was asked about the charges made as to Hearst's personal life, particularly that of his being a debauchee of a peculiarly depraved type. To this Brisbane replied: "I know that this charge has been widely circulated. But I lived in the same house with Mr. Hearst for three years, and I know of nothing whatever to support it. He is a man who never drinks, and works hard every day until two or three o'clock in the morning. He is a big strapping fellow, a man of domestic habits, and his little boy is a marvel of health and vigor."

When the average congressman entrains for his new job at Washington it is worth a half column in the local paper. But when William Randolph Hearst took his seat it was front page news in every Hearst paper from coast to coast. Brisbane saw to that.

Long before the session opened, Hearst, Brisbane, Carvalho, and Shearn, Hearst's attorney, planned the bills he wanted to introduce. Shearn prepared them in proper legal form. Brisbane opened up a series of broadside editorials to "educate" his public to the need for such legislation. Then, at the proper moment, would come the bill itself, introduced by the publisher. That many of these bills were progressive and worthwhile cannot be denied. But Hearst made no attempt to carry them beyond their original introduction. They died in committee. The big thing was to have them introduced so that his papers could carry on the campaign on his behalf in preparation for the presidential nomination of 1904. During the first and second sessions of the fifty-eighth Congress, Hearst answered the roll call only nine times. He seldom voted on any measure.

The best picture of Hearst and the Hearst brigade was furnished by Charles Willis Thompson, a contemporary newspaper man.

Thompson first compares Hearst with Bryan. Bryan he

admits is a radical, "but between his radical Democracy and the unconcealed Socialism of Hearst, there lies the widest gulf. Bryan is a conservative compared to Hearst." The millionaire radical was in Congress to make himself a leader, not a follower in the ranks. "He seeks to be the captain of the forces of social discontent and plans to reap a harvest following the next panic. He cares nothing for bills about improving creeks or removing desertion records" but is on hand only when "there was any chance to advance his socialistic principles."

In the first session of Congress the Hearst brigade consisted of about six men. But by the second, it had grown to more than a dozen. Most of the Democrats had at first looked upon him with contempt. This soon changed to hatred. "That hatred may soon be intermixed with fear; not fear of what he can accomplish in Congress, but fear of what he may do to the Democratic party outside of it."

When Hearst desired a place on the Labor Committee, House leader Williams had already made up his slate and good naturedly explained his regrets to the would-be candidate. Hearst took the decision quietly and made no comment. "Shortly thereafter petitions from labor unions all over the country began to pour in on Speaker Cannon and Mr. Williams to put Hearst on the committee; meetings began to be held, and organized labor appeared to be in state of volcanic eruption. Cannon and Williams remained firm, but one of Williams' appointees bowed to the storm. This man gracefully resigned in Hearst's favor and the Labor Committee was completed accordingly."

Most of the Hearst brigade of those days have long since passed into oblivion. One, alone, continued in public office and gained greater fame. He was Garner of Texas, vice-president in the Franklin D. Roosevelt administration.

To woo the labor unions for the cause of the Hearst candidacy, Brisbane editorialized again and again on their behalf. One of them read: "You see a horse after a hard day's work grazing in a swampy meadow. He has done his duty and is getting what he can in return.

"On the horse's flank you see a leech sucking blood.

"The leech is the trust.

"The horse is the labor union."

Day after day the outpouring continued—a clamor for cheaper milk, cheaper ice, cheaper transportation, public ownership, good government, control and regulation of the trusts. Frederick Palmer maintained that Brisbane had probably influenced more votes than any other writer: "His outpourings in the evening edition had the quality of being spoken at your elbow . . . they do not read well when you rise fresh in the morning equipped with the optimism of dawn for your day's work; for they are feverish. Their potency is to the man hanging to the strap in a crowded streetcar, after the day's disappointment when his mind is most sensitive to the preaching of discontent."

With the gift of a novelist, Brisbane, editorially, could put himself in the place of the Italian immigrant workingman, the horny-handed farmer, the small shop keeper, or the Wall Street customer's man. He knew how to direct his appeals to the specific group he wanted to reach. "Historical and scientific comparisons, quick conclusions from premises swiftly arranged to suit his contentions, come racing from his mind in the form of smart sentences."

"The French have money to buy our railroad bonds," he said when the Pennsylvania floated its five percent bonds in Paris; "because they are not robbed by their own railroads as we are."

"That sounds so well that you might not stop to think

that it was bad political economy if you were tired and wanted a cocktail in printed form. Or if you did stop to think, he would have caught your eye with the freshly minted gleam of another piece of coinage before you had time fully to test the first as a counterfeit. If the moneyed oligarchy could get Brisbane as a press agent, he could, when in the mood for composition, talk more arguments in favor of trusts in half an hour into a phonograph, than Rockefeller has conceived in all his life."

It was Brisbane who induced David B. Hill to insert into the New York state democratic platform of 1902 the plank declaring in favor of the ownership of the anthracite coal fields by the government. Conservative magazines like *The Outlook* feared for the future of the country and charged the Hearst-Brisbane movement with harboring social revolution as its goal. Of Brisbane it said, "the illustrious father failed; the son is following in his footsteps."

The importance of what Hollywood today calls "leg art" had been learned by Hearst in his early days on the *San Francisco Examiner*. Circulation jumped in the direct proportion to the shortness of the gowns worn by the comely young ladies illustrating his columns. Brisbane, as editor of the *Journal*, saw to it that leg art was adequately developed in that paper. A favorite method was to write an indignant moralistic editorial denouncing such methods and then to have the editorial profusely illustrated with examples.

The holier-than-thou attitude of the *New York Journal* left a bad taste in the mouth of most newspaper men. Frequently one would find an editorial preaching temperance backed up by an inviting advertisement for whiskey. Or, on the back of a Brisbane blast favoring high ideals, clean living or, perhaps, better education of our youth, would be the claims of quack doctors, patent medicine artists and all those who pander to public degeneracy or ignorance. Anthony Comstock, the self-appointed snooper and defender of public morals, was held up to ridicule by most New York papers. Brisbane knew that tens of thousands of would-be Anthony Comstocks would rally behind a paper supporting them. When through Comstock's efforts the magazine of the Art Students' League was suppressed, because of its illustrations of nudes, Brisbane righteously defended Comstock as the guardian of the home and of morality.

Before cigarette advertisements became a lucrative source of income for publishers, Brisbane was perhaps the most violent denouncer of cigarette smoking. When a New York restaurant changed its policy and openly permitted women to smoke there, it was Brisbane alone, of all editors, who thundered forth denunciations of such immoral acts and joined hands with the Comstocks to prevent this from taking place. In 1906, when Hearst began his campaign for Governor of New York, Brisbane opened up an attack upon the lewdness of the personal column appearing in the *New York Herald*. He charged that demi-mondaines and houses of ill fame were able to peddle their wares in this way. The attack made for new circulation and tended to act as a lightning rod to ward off the attacks upon the personal character and life of Hearst and Brisbane.

Journal reporters under the watchful eye of moralistic Arthur learned how to exploit a scandal, a mystery, or a murder. Every suggestive detail was handled so as to cause the semi-moronic readers to crave more. Their minds were inflamed and their appetites stirred by the juicy bits told, and their imaginations titillated by the suggestions of what was left unpublished. Frederick Palmer says the editors of the *Journal* boasted that in the Para Nova case they never spoke explicitly of lewd details because "they did not have to speak of them in order to make their readers think of them. Through the pages on pages of nauseating psychological comments and suggestions, they aroused the imagination of the masses who pursued strainingly the hope of a salacious revelation, and then busied their minds in hypothesis about the things which they were not told." The same could be applied to the celebrated Stanford White murder by Harry Thaw.

As Brisbane began hitting his stride editorially, he turned his eyes to other fields. New methods must be devised to bring advertisers to the paper. Brisbane was a wizard in this field, too. The Hearst chain grew to include papers in Boston and Los Angeles. Brisbane would be sent out to look them over and plan the methods for building circulation and advertising. He was invariably successful. Chicago became the proving ground for many of his theories. Some of the methods developed there are still recalled by advertising solicitors of the *Chicago American* with gusto.

One of the large Chicago department stores persistently refused to advertise in the Hearst papers and finally notified the Hearst management not to send any more solicitors.

Through the connivance of a physician the Hearst outfit found a young girl who was in the incipient stage of smallpox. They managed in some way to get her a job as saleswoman. Toward the close of her first day's work, a physician, sent there for the purpose, strolled through the store, saw the girl, talked to her a moment, looked at her tongue, felt her pulse, and told her that she had smallpox and must come away at once.

A few minutes later, the store management was called by a Hearst editor and asked for additional information as to the prevalence of smallpox in the establishment. The story had already been set and a reporter would be sent around so that the management could make such corrections as to facts as might be necessary. The story had a five column head, a picture of the girl, a picture of women crowding around a counter. The accidental discovery of the case by a physician was described and the girl's being sent to a small-pox ward of a hospital was recorded. In addition to this front page spread, an editorial had been prepared calling upon the city health authorities to close the store while a thorough investigation of small pox conditions in it were made. "After all, other employees might have the disease."

The store's manager was frantic at the sight of all this. Owners and managers alike rushed to the newspaper office. Not one line of the story or the editorial appeared. But within twenty-four hours a big advertising contract had been landed.

Another case concerned a leading Chicago hardware dealer. Though a large advertiser, he was disgusted with the Hearst papers and refused to give them a single line of business. The advertising solicitors from the Hearst press were told in no uncertain terms that he viewed the Hearst readers as the scum of the earth. When word of his remarks came back to the newspaper management, two advertising solicitors (one of them a disguised reporter) were sent again to obtain his advertising. They received instructions to goad him into saying something which would look very bad in print. This was easily accomplished. The hardware man became so wrought up he declared he didn't want any reader of a Hearst newspaper to enter his store. He wanted no dealings with them. They were a set of bums sitting on park benches; they had no money to spend anyhow. His callers reminded him that the Hearst newspapers had been endorsed by nearly all local trade unions and that he sold tools. The Hearst papers were read by carpenters, tinsmiths, bricklayers, and other mechanics who used his products. But the information failed to register in the heat of the discussion.

The next day the young men came back and spread out the proof. There was an affidavit, sworn to by both of them, in which the hardware man's remarks were set forth verbatum. A big headline informed the world that Mr. X. did not care to sell anything to the readers of the Hearst papers.

"We didn't come here yesterday to get a news story," the young men explained, "but the interview turned unexpectedly into news. It will certainly be surprising news to most of the craftsmen of Chicago that you do not want to have anything to do with them. This is to be published tomorrow, and the editor wants you to go over it to check up on possible errors. He told us that he would make some editorial comment."

The hardware man exploded. He grabbed the phone, called his lawyer, charged that he was being blackmailed and would get even with the Hearst papers. The young men left.

Late that afternoon the hardware man's attorney appeared at the newspaper offices and meekly asked what could be done to straighten out the whole matter. It was straightened out. The article was never printed, but from that day on the hardware store placed plenty of advertising.

In this instance the Hearstian technique at least proved successful for the advertiser. The promotion department of the paper helped him prepare his advertisements to fit the Hearst clientele. His volume of sales went steadily up month by month and the whole thing turned out a success. In fact, the hardware man became so enthusiastic that on his own account he wrote personal letters to other merchants advising them to advertise in Hearst's newspapers.

Brisbane, as we have already noted, had won recognition as the spokesman for the underdog. He was strong for labor unions. In Chicago the staff of the *American* joined a reporters' union. But this time there was no friendly reception from the boss, or the son of Albert Brisbane. Word had been passed down the line that Mr. Hearst and Mr. Brisbane disapproved of such a union. Those who failed to resign lost their jobs.

Methods of local newsgathering were introduced that remind one of the early days of the *Journal*, which stole or rewrote all local news from Pulitzer's *World*.

William Salisbury, a reporter on the *Chicago American* at this time, remarked: "I soon learned how the paper got most of its news. Among the reporters was one who talked like 'Chimmie Fadden.' The first night, when I heard him remark, 'Oh, wot's de use of woikin' hard on dis paper?' I wondered that such a person should be one of us. At two A. M. the reason was shown.

"I saw him run into the editorial department from the back stairway. He was breathing hard. From under his coat he pulled copies of the other Chicago morning papers, still damp from the press.

" 'Gee! I had a fierce tussle makin' a getaway dis time,' he panted. 'Dey're gettin' on to me. It was hard woik gettin' dese foist editions from the delivery wagon. I guess I'll make Mr. Hoist raise me, or else buy me a armored soot.'

"The rest of us were given clippings from the papers he brought in, and were told to rewrite the news from them as quickly as possible. 'Just a few lines of introduction will do—paste the balance on,' was the order."

The unscrupulous methods in Chicago were likewise

carried on in New York under the direct responsibility of Brisbane. Thousands of readers of the *Journal* wrote in to criticise its policy, its editorial injustices, or to complain how they had been defrauded by the advertisements of fake concerns. These letters were never published—that is, unless one of them, because of its poor grammatical construction or spelling, made it possible to discredit the writer.

Young women were lured into telling their tales of disappointed love to female reporters under the promise of absolute secrecy and aid. Once the stories had been obtained, they were built up and served out to the *Journal* readers hot from the griddle. Those who dared bring suit against the *Journal* discovered it was a long and costly process.

While these things went on, Brisbane continued writing editorials on THE LITTLEST WOMAN IN THE WORLD—ONCE SHE WOULD HAVE BEEN THE KING'S PLAYTHING. SHE IS THE PEOPLE'S AMUSEMENT NOW. HER CAREER ILLUSTRATES THE FACT THAT THE PEOPLE HAVE BECOME KINGS. Or he would address his readers on the problem of "IMMORTALITY OF THE INTELLECT—IT CAN BE ACHIEVED ON THIS EARTH. The teacher's life is renewed and strengthened in that of his pupil; the father's in that of his son." Or he would deal with THE PRISONER OF THE BOTTLE—a half-page illustration showed a man imprisoned in a bottle. An ape representing the past was on one side; a tiger representing the future, on the other. Brisbane went on: "How willingly he would leave his prison and escape from the bottle forever, but hatred of the past and dread of the future combine to keep him where he is."

Turning from these speculations to more economic problems, he would write on DON'T DO JUST ENOUGH TO EARN YOUR PAY. Interspersed among all these would be editorials on the Legislative programs Hearst was advancing as well as continuous paeans of praise for Hearst himself. Since his master was aiming for the Presidency, "his dress of late has been the usual uniform of American statesmanship, combining the long-tailed frock coat and the cowboy's soft slouch hat."

His boost for Hearst extended beyond the realm of the Hearst press. Brisbane, (as did Charles Edward Russell and other leading Hearst writers) contributed to the *North American Review*, *The Bookman*, *Cosmopolitan*, and other magazines. Then he tried to push his candidacy and sing his praises. Thus, Hearst was not interested in any money-making scheme. The power of money merely enabled him to scatter ideas through the newspapers. "This seems important, for while it is difficult to conceive that a man of any intelligence should be interested in money except for the work that can be done with it, we know that the best energies of our country at this moment are diverted to aimless money-making . . . It can truly be said that the property which Hearst owns has not in any way controlled his opinions."

It was Brisbane and Hearst's paper pulp and ink that made Hearst in the eyes of the reading public, the outstanding progressive of that day. The attacks upon the methods of Yellow Journalism employed by the Hearst-Brisbane combination fell largely on barren ground. Brisbane eagerly defended Yellow Journalism.

"It is," he claimed, "the power of public opinion, the mental force of thousands or millions of readers utilized with more or less intelligence in the interests of those readers.

"The yellow journal is the successor of the open spot where citizens of the Greek Republic met to settle public affairs . . . I have no doubt that Hearst (and his influence on public thought and action) is the most powerful man in the United States today. That is because he owns the present meeting place of the people—the yellow journal—and he presides at all the meetings."

The Hearst steamroller had its effect. Mossback country politicians in the South and Southwest knew of Hearst only as the one New York editor who had supported Bryan in 1896, so they supported him. In the open the machine worked with the radicals, liberals, and progressives; but behind their backs, it made deals with unscrupulous political leaders.

It was at the beck and call of the organized labor movement of Los Angeles that Hearst launched his first paper there, *The Examiner*, in 1903. Organized labor declared a holiday and paraded thousands strong to the *Examiner* building to celebrate the arrival of its friend and champion in the open shop center of the Pacific Coast. Leaders of labor unions who had not come into close contact with the Hearst-Brisbane machine, but had gained their information through its editorials and news columns, backed him for the Presidency. Radicals—even a great many Socialists—dashed to the banner of Hearst.

When the Democratic national committee met in Washington at the Hotel Shoreham it was overrun by troops of radical politicians who flooded the swanky hotel's corridors and truculently read the riot act to their national committee. They wanted the convention held in Chicago. They swore and spat and thumped on tables and chairs.

The cautious Democratic leaders took fright.

"This is a mob," they said. "Or rather the conjunction of the mob and the payroll. If it so vociferously swaggers here at the Shoreham, what will it do at the Chicago Convention?"

The Hearst machine was strong in Chicago. The old time

politicians feared the convention would be ruled by the gallery and the gallery would be ruled by Hearst. To save themselves and their party from Hearst control, they changed their minds and arranged for the convention to meet at St. Louis. They had had a glimpse of the subterranean workings of the Hearst movement. They were not scared—at least so they said—but they would take no chances.

Oswald Garrison Villard suggests that he and his chief editorial writer, Rollo Ogden, through the medium of the *New York Post*, played an important part in defeating Mr. Hearst at the Democratic convention as well as later, when he ran for Mayor of New York. Ogden wrote a long editorial "giving a complete picture of the rascality of both Hearst and Brisbane. This editorial was then reprinted as a pamphlet and distributed in tens of thousands of copies." Brisbane launched vicious and personal attacks against Villard as a result of this, and accused him of "all the crimes in the calendar."

An interesting postscript to this campaign of vilification was made by Villard. In 1906 Villard was seated at the speaker's table of an Associated Press dinner when Mr. Ogden came up to him and said, "Mr. Brisbane wants to meet you." Villard replied, "I will not meet Mr. Brisbane *now, or any time*." Brisbane, who was directly behind Ogden when this was said, came forward and remarked: "I don't blame you at all. I would have done the same thing myself in your place." Brisbane and Villard never did meet after that.

At the St. Louis convention it looked for a while as though Hearst would be nominated. He managed to get as many as 263 votes for his nomination. Bryan, who had been supported by Hearst in the early days, and was later kicked about by him, threw his influence behind Alton B. Parker. Parker finally received the nomination.

Hearst and Brisbane had suffered their first serious political defeat. Brisbane's dreams of himself as secretary of state had to be postponed for at least another four years. Meanwhile, the work had to go on. New York City was soon to elect a Mayor, and the state a Governor. Why not try for those offices as stepping stones to the White House in 1908?

7

WORLD'S HIGHEST PAID NEWSPAPERMAN

"FORTY YEARS AGO," said the *World's Work* in October, 1906, "such a forceful personality as Mr. Brisbane would have stood before the public as the great editors of those days did. Now his financial recompense is much larger than theirs, but his personal fame has been swallowed up in the Hearst myth."

That myth was making of the publisher an omniscient personality, combined with the patriotism of a George Washington, the humanitarianism of an Abraham Lincoln, and the drive of a Theodore Roosevelt. His subordinates were mere automatons, catapulted into prominence and the public eye by Hearst, where they remained shining by his reflected light. The well oiled publicity machine of the multimillionaire publisher did its best to promote this myth.

But among the skeptics another myth was in the making. They contended that Hearst had money, but no brains. He hired the brains which made his papers great. A triumvirate consisting of Arthur Brisbane, Solomon S. Carvalho and Clarence J. Shearn, according to this theory, constituted the power behind the throne, ably supported by other writers and executives like Morrill Goddard, Sam Chamberlain, Andrew Lawrence and Max Ihmsen.

Brisbane, by unanimous consent, was voted the most important of the triumvirate, the journalistic brains behind Hearst. So long as his employer was willing to pay him handsomely and permit his name to appear on the masthead of the Hearst papers, Brisbane had no objection to crying the wares and proclaiming the virtues of his master. He was considered the expert propagandist.

Carvalho handled all the details of advertising, circulation, distribution and mechanical production. He was the one who arranged for the widespread circulation of Brisbane labor editorials in factory towns and other sections where circulation canvassers could best use them. Shearn—the third leg of the tripod—was Hearst's attorney. He defended the *Journal* in its numerous libel suits. He drafted the many pieces of reform legislation (Hearst Railroad Rate Bill, Hearst Anti-Trust Bill, Hearst Gas Bill, etc.) on which Arthur Brisbane wrote editorials so eloquently and effectively.

It remained for Lincoln Steffens to upset this theory of the triumvirate. Hearst, he contended, *did* have brains. To support his contention he argued tht different men edited the Hearst papers in New York, Chicago, and San Francisco—but the tone and spirit were all the same. Steffens admitted the importance of the Brisbane-Carvalho-Shearn combination, but insisted that back of them at all times was Mr. Hearst himself, pulling the strings and giving the orders. For source material on the great publisher, Steffens had gone to Brisbane, which had infuriated Steffens' co-workers on the *American Magazine*. Finley Peter Dunne charged him with having fallen under the spell of Brisbane. "But Brisbane knows more about Hearst than you do," protested Steffens, "and he is fairer." Nearly thirty years later, Steffens still felt this, for in his *Autobiography* he added: "Brisbane was clear on Hearst, both his strength and his weaknesses, and he gave me and he illustrated a fine, balanced analysis of the man without any prejudice that he cared to put over on me."

Notwithstanding his protestations, Steffens was taken in by Brisbane. In his article "Hearst—The Man of Mystery,"

Steffens describes him as a great man "both self-dependent, self-educated," driving forward toward his unannounced purpose, "to establish some measure of democracy, with patient but ruthless force. He had ambition not to sit in offices he ran for, but to do something in them, to do himself things which his candidates never did satisfactorily." It was Steffens' firm belief that Hearst proposed to give the American people democracy, as other rich men gave to charity or to an art museum.

This analysis was derived directly from Brisbane, who had been telling his readers the same thing for several years.

Joseph Pulitzer had tried to teach young Brisbane that the moment the owner of a great newspaper craved official position he surrendered the heart of his calling as a publisher of the truth and made of his columns merely an organ for his personal ambitions. This might apply to common men, thought Brisbane, but never to his new master, William Randolph Hearst. He kept repeating: "Hearst did not enter journalism to make money." That he did make money was a secondary fact. So, too, Hearst in entering politics had no interest in personal office for glory. He was serving a cause —the cause of mankind. "There is no doubt Hearst will be elected president if he lives. He is the most popular man in the United States today."

No phrase was ever coined to apply to Hearstian political life as "yellow journalism" did to his newspaper activities. Had such a phrase been concocted, Brisbane would have been the first to accept it willingly and joyously, just as he gloried in the term "yellow journalism."

"Hearst is the yellow editor of the day. Nobody disputes his claim to the title, although not a few imitate him more or less ably, without ceasing to decry his objectionable activities . . .

"Far more important than anything else is the work of the yellow journalist in influencing the community in its *thought*, stimulating and supporting it in fighting the encroachment of class war, of capital upon the popular rights . . .

"Yellow journalism is important to the peaceful stability of society, BECAUSE IT ACTS AS A SAFETY VALVE FOR PUBLIC INDIGNATION."

The editors of *The Bookman*, commenting editorially upon Brisbane's article which appeared in their issue of June, 1904, remarked, "However we regard what yellow journalists are *doing*, we cannot help being serious as to what they *think* they are doing. Men's views of their own deeds are often so delightfully romantic."

Brisbane was undoubtedly the most important person in the whole Hearst organization. He was Hearst's Man Friday. He believed in his employer's methods; and this belief was strengthened by the increasing salary he received. His outlook, at the time, was a hopeless jumble of half-digested socialistic ideas (imbibed in part at his father's knee), augmented by the ruthless, unscrupulous methods used to achieve success by politicians, speculators, and grafting industrialists of the day.

Frederick Palmer, who knew Brisbane and Hearst well, charged the editor with being not *insincere* but *unsincere*, even as his employer was not *immoral* but *unmoral*. "In Brisbane's mind," he added, "there are no steady watch fires. There are only rockets, and he wonders why anyone should like watch fires anyway, when rockets are so easy to send up and they break into such wonderful stars, and you may vary the sensations if you please by having roman candles and pinwheels, and finally you may have William Randolph Hearst in a set piece go off with a fizz of surprise."

In the spring of 1905, Arthur Brisbane made a broadside attack upon Mayor George B. McClellan, of New York City. McClellan was the Tammany mayor. Hearst was determined to get the office himself, but Charlie Murphy, Tammany's big chief, would not agree. The friendly relations of the past three years were broken off.

The new campaign was conducted under the auspices of the Municipal Ownership League, made up of Hearst employees and satellites. Every edition of the *Journal* hurled a volley of Brisbanian thunderbolts at the city administration. The city must be saved from the tyranny of Tammany Hall and its corrupt leadership, he said. Meanwhile the other members of the staff built the political framework of their League and prepared the day for the big mass meeting where Hearst was to receive the independent nomination for Mayor. This took place on October 4, 1905. Hearst himself was one of the speakers, but made no mention of his desire for office. Instead, he challenged his audience: "You are a sleeping majority, pledged by pigmies. Wake up. Nominate independent men—men who will lead you to victory and restore this city to a government of the people, by the people, and for the people."

Before the applause had died down, Hearst men were leaping to their feet placing the name of their employer before the mass meeting as candidate for mayor. The nomination was made unanimous. But Hearst, seemingly amazed at the decision of the mass meeting, pleaded for time in which to make up his mind. Gently, he refused the honor. But his loyal employees would not be denied. Brisbane, Shearn, Ihmsen, and Carvalho continued their pleadings through editorial broadsides or as representatives of the Municipal Ownership League. Hearst could not fail his "public," so he wrote: "I am absolutely unable and unwilling to accept the omination you have offered me, but I have at length de-ided to defer to your wishes and not to shirk a task that resents itself to me as a public duty."

Brisbane plunged wholeheartedly into the campaign. The *Jew York Journal* became a vast electioneering sheet on ehalf of Hearst. The campaign itself, as conducted by Bris-ane, centered around three points. First, the attack upon Murphy and Tammany Hall. "Murphy is as evil a specimen f a criminal boss as we have had since the days of Tweed." Murphy is as bold a buccaneer as ever sailed the political cene." No charge was too evil to be made against the Tam-nany Boss and Mayor McClellan.

The second phase of the campaign was to meet the harges against Hearst's personal life by adorning the pages f the *Journal* with photographs of young George Hearst, is mother, or the family in happy gatherings. With great noral indignation, Brisbane attacked sexual depravity, ambling, motion pictures, and prize fighting. Editorially, ne Hearst papers became paragons of virtue.

To garner the Catholic and Italian vote, a large portrait f His Holiness the Pope was reproduced, inscribed with a ersonal message of thanks to Hearst for financial aid to the talian people during one of the erruptions of Mount Ve-uvius. Careless headline readers would easily assume that ne Pope himself was blessing Mr. Hearst and his candidacy.

The third phase of the campaign was to point to the many nunicipal reforms needed. Municipal Court Judge Samuel eabury had written a small pamphlet entitled, "Public Ownership and Operation of Public Utilities in New York." eabury was at once drawn into the Hearst machine and his leas were incorporated in the speeches and articles of the Municipal Ownership League and editorials in the *New York Journal* and *American*. The campaign sped on to a frenzied finish. Murphy was wrought up when he saw hir self depicted in prison garb in the columns of the *Journa* The verbal lashings administered to the Tammany men ger erally by Brisbane and his underlings made them determine that Hearst must under no circumstance be permitted to wi the election.

The Hearst forces, on the other hand, were confident c victory. So confident, in fact, that Brisbane himself wrot the headlines for the victory edition of the *Journal* befor the voting ended. In the largest of large type, the headlin ran: "HEARST WINS!" Then bethinking himself th there might possibly be a reversal, he wrote another hea to be used should Hearst be defeated: "ELECTIOI STOLEN BY TAMMANY."

Murphy's bruisers, obeying instructions, mutilated an kidnapped Hearst workers and intimidated untold thousan of voters. Brisbane and all other Hearst lieutenants wer frantic with excitement. Hearst alone kept perfectly coo In his cold, small voice, he issued the orders to attend to th wounded or send reinforcements wherever needed. Earl reports indicated a Hearst landslide, but as the precinct from Tammany controlled districts poured in, the vote be came closer and closer. Finally came the word that Hears had been defeated by 3,000 votes.

The demand for a recount was announced at once. Bri bane ordered one of his cartoonists to depict Murphy i prison stripes with a convict's close-cropped hair. This wa published on the front page the day after the election. Be low it, in bold-face type, appeared Brisbane's editoria "Every honest voter in New York WANTS TO SEE YOU I THIS NEW COSTUME. You have committed crimes against th people that will send you for many years to state prison, the crimes can be proved against you. Your dull mind car not conceive of any REAL public opinion. But an awakening is ahead of you. YOU KNOW THAT YOU ARE GUILTY. THE PEOPLE know it. You have swindled the poor as their employer; you have swindled the voting public as political manager of your miserable little gas tool. The people have found it out. If you persist in your efforts to rob the city, your friends will soon find you in state prison.

"Don't be such a fool as to repeat Tweed's question. He only stole MONEY. You have stolen VOTES. There could not be found in New York at this moment a jury to ACQUIT you. YOU KNOW THAT.

"Look out! If you ever sit in the prisoner's dock you will not come out, except in striped clothing. You were warned before election. Be warned now—or follow Tweed and the men BETTER THAN YOU that have worked for the state prison after working against it in public office."

Tammany did the recounting and McClellan was elected.

Many years later, Brisbane retailed a story about that campaign told to him by Thomas Foley, the Tammany leader in whose district Brisbane voted. "You know," said Foley to Brisbane, "that in every election we have a certain number of Bowery derelicts that we take care of before election day. We put them in lodging houses, then see that they have all they want to eat and drink, Then we register them in different places and vote them. But the ballot is secret, and while they would always vote for us ordinarily, because we gave them their money and their whiskey, we didn't dare vote them when Hearst was a candidate, knowing ten to one every one of them would turn against us and vote for him. That was because he did so much for poor people, sending out on snowy days some of his men, with money, up and down the Bowery to keep men from sleeping out of doors when there *wasn't* any election.

"So we kept all our bums in the lodging houses where they couldn't move; and we got other trained repeaters to vote the name under which we had registered them. We took no chances on being double-crossed." Brisbane added, "I stood in line at the polls with a stream of those repeaters ahead of me."

The election ended, Brisbane reverted to standard edi torials on "Honesty," "Virtue," "How To Make Peopl Think," "Lessons From the Great Philosophers," and th like. Behind the scenes he and Hearst repaired their politica fences, and organized new alliances to put Mr. Hearst into the Governor's chair at Albany in 1906.

The idea that Brisbane was the power behind Hearst con tinued to grow. *World's Work*, for example, in its April 1906, number declared: "The Hearst of today is, in a degree the product of Mr. Arthur Brisbane. Mr. Brisbane is a cleve journalist and something more. He has a creed that look kindly at the underdog . . . Mr. Brisbane is capable of play ing a part, capable even of cynicism . . ." This magazin which had attacked Hearst repeatedly now insisted "he i sincere and is very much in earnest."

The obvious candidate for the Republican nominatio was Mr. Charles Evans Hughes, who had won great fam as counsel for the Armstrong Committee in his investigatio of insurance rackets. The year before, Brisbane had laude Hughes for his good work. "No one in New York Stat will question the excellence of the work done by the counse of the people, Mr. Charles E. Hughes. He has drawn from the management of the companies under litigation admis sions which have damned them in the eyes of the public . . He has done perhaps everything that could be done during the time at his disposal. If there should be no extension o time, Mr. Hughes can retire with perfect certainty that hi work has had the approval and aroused the commendation of the people."

The Municipal Ownership League became a state-wide organization, and changed its name to the Independence League. It recried the fact "that a corrupt non-partisan alliance exists in the state of New York between Political Bossism and Private Monopoly resulting in the present reign of graft and threatening the perpetuity of popular government as established and maintained by Jefferson and Lincoln." The document was obviously a Brisbane product.

While the Independence League was being used as a special pressure group upon the old parties as well as a catch-all for unaffiliated progressives, radicals, and liberals, arrangements were simultaneously going ahead to obtain the gubernatorial nomination from the Democratic Party. All of Hearst's lieutenants aided in this work. Secret negotiations were begun with the erstwhile "political criminal" Murphy to win the support of the Tammany machine for Hearst's gubernatorial ambitions. Brisbane was an active participant in these negotiations. Murphy finally agreed, with the understanding that Hearst was to contribute a substantial sum in payment, estimated by some political commentators as high as a half million dollars.

The editors of the *New York Times* were particularly naive and believed the idea of Hearst's nomination by the Democrats at their Buffalo convention would be as fantastic as an endorsement of him by the Republicans. Pulitzer, far wiser in the ways of politics, wired his editors: "Hearst's chances to obtain the Democratic nomination excellent, almost probable, as far as anyone can see today. Of course, seven weeks yet before Buffalo, September 25, and many things may happen, but no sign of any opposition whatever; Hearst getting things by default; Democratic machine rotten to the core . . . ; no leader has raised his voice yet, no activity or organization against him; ceaseless energy and work in his favor by his agents day and night all over state. Venality of Democratic bosses big and little; these are all in his favor, but above all the fact that corrupt and unprincipled persons like Murphy and McCarren will control at least half the membership of the convention voters . . . Whether Mr. Hearst is sincere or not in his profession is no more the question than whether Mr. Murphy is sincere in his alleged Democratic principles. The main question is who teaches more independence in voting, who awakens more indignation against corruption and mis-government, who comes nearer presenting the real truth, who is more against party humbug, who is against fooling the people. We sincerely hope Mr. Hearst will receive a large vote. If Henry George could receive 65,000 votes in the then smaller New York, without Brooklyn, it is an interesting question how large a vote Mr. Hearst will receive in greater New York, with an electorate practically three times as large as that when Henry George ran . . . The idea is to approve his candidacy without approving his principles and character, or that of his unprincipled good work in connection with the tax franchise bill originated and pushed by the *World*."

Pulitzer, in a later telegram to his editors, enlarged upon his point of view. "If he (Hearst) will give vigorous articulation and organization to the deep conviction among all intelligent Democrats that the name, spirit, spell and fame of the ancient Democratic Party was used by unscrupulous bosses and politicians purely for money making for their own pocket all the time, the Murphys, McCarrens, etc., he will render a public service, whatever his motives. If he will detach from the blind followers of the Murphy machine a large body, if he will teach the voter that his first duty is to vote in accordance with his own conscience and as a free man, he will render a service to the cause of independence and intelligence and show the way . . . Murphy has already seemingly made alliance with Buffalo bosses who are all for Hearst. Irony of fate, humorous situation that Hearst denounces Tammany boss, owes his popularity to this denunciation, received at least half of his votes (for Mayor of New York City) last fall simply because the people wanted to smash Murphy and McCarren, whom Hearst with extraordinary boldness and great ability, held up to public infamy; that now Hearst is apt to receive Murphy's support and through that support regular nomination for Governor and not only the anti-Tammany and anti-Murphy sentiment but also candidate of Mr. Murphy and Tammany Hall itself."

Murphy and McCarren lived up to their part of the bargain. They steamrollered the Buffalo Convention into accepting Hearst as the candidate for governor on the Democratic Party ticket. Once Hearst had the Democratic nomination safely tucked away, the Independence League was dismantled and junked.

Brisbane's laudations for Hughes a year previously now gave way to the most violent and vitriolic denunciations. He felt the weight of his responsibility as mouthpiece and keynoter in the campaign. The defeats of the past must now be the basis for victory. Every trick that had failed in the past was discarded; every one that had thrown confusion into the enemy was carefully studied, revamped, and refined to suit the current campaign. Brisbane ordered his staff to turn every bit of news into campaign material. Hearst must be elected, Hughes defeated—no matter what the cost!

Special editorials and editions were prepared for the upstate farmers. Deals were made with local and county politicians. Each was promised what he most wanted. Once again, Brisbane had special appeals made to Catholics, Protestants, and Jews. To labor groups he pictured Hearst as the friend of the underdog; to business men his candidate was described as a rich and successful business man who would ease their taxes and stop the looting of the public treasury.

Hughes was accused of being the tool of Ryan, the traction magnate and financier. Caring little for fact, Brisbane unsparingly applied his verbal brush to the opposing candidate. *The Outlook* indignantly observed: "Recently a Hearst paper stated on its editorial page that Mr. Hughes, after receiving a retainer from the Attorney General of the state to help him argue a motion in a gas suit, took the money and went to Europe. Not only has the Attorney General denied this, but Mr. Hughes has explained that he prepared the arguments and argued the case, and has not asked or got a cent. And yet Mr. Hearst up to this week has refused to put Mr. Hughes right before the community on a matter that concerns his personal and professional reputation."

The Hearst platform—once again largely penned by Brisbane—of anti-monopoly and Americanism sprinkled heavily with reform issues, prompted *Collier's* to suggest, "Why not reform yourself, Mr. Hearst? Why not do one act of beneficence with no advertising tag attached . . . Give some men credit, sometimes, beside yourself, for ordinary human virtues. Try to see to it that the trunks of murderers less often contain collections of your papers. Teach love. Rely on truth. Don't cry Ryan! at everybody who opposes you, whether it be Mr. Murphy one month or Mr. Hughes another. Don't lie about men to beat them. Beat them, if they deserve defeat, but by no weapon but the truth. *Ask Mr. Brisbane to try this principle even in such little matters as printing an old photograph, with smoke added, for the San*

Francisco fire, or one of the same photograph, in different pages of the very same issue, to represent a clergyman in Pittsburgh and a bogus baron in New York. Although contempt for truth may be worse in larger matters, it is better not to instil it insidiously even in detail."

The Plunderbund, as Brisbane called the corporation heads, were unmercifully attacked by him. The corporations, he charged, were really undermining the very basis of modern republican government. "Corporations control the primaries where candidates are nominated. Corporations control conventions. Corporations count the votes and own the bosses and select officials." This applied at Albany as it did in Washington. The public was plundered. Laws were passed for the benefit of corporations, interpreted in favor of corporations by corporation attorneys and corporation judges.

Mr. Hearst in a telegram to Brisbane had suggested attacking the courts, though cautiously. The people must be taught how they were governed by the judiciary. "The fight must be made for honest judges, and it is only a phase of the fight against boss rule and corporation rule which is the great issue of today. We do not want the judges appointed either by legitimate executives or by corrupt bosses or by criminal corporations. We want them elected by the people, responsible only to the people, and replaced at sufficiently short intervals to make them realize their responsibility. The people must appreciate the importance of the judiciary as well as the corporations realize it. They must own their judges, limit their power, and make their impeachment easy . . ."

Brisbane did as he was ordered. The attack on the courts and their corporation masters went on daily, unhampered by the fact that Brisbane not only knew of but actually assisted in setting up a series of corporations to protect Hearst, using dummy directors and other tricks of incorporation.

The *Morgen Journal* was separately incorporated. Mr. Hearst could not be held for its obligation, and as its debts were about three times the amount of its assets, to sue it for libel would be a complete loss. The *Evening Journal*, which carried Mr. Hearst's name as publisher and Arthur Brisbane's name as editor, was also the property of a separate corporation with more debts than assets, and the *New York American* was published by the Star Company "with its address in a lawyer's office, containing no one connected with the company." Even the sheriff was unable to find anybody there representing that corporation. What if he had? "It has, according to its own statements, no accounts receivable; no goods, wares, or merchandise; no machinery or plant; no cash on hand or in the bank. . . ." Its offices were in the same building with those of the Standard Oil Company, the Ice Trust, the Lighting Trust, the Book Trust, Mr. Harriman's Security Company, various sugar and coal companies and the rest of the huge corporations which Mr. Hearst and Mr. Brisbane were so regularly attacking. Said *Collier's:* "He (Hearst) attacks wealth and makes a million a year from a betting fraud. He attacks corporations, and uses nearly half a dozen of them for swindling purposes in publishing his American. It is the corporation plan perfected by Rockefeller, used by Hearst to avoid responsibility and cheat people with honest claims, like the claim of the poor woman recklessly run down and injured by a *Journal* delivery wagon."

The flood of Brisbane editorials throughout the state was having its effect. It appeared as though Hearst might win the election. President Roosevelt, in an effort to save the day, sent his secretary of state, Elihu Root, back to New

York to campaign for Hughes. Root, as the President's official spokesman, declared "that he, President Roosevelt, regards Mr. Hearst as wholly unfit to be governor, as an insincere self-seeking demagogue who is trying to deceive the workingmen of New York by false statements and false promises. And I say to you, with his authority, that he considers that Mr. Hearst's election would be an injury and a discredit alike to honest labor and to honest capital and a serious injury to the work in which he is engaged of enforcing just and equal laws against corporate wrong doing . . . President Roosevelt and Mr. Hearst stand as far as the poles asunder."

Pulitzer and the *World* campaigned on behalf of Hughes. So did most of the other papers. But the factor which turned the election against Hearst was the enmity of State Senator Pat McCarran, the Democratic boss of Brooklyn. He ordered his followers to scratch the Hearst name on the ballot. They did this in such numbers that Hearst lost out.

Brisbane's readers in the days following Franklin D. Roosevelt's reelection in 1936, were startled by the announcement: "Let's forget politics—read the *Journal* for fun." This idea was developed originally thirty years earlier. Immediately after Hearst's defeat for the governorship of New York in 1906, Brisbane addressed his following: "You will be pleased to learn, friendly readers, that this column of the *Evening Journal* will try to forget politics and politicians for a while. A majority of the votes, or a majority of the Dollars (it seems to be about the same thing in this happy land) have declared for a continuation of Trust Government."

For the next thirty years, the Brisbane-Hearst-Tammany alliances would alternate with long periods of bitter enmity. During one of the latter, Mr. Brisbane's under cover man for the *Journal* bribed a chambermaid at a resort in Mt. Clemmons, Michigan, where Murphy was taking a cure. Her job was to bring him the contents of Murphy's wastebasket day by day. From these contents were obtained copies of letters which had passed between Murphy and Mayor Gaynor, on matters of patronage. These were then featured in the *Journal*. Shortly thereafter, Brisbane met Murphy at Delmonico's restaurant and offered to shake hands with him. Murphy refused. They almost came to blows.

The following year, Brisbane was principal speaker at the dinner of the Genessee Society at the Waldorf-Astoria Hotel. James W. Gerard, the toastmaster, had introduced him as "righter of wrongs," and a revealer of "scandals in the lives of mosquitoes." Brisbane, unaware that a great many members of the audience were "big shots" in the Tammany Hall organization, launched into an attack upon Tammany and a defense of his paper, *The Journal*: "The newspapers do libel people; they do say things that are not true, that hurt people and can't be helped. But it is the little fellows that are hurt by falsehoods in the press, big people are hurt by nothing except the unpleasant truth. Therefore we try to be truthful about the little people. But the harm done by libel is not commensurate with that which would be done should the newspapers be interrupted in the fearless or even hasty conduct of their business.

"*The Journal* . . . published recently some interesting letters. I don't know where they came from . . .

"But you do know that the chief objection to the Hearst letters was that they were being published. And if they were stolen, as some say, was it not a plain duty to steal these records of that medley of corruption, Tammany Hall, and of those rascals with the red faces and thick necks who compose it?"

State Senator Thomas F. Grady, who followed Brisbane, and who, at the behest of Murphy, had sought to unseat the anti-Hearst delegate at the Democratic Convention of 1906, said: "As one of the gang of red-faced, thick-necked, grafters, I rise to reply. Nobody thinks that the Hearst letters were stolen. The proceeding was much more dignified. The chambermaid was bribed to save the fragments of the waste basket that they might be pieced together."

Brisbane had no reply to make.

Bribing chambermaids was only one of the methods used by *Journal* reporters under Brisbane's tutelage. The famous Standard Oil letters which were to create such a sensation in 1908 and again in 1912 had been purchased by the *Journal* from Willie W. Winkfield, the negro doorman, and Charles Stump, a white porter who had access to the office of John D. Archbold, vice-president of Standard Oil. The purloined letters were first offered to the *New York World*, which turned them down. Hearst denied before a United States Senate Committee that he paid anything for them, but *Collier's* later discovered that $12,000 had been received by the two men. The Standard Oil Letters were the sensation of the 1908 election. Senator Foraker of Ohio suffered a political death blow. The whole Standard Oil crowd was worried. Even President Roosevelt was concerned about them.

The Hearstian method of muckraking differed fundamentally from that of Lincoln Steffens, Ida Tarbell, Ray Stannard Baker, David Graham Phillips, or Upton Sinclair, who were tireless in documenting their evidence. Hearst found it much easier simply to trust his own imagination or that of Arthur Brisbane and his subordinates, with the result that much of the muck which he raked up was muck which he himself deposited.

The ill luck attending his mayoralty campaign of 1906 left Hearst cold on the Democrats. The following year he promoted a Republican-Fusion deal to elect Max Ihmsen, his political manager, as Sheriff of New York. But the new alliance, though ably supported by Brisbane broadsides, failed miserably.

The boy wonder of Nebraska, William Jennings Bryan, who had twice been Democracy's presidential nominee and twice been defeated, received the nomination for the third time in 1908. Hearst and Brisbane, who had profited so much from the work of the "Great Commoner," fought him tooth and nail in the election. They put an Independent League ticket in the field, the effect of which they hoped would be to split the Democratic party and render a Republican victory certain. Thus did Hearst reply to Bryan's eulogy of his party loyalty three years before.

As for Arthur Brisbane, it was in large measure due to Bryan that his name and editorial acuteness had been made known to hundreds of thousands of people in the smaller towns and cities of the east and middlewest. But Brisbane's aversion to Bryan became as great as that of his publisher. He instructed his reporters to goad his erstwhile political champion, and his artists and cartoonists to make Bryan look thoroughly ridiculous in the eyes of the reading public.

"If you want to get into trouble," the editor warned, "elect Bryan. He doesn't understand how to conduct any kind of business. Before he started *The Commoner*, he might have fooled me into thinking he could run a newspaper but it is a mass of stupidity and egotism. I have run a newspaper and Bryan could not be office boy on my paper. Bryan is an ignorant man. You need in the White House a good brain, and you don't need a mouth. Bryan is a mouth."

A sidelight on political mud-slinging of the day is furnished in the exchange of epithets between William Travers Jerome, popular District Attorney for New York, and Messrs. Brisbane and Hearst. Jerome was described by Brisbane as "this man, with the shaking hand, the uncertain, inflamed mind, the almost lunatic conceit of arrogance . . . He is the man who has made it safe for the big criminals to rob the millions of smaller people."

Jerome had retorted in kind, implying that the editor of the *Journal* (whom he viewed as the real power behind Hearst) was mentally deficient. He won applause by demanding that his opponent "go to Brisbane and find out what his own platform meant." Hearst he described as, "intellectually sterile, socially vulgar, and morally obtuse."

The Hearst Independent League Ticket was a complete disaster. Hisgen, the presidential candidate, polled a mere 83,628 votes, while John Temple Graves, a Hearst feature writer who was vice-presidential candidate, obtained only 77 votes in his own home state of Georgia.

Successive defeats for himself and his candidates over a period of six years did not daunt Hearst. In 1909 he threw his hat a second time in the ring for Mayor of New York. His opponent this time was Judge William J. Gaynor, who was supported by Tammany. In the preliminary political skirmishes, Hearst had been a strong backer of Gaynor and suggested him as the Fusion nominee against Tammany Hall. But Murphy picked him for the job as Tammany's representative and Gaynor accepted. Brisbane was furious at what he considered a double-crossing. Hearst then had himself nominated for the office on his own brand of Republican-Fusion ticket. The regular Republicans nominated Otto Bannard, a political unknown.

A unique bit of political strategy was then engineered by Brisbane in the 1909 election, when he wired to Mr. Pulitzer in Berlin: "Should be glad to contribute two columns a day over my signature to *Evening World* during campaign if acceptable. Thought you might like to give our side. If you accept proposition, I shall write no other signed articles except for *World*." Pulitzer thought it over and wired Seitz: "Might make good feature but you alone must decide and let him know." Seitz accepted the offer. Pulitzer again advised his editor: "Be careful in announcements to avoid editorial identification with Brisbane's views. Might be good idea to have another column representing Tammany's views answering Brisbane. And another column representing Republican views as equal chance for all."

In his biography of Pulitzer, Don Seitz remarks, "He Brisbane, attacked Gaynor with such virulence that the Judge sued the *World* for libel—a proceeding without precedent—in view of the stout support of his candidacy. There was consternation in the office as to the best course to pursue. Some were for instant repudiation of the candidate, but Mr. Cobb very amiably met the crisis with this admirable editorial: Judge Gaynor's libel suit against the *World* for the publication in its evening edition of one of Mr. Brisbane's entertaining articles in behalf of Mr. Hearst is to be accepted as further proof of the Democratic candidate's militant independence.

"If Judge Gaynor, in the midst of the campaign, brings suit against the *World*, which is his chief newspaper supporter, we have high hopes that as Mayor, he would be equally courageous in starting litigation in the public interest. That kind of a man could bring all the tax dodgers to time, collect the franchise taxes that the corporations have evaded for years and compell the traction companies to fulfill their contract obligations. That is what we want a Mayor to do.

"New York needs a Mayor who is not afraid to start law-uits against anything and anybody and who will not be werved by personal considerations of any sort."

The *World* gained tremendous prestige as a result of this ction while Brisbane's denunciations of Gaynor added little uster to Hearst's candidacy. His employer was on the po-itical skids. Gaynor won by a large plurality. His vote was 50,387. Hearst received 177,304, and Bannard, 154,187. Thus ended for the time being the political hopes of Bris-bane's Man of Destiny. The *New York Post* estimated that he eight years of political campaigning had cost Hearst pproximately two million dollars.

Meanwhile, Arthur Brisbane's income continued to rise teadily. By 1910, he was the highest paid editor in the world, and proud of the title. His salary was as large as that of the President of the United States and his cabinet com-bined. Early in 1907, he purchased the deserted village of Allaire, New Jersey for $25,000. It covered about 600 acres nd was close to his old boyhood home of Fanwood. There he built himself a palatial residence, established a fine racing table, and announced a model farm would soon be in opera-ion. Allaire became his permanent abode.

The original six hundred acres proved only a beginning. Brisbane was as land-hungry as his grandfather James. He nstructed his agents to buy up more and more of the land urrounding the original estate. Two years later, he told William Inglis, a writer for *Harper's Weekly*, "I guess I have ten thousand acres down there. The old official survey made it about seven thousand acres, but experts tell me that t may run up to ten or twelve thousand acres."

When Inglis asked him what he was going to do with it all, Brisbane answered: "Sell some and keep the rest for farms. I'm going to help that country grow if I can. It's a beautiful country. I have a dozen horses down there and they are doing well. Just now there are only forty working men on the place, but they are all enjoying life, working decent hours, for fair wages, and occupying comfortable houses with their families. They get milk and potatoes free; so the more children a man has, the better off he is."

His Long Island estate at Hempstead had also been enlarged. The new automobile speedway, built privately by William K. Vanderbilt and other New York millionaires, skirted Brisbane's place. The private speedway had been fenced off with stout locust posts and strong wire netting. To an acquaintance, Brisbane remarked proudly: "I sold them all those posts. They were all grown on my place at Allaire."

Brisbane's enthusiasm for real estate knew no bounds. He wrote about it in his column. He spoke of it in his lectures. Friends, acquaintances, even strangers were urged to buy! buy! buy! "You ought to buy a place down here," said he to a reporter who had come to interview him. "It's very healthy country and the land values are going to boom as soon as the Pennsylvania Railroad finishes its tunnel and gives Long Island real rapid transit. Even today values are far above what they were a few years ago. Why, the man who sold me this property threw in fifteen acres of pasture land as an inducement. Just like putting thousands of dollars in my pocket now."

The highest paid editor in the world was still a bachelor. His sister, Alice, lived with him and looked after his home. Other friends and relatives stayed with him from time to time. But the household was run for him and for him alone.

Like his father before him, he had certain queer notions regarding health and diet. He had read about the wonderful cures of tuberculosis and other diseases effected by keeping patients out of doors all the time whether waking or sleeping. "If that sort of thing makes sick men well," he reasoned, "why shouldn't it be even better for well men?" So he had built on the roof of his house a room whose walls were of glass windows which could be opened wide to let in sunshine and fresh air. There in his pent-house—the grandfather of pent-houses—he slept the year around, fair weather and foul. In winter he wore woolens and a cap and was covered with a woolen blanket. In summer, to avoid being awakened by the light of early morning, he would tie a black silk handkerchief over his eyes.

Brisbane was an indefatigable reader and would devote one or two hours to some classic before he retired. Almost invariably these were the works of the French Encyclopedists, Voltaire, Rousseau, Moliere, or the scientific classics of the nineteenth century—books by Charles Darwin, Herbert Spencer, Ernst Haeckel. At other times he would sample Shakespeare, Heine or Goethe. Hundreds of books poured into his office and his home. Some of them he read. Most of them he merely glanced at.

The economic, sociological, and scientific achievements of the late nineteenth and early twentieth century never really appealed to him. In spite of his continuous editorializing about looking forward into the future, Brisbane always did so with the eyes and outlook of a person of the eighteen-seventies. His mind was cluttered up with innumerable stray bits of facts and information mixed with half-baked theories and acute observations.

He spoke his comments on the happenings of the day with great ease into the machine given him by his friend, Thomas Alva Edison. As he talked into the mouthpiece of this strange contraption fragments of French philosophy, Continental history, English nineteenth century evolution, a hodgepodge of mental bric-a-brac would be transferred from his mind to the cylinder, interspersed with comment on the news of the day.

Part of Brisbane's astounding success may have been due to the fact that his mind mirrored so completely the mind of the average man. It, too, was a jungle of half-digested and half-remembered fact and fiction. Brisbane's editorials were like the conversation carried on by an average group of persons, who, in the space of a few minutes, have covered personal feelings, business affairs, problems of the day, sex crime and politics. Each point is interesting, but only for the moment.

"At one moment he is busy with the editorial thirteen-inch shells he hurls against the predatory rich; the next he is al wrapped up in the fate of the nest of helpless little blind mice who might die because their mother has been trapped or gravely and reverently discussing the character of God or urging men who criticise others to find out their own faults first, or speculating about the happy future when we shall easily work and play and live upon the floor of the ocean."

Typical of Brisbane's specious logic at the time was his statement to the students of the Columbia School of Journalism in 1907, that Henry Ward Beecher was "the yellow journalist of the church, for his spectacular methods, especially in putting a runaway slave girl in the pulpit and selling her a public auction—the proceeds to be used for freeing the slaves."

Though his analogies often limped and his observations were frequently superficial and banal, no such charges could be made against his techniques of attracting attention quickly and effectively. "You know you can't drag people up to a subject and make them think about it. You've got to talk to them about things they really care about. Suppose you want to catch the attention of a woman who has a baby with red hair and cross eyes? Of course, you explain to her what a wonderful thing it is for a baby to have red hair and cross eyes. Then you've got her, and you can tell her about something else."

Brisbane worked on the theory that man was interested first in himself, then in his family, and last in his race or country. "Hang your idea on a peg that all can reach," he used to say. Discussing this with Gilbert Seldes, years later, he illustrated it as follows: "If you have to write an article on 'The Dietary Laws of the Ancient Hebrews and their Connection with the Social Customs of the Time,' call it, 'Don't Blame Moses—He Had No Ice Box.'"

Knowing that man is usually selfish and greedy, Brisbane used these sentiments to fortify his editorials. But he also knew that man likes to think of himself as an idealist—that his thoughts and actions are inspired by higher and nobler motives than those of selfish gain. These chords, too, Brisbane would play upon in other sections of his editorials. He sounded the slogan of *service* long before our service clubs had become the established institutions they are today.

The future looked bright to him. Enlightenment would put an end to war: "We've developed a long way beyond the primitive days when men rushed out with clubs and stones to brain every stranger they saw . . . Implements of war will be as great a curiosity to future generations of really intelligent men as the rack and the thumb screws and the Iron Maiden are to us now." The struggle for individual gain and power, too, would some day end. When that day came, "you'd find men working as hard as ever but working for the common good, the ablest men proud of their ability to do more than the others. That spirit is in us now. All it needs," he added, "is development and encouragement. Look at the boys who play football for the colleges. Men in the prize ring fight hard for fame and big purses. Football players are pounded twice as hard, train harder, work harder, risk their lives. Why? For the glory of their college—not for individual fame. You couldn't hire men to take all that punishment! Transplant that spirit into business life, and we'll find the big men working their hardest for that kind of glory. It's coming! It's bound to come! The right kind of education will do it. Make men think, convince them. They'll do the rest."

The campaign for enlightenment was demonstrated every day in the newspaper which Arthur Brisbane edited. Consider, for example, the issue of March 3, 1907, with its twelve pages of illumination for the masses. The editors of *Collier's* summarized its content as follows: "The first page contained a photograph of a painting of the rape of the Sabine women and a large and gruesome picture of similar doings in Alaska. The second was mainly devoted to an illustrated discussion of the question: 'Is Woman Human or Animal?' The third was occupied with a tale of a 'Woman With a Past,' and an 'Infatuated Weekly.' The fourth described a torture chamber. The fifth was devoted to 'The Black Spectre That Frightens Fashionable Brides at the Altar.' Although the sixth and sevetnh were supposed to be given up to science, there was a chance for a female figure to hold up her dress while walking through a sewer. The eighth represented 'The Gruesome Enigma of a Dead Hand.' On the tenth, a gentleman explained: 'How I Fascinated Over Twenty Different Women,' and gave examples in the art of Bigamy. The eleventh combined fiction about 'Love, Intrigue, Tragedy, and Mystery,' with some of the most indecent and contemptible advertisements known."

Four thin volumes constitute the sum total of Brisbane's wisdom between the covers of books. Three of them are already completely forgotten—museum pieces referred to on rare occasions by students of journalism. The fourth, entitled "Mary Baker Eddy," is still sold occasionally by the Christian Science Reading Rooms.

Arthur Brisbane interviewed Mrs. Eddy at her home in Concord, New Hampshire, June 8, 1908. This interview was published in every Hearst paper. In later years Brisbane considered it one of his finest pieces of reporting. Brisbane was no Christian Scientist, "but a believer in material science, in non-sectarian government, and in the absolute right of Christian Scientists to believe whatever they choose." The great editor turned reporter described minutely Mrs. Eddy's home, her furniture, her appearance, and waxed lyrical in his praise of her. "Where there is a big effect there is a big cause. When you see flames, lava, and dust coming up from the mouth of Vesuvius, you know there is power below the crater.

"When you see millions savagely fighting in the name of one leader, or patiently submissive and gentle in the name of another, you know that there was power in those men.

"When you see tens of thousands of modern, enlightened, human beings absolutely devoted to the teachings of Mrs. Eddy, their leader, and beyond all question made happy and contented by her teachings, you know there is a cause underlying that wonderful effect."

Brisbane then described his meeting with the founder of Christian Science: "Beside a writing desk, in her arm chair, sat a white-haired woman who rose and walked forward, extending her hand in friendly greeting to a stranger. That was Mrs. Eddy, for whom many human beings in this world feel deepest reverence and affection and concerning whom others have thought it necessary or excusable to write and to say unkind and untruthful things.

"It is quite certain that nobody could see this beautiful and venerable woman and ever again speak of her except in terms of affectionate reverence and sympathy. There are hundreds of thousands of Christian Scientists who would make almost any sacrifice for the privilege of looking upon Mrs. Eddy's face . . . A face made very beautiful by age, deep thought, and many years of exercise of great power. The light blue eyes are strong and concentrated in expression . . . The forehead is high and full, and the whole expression of the face combines benevolence with great strength of will. Mrs. Eddy has accumulated power in this world. She possesses it, and she exercises it, and she knows it. But it is a gentle power, and it is possessed by a gentle, diffident, and modest woman."

When Brisbane asked her about the lawsuits (then pending against her which sought to take away from her control of her money and her actions) she replied, "in a deep, earnest voice that could easily have been heard all over the biggest of her churches: 'Greed of gold, young man. They are not interested in me, I am sorry to say, but in my money, and in the desire to control that. They say they want to help me. They never tried to help me when I was working hard years ago and when help would have been so welcome.'"

Brisbane described at length how young she looked, how firm her tread, how clear her eye, how good her health, and how keen and penetrating her mind. So flattering was the picture that, reading it today, one begins to wonder what was behind it. "The lawyers who oppose her would like to show that Mrs. Eddy is not fit, mentally or physically, to take care of herself or of her fortune, which is considerable. They would like to remove her from her present surroundings, and make her physically subject to the will of others appointed to control her. Success in this effort, in the opinion of the writer, would be shameful, a degradation to all womanhood and old age." Brisbane was thoroughly impressed when Mrs. Eddy said to him: "Young man, I made my money with my pen, just as you do, and I have a right to it." To which Brisbane adds, "Mrs. Eddy not only has a right to it, but she has the mind to control it."

But why this tremendous interest in the affairs of Mrs. Eddy? The key to it is perhaps found in the statement made by Mrs. Fremont Older in her authorized biography of Hearst: "In 1907, another son was born to the William Randolph Hearsts. He was an attractive, intelligent, blue-eyed child, his father's name-sake, William Randolph Hearst, junior. When the baby was about a year old, he fell ill with pneumonia and the distraught parents feared that he was dying. Mrs. Morrill Goddard, wife of the editor of the *American Weekly*, was a Christian Scientist and very devoted to her faith. She treated William Randolph Hearst, Junior, and he recovered.

"The healing of his son brought a new spiritual interest into Hearst's life. From that day, the publisher had a friendly interest in Christian Science. When *McClure's Magazine* attacked Christian Science and Mrs. Eddy, Hearst sent Arthur Brisbane to write articles concerning the leader of the movement. They proved to be a defense of Mrs. Eddy."

Brisbane did his job so well that when Mrs. Eddy died he was the only non-Christian Scientist who functioned as an honorary pall-bearer.

Another outstanding personality of the day about whom Arthur Brisbane wrote was the King of the meat packers, J. Ogden Armour.

Hearst investigators in 1905 and 1906 made a drive against

the big meat packing houses of Chicago. Brisbane had these stories featured in the *Journal*. They made spicy reading, built circulation, and threw the fear of the Hearst press into the hearts of Swift, Armour, Cudahy, and Morris. Upton Sinclair, one of the investigators of the period fictionized his findings in his novel, *The Jungle*, which was published by the Hearst press. It created a sensation. President Theodore Roosevelt called for action. A federal grand jury indicted most of the packers.

At this point Mr. Hearst's publications lost interest in the issue. Shortly thereafter, Brisbane began to play down the exposures. Writing in the February, 1909, *Cosmopolitan*, he chided Sinclair for his cries, groans, lamentations, and conclusions. "Mr. Sinclair acted as a little girl does when she walks into the garden and finds a green slug eating her pet tomato vine.

"Such conduct on the part of the slug seems horrible and unbelievable to the little girl. And everything in the business of killing animals seems horrible and unbelievable to kind hearted Sinclair, who is a poet, a vegetarian, and the gentlest of all gentle dreamers."

His story of the king of the meat packers, Brisbane assured his readers, would differ from the type then in vogue. "This is not to be the usual delightful, daring and dashing flogging. No shivering, cringing money king is to be dragged up to the magazine whipping post and lashed remorselessly while all the world cries bravo!"

"That work has been done, well done; it would be ridiculous to do it over again badly. It has been done by Upton Sinclair in shrill spiritual falsetto; by Lincoln Steffens in grumbling, rumbling bass; by Alfred Henry Lewis with Texan foam and fury; by Ray Stannard Baker in lawyer-like reportorial-like coolness; by Ida Tarbell with Lady Macbeth fury and Charlotte Corday devotion. Why do it all over again feebly?"

Brisbane discovered J. Ogden Armour to be an amazingly capable man. To be sure, he was one of the great money kings of the twentieth century. But these money kings, he found, were great human benefactors. "They are showing the people how to do the things that the people must do for themselves in the future." Armour received a clean bill of health and was heralded as a pillar of progress and enlightenment.

Immediately after the meat packing investigation, an issue of vital importance to the nation as a whole, but especially to the underprivileged masses who were heavy consumers of medical nostrums and canned foods, came to the fore—the Pure Food and Drug Bill then before Congress.

Brisbane did not seize upon this issue; instead, he fought shy of it whenever possible. The editor's only active part during this campaign was in the form of a concession to the groups which the bill condemned. He satisfied the patent medicine interests and at the same time yielded to pressure from the public by preparing the advertisements of the patent medicine groups as news or editorials—never forgetting, however, to collect on the basis of the current advertising rates. Had he attacked the enemies of the bill, he would have alienated some of the *Journal's* best advertisers who paid top rates to misinform the American public on the merits of their miraculous cures. As in 1906, Hearst and Brisbane again protected the patent medicine interests against the public in 1934 when the Tugwell Bill was before Congress. This policy on the part of the Hearst press met with considerable criticism.

Norman Hapgood, editor of *Collier's* at the time of the Food and Drug Bill agitation, ran a series of startling articles on the patent medicines of the day and described the type of material prepared by their central association, The Proprietary Association of America. In the opinion of Hapgood, most leading newspapers refused to accept the canned editorial articles of the Proprietary Association. There was one conspicuous exception—Mr. William Randolph Hearst.

"Mr. Hearst defends the patent medicine people, as should be expected. He (or Mr. Brisbane for him) repeats the stereotyped and ready made arguments of the Proprietory Association. . . . Mr. Hearst (or Mr. Brisbane) is able to explain why he publishes gambling tips while attacking gambling; he is able to explain why the doctors are the real villains, not the Proprietary Association of America." Somewhat later, the Hearst Press announced that it was going to cease accepting so-called objectionable medical advertising, but a glance through the issues of the *New York Journal* reveals their continuance for years afterwards.

A new field to which Brisbane now turned his attention was that of theatrical advertising. Notwithstanding the immense circulation of the *New York Journal*, it was considered a poor medium for such advertising because it was believed its readers constituted a very small portion of the easy-spending Broadway audience type. It never printed legitimate theatrical criticism.

Broadway money was always easy money. Why shouldn't the *Journal* get some of it? Brisbane decided upon a new policy. Ashton Stevens, who had been writing dramatic criticism for the *San Francisco Examiner*, was transferred to the *New York Journal*, where he founded a dramatic department. But Stevens was not a conscious agent to the scheme worked out during the next three years between the advertising and news department of the paper.

The Christmas season of 1907-1908 saw the inauguration

of the new plan. Brisbane began with a series of editorials announcing the new policy regarding theatres. His first, on December 13, 1907, was entitled HOW TO CRITICISE MEN, ACTORS, CHILDREN, ALL WORKERS. From this time on, the *Journal's* attitude toward Broadway would be that of "constructive criticism." Instead of tearing down, it would seek to build up. "It is the intention of this newspaper in criticising books or plays to tell the public about those that are GOOD AND WORTH SEEING, and leave the others to their natural fate, WITHOUT KICKING AN UNHAPPY FAILING MAN OR WOMAN. . . . We want our readers to know that if they read extended criticism of a play in this newspaper, IT IS ONLY BECAUSE IT IS A GOOD PLAY AND ONE THAT, FOR REASONS STATED, WOULD AMUSE THEM OR INSTRUCT THEM. Why do we not imitate the sun that warms, develops, and brings out what is good?" asked Brisbane.

The warming rays of Brisbane's editorials were soon to begin.

Meanwhile the *Journal* had also begun what was known as "Zittell's Vaudeville Racing Chart." Vaudeville was then in its heyday, and Mr. Zittell imitated the regular form sheet used for horse-racing, applying it to vaudeville. The theatres were listed as the tracks and the performers as the horses. Each Saturday, "Zit" would arrange the numbers of each house into winners of first, second, and third places together with the "also ran." The scheme, in modified form, has been followed by movie reviewers in recent years. The racing chart, which was a bid for vaudeville advertising, succeeded from the start. Within a month, the racing chart page was filled out with announcements and "cards" of acts.

The first number of "Zit's Chart," which appeared January 18, 1908, was evidently unaware of Mr. Brisbane's "constructive criticism," for it read: "Mlle. August & Co.

gave one the cramps. Of all the Kosher cheese acts ever offered in vaudeville, some parts of this one should be sent to the Board of Health."

During that winter and spring many favorable editorials appeared in the columns of the *Journal* about plays, playwrights, and actors. But not until the following fall, as the new theatrical season got under way, did the "constructive criticism" really start.

The leading editorial of November 6, 1908, was entitled: A GREAT PLAY—TWO POWERFUL MEN COLLABORATE. Brisbane urged his readers: "Go to see it. It will make you think . . . It contains a lesson for husbands and wives and others." The play was "Samson" by Gillette.

The next day, a full page advertisement appeared in the *Journal* for the play.

A few weeks later, December 30, another lead editorial was entitled: THE BATTLE—INGENIOUS PLAY INGENIOUSLY ADVERTISED, followed by the usual Brisbane approbation.

Three days later, "The Battle" was advertised by a full page in the *Journal.*

On January 9, 1909, an editorial appeared: A GENTLEMAN FROM MISSISSIPPI—"This is one of the plays that has a PURPOSE—may its success breed imitators." As the warming rays of the sun cause seeds to sprout and grow, Brisbane's warming rays of constructive criticism brought about a sprouting of full page advertisements. "A Gentleman From Mississippi" responded with a full page advertisement the day after the editorial appeared.

During the balance of that theatrical season, four warming editorials from the pen of Brisbane applauded Broadway productions. Each was followed by full page advertisements.

Will Irwin, who first exposed these practices of Brisbane

ı the June, 1911, issue of *Collier's Weekly*, reported: "The ew advertising policy of the *Journal* was public property ı the theatrical district, where gossip travels as in a little illage. Every manager knew that the *Journal* offered a paid dvertisement and a Brisbane editorial for a thousand dollars. : was remarked that Brisbane would not 'boost' under this rrangement any play which he did not like—but his tastes re catholic. Just as well was it understood that for five undred dollars, the *Journal* would give a half page advertisement, and a 'special' with illustrations by Nell Brinkley, ›gether with liberal 'news notices.'

"The *Journal* generally signed no contracts for these ansactions; it was just a gentleman's agreement between ›licitor and manager. Of course what the managers really anted for their thousand dollars was not the advertisement ut the editorial."

Miss Brinkley's pen and pencil sketches on theatrical or audeville attractions appeared about forty times during ıe 1909 season—almost without exception accompanied y a half-page advertisement. Sometimes Brisbane arranged ›r other feature writers or artists to do the "constructive riticism" or the illustrations—Beatrice Fairfax, Merle Johnon, or "Tad." The policy continued through the year 1910.

When the theatrical managers arranged to use the columns f the *Journal* for advertisements, all was well editorially. ut those who failed to comply fell under an eclipse. Thus, hen one of the great circuses of the day came to Madison quare Garden and refused to buy the space demanded by ıe solicitor for the *Journal*, it was told it would get no pubcity in the paper. The circus remained in New York for ı entire month. Every other paper published many stories bout it. Only one appeared in the *Journal*—a notice that the ircus had opened and that a performer had broken his wrist!

The *Collier's* article caused a sensation. Hearst and Bris
bane were furious. They threatened both criminal and civ
libel suits. Hearst did in fact file a civil suit for $500,00
Collier's was not worried. It announced editorially tha
Hearst "was shrewd enough, however, not to bring th
threatened criminal action, so he can safely circulate hi
$500,000 bluff, knowing that he can wait three or four year
and then drop his case. Probably he suspects, that, followin
our custom, we have not discharged all of our ammunitio
in the first engagement."

Collier's was right. The suit was dropped. No denial wa
ever made to the charges but the policy of "constructiv
criticism" in the *Journal* ended.

8

AMERICA FIRST

Only three American presidents since the days of Abraham Lincoln may safely be called leaders of progressive thought and legislation—Theodore Roosevelt, the Republican; Woodrow Wilson and Franklin D. Roosevelt, Democrats. Yet these three progressives received the most damning vituperation from Arthur Brisbane and William Randolph Hearst. Praise was reserved for such executives as William Howard Taft, Warren Gamaliel Harding, and Calvin Coolidge.

Leading candidates for the Democratic nomination in 1912 were Champ Clark, speaker of the House in the sixty-second Congress, and Woodrow Wilson, Governor of New Jersey and former president of Princeton University. Clark was a machine politician allied with New York's Tammany crowd. Wilson, on the other hand, was the ardent advocate of those reforms which had been demanded editorially so often by Brisbane. But Hearst and Brisbane could not and would not throw their support to Wilson.

The presidential bee no longer buzzed so loudly in Hearst's bonnet. He saw himself instead as the Warwick of American politics. Aspiring candidates must come to him and bid for his favor. They must accept his advice. The Hearst chain would become the official mouthpiece of the administration and Brisbane editorials would voice the desires and shape the policies for the new president.

Woodrow Wilson called Hearst a "sham progressive"

and, as far back as 1910, had joined Mayor Gaynor of New York in denouncing him. Hearst had invited Wilson to dinner to talk things over. Wilson told his friends: "I want the Democratic Presidential nomination and I am going to do everything I can, legitimately, to get it, but if I am to grovel at Hearst's feet. I will never have it."

The month preceding the Baltimore Convention of the Democratic party was devoted to a continuous series of attacks against Wilson. Brisbane personally took the lead in this campaign of mud-slinging, ably seconded by John Temple Graves (Hearst's hand-picked vice-presidential candidate in the 1908 election) and Alfred Henry Lewis, a veteran Hearst man who could blow hot or cold on any issue.

Wilson was depicted as pro-English, as a snob and a poseur. He was charged with being a lady's man while a professor at college. Every conceivable point that could be built up to prejudice opinion against the candidate was carefully developed. Hearst readers were told that among Wilson's crimes was that of accepting a Carnegie academic pension.

At the Baltimore Convention, Champ Clark took the lead from the start, with Wilson a poor second. William Jennings Bryan, himself no longer a candidate, but a force in the party nevertheless, finally obtained passage of a resolution pledging the convention not to support any candidate backed by Tammany Hall or the Illinois delegation under Sullivan. The Hearst-Brisbane machine was working hand in glove with both of these groups; they in turn were tied up with the traction interests and real estate operators headed by August Belmont and Thomas J. Ryan.

Arthur Brisbane covered the convention for the Hearst chain. His articles had a definite anti-Wilson, pro-Clark bias. Day after day the hot, tired delegates balloted while behind the scenes political manipulators attempted to arrange a compromise. This would have been possible, according to a *New York World* editorial, "until it became apparent to every intelligent man that the Ryan-Murphy-Belmont-Hearst coalition had set out to strangle Progressive Democracy, destroy Mr. Bryan politically and prevent the nomination of Woodrow Wilson at any cost."

After fifty-eight ballots, Wilson won. America's self appointed Warwick lost his first major engagement.

Unable to support the Democratic nominee, Brisbane and Hearst found it equally impossible to support Theodore Roosevelt's Progressive Party, so they whooped it up for Taft and the G. O. P.

The attacks against Wilson continued after his election as President. Wilson's personal appearance before Congress to read his message was denounced as a "mere adaptation of the British usage of a speech from the throne." Another serious charge was that "Mr. Wilson has only comparatively recently delivered an address in which he declares that he gets his information on world events from the columns of the *London Weekly Times*." Surely no more devastating accusation could be made!

But this perfidious crime had its antecedents. Had not the Chief Executive gained his degree of Doctor of Philosophy by an essay "which contended flagrantly in the face of fact, that the English parliamentary form of government was superior to the American Congressional system?" And to top it off, Mr. Wilson was found to be "an English free-trader."

The Anglophobia of Brisbane and Hearst had been obvious for many years. It was good business, for the Hearst readers were made up largely of those whose elementary education in American schools had been colored by the red-coat theory of British aggression. The Irish, German, and Italian populations in New York, Boston and San Francisco who composed a large sector of Brisbane's readers likewise gloried in attacks upon John Bull.

Winsor McKay, star cartoonist for the *New York Journal* and the special cartoonist for Brisbane's Sunday editorials, would depict Wilson as a graceless school master misrepresenting to his pupils the patriotic events of American history. Brisbane gloried in his newly found task of "exposing" Wilson. These attacks, both in editorials and news columns, became so vicious that the *New York World* charged they were "more malicious, mendacious, and incendiary" than those upon McKinley prior to his assassination. Every rumor or insinuation was built up into a charge against him.

Immediately after America's entry into the World War Mr. Brisbane, fearful that he would be forced to desist from his attacks, wrote Wilson a letter asking if the Espionage Act before Congress would be used to shield the President against criticism. The reply dated April 27, 1917, is a noteworthy document of the Chief Executive of a country in time of war. To the present day world it is especially significant in the light of the actions of Mussolini, Hitler, and Stalin, with their blood purges, mass executions, and punishment of those who dare oppose their whim.

"My dear Mr. Brisbane:

"I sincerely appreciate the frankness of your interesting letter of April 20, with reference to the so-called Espionage Bill now awaiting the action of Congress. I approve of this legislation, but I need not assure you and those interested in it, that, whatever action Congress may decide upon, so far as I am personally concerned, I shall not apply or permit any part of this law to apply to me or any of my official acts, or in any way to be used as a shield against criticism.

"I can imagine no greater disservice to the country than to establish a system of censorship that would deny to the people of a free republic like our own their indisputable right to criticise their own public officials. While exercising the powers of the office I hold, I would regret in a crisis like the one through which we are passing to lose the benefit of patriotic and intelligent criticism.

"In these trying times, one can feel certain only of his motives, which he must strive to purge of selfishness of every kind, and wait with patience for the judgment of a calmer day to vindicate the wisdom of the course he has tried conscientiously to follow. Thank you for having written me.

"Cordially and sincerely yours,

"Woodrow Wilson."

British Imperialism was to be feared and fought, but American Imperialism was to be encouraged. So long as Porfirio Diaz ruled Mexico with an iron hand, the attitude of the Hearst papers toward the Republic to the south of us was most friendly. Diaz had been a close friend of the elder Hearst and had given him, almost as a gift, nearly six hundred thousand acres of land. George Hearst had likewise acquired the huge Babicora ranch of nine hundred thousand acres in the state of Chihuahua during the Diaz administration. William Randolph Hearst inherited these properties and still holds them.

When the Mexican people finally rose in successful revolt against their oppressor and drove Diaz from the country, the Hearst papers began a campaign against the Mexican people and their various governments which, with slight interruption, has continued to the present day.

Francisco Madero led the forces of revolt against Diaz and forced him to sign his own abdication May 25, 1911. Madero was a liberal and an idealist. He wished to improve the lot of the impoverished Mexican people. Brisbane lent his services to a campaign against him. In 1913, Madero was shot by Victoriano Huerta, a general who promised to restore the ancient regime and give protection to foreign concessionaires and interests. President Wilson refused to recognize the Huerta government. Huerta was overthrown by the victorious forces of Carranza on August 20, 1914. From then on for a period of years, Mexico continued in turmoil. Francisco Villa, a Mexican "Robin Hood," conducted his own private warfare against the new government. He captured and shot eighteen Americans on January 10, 1916 and soon thereafter crossed into New Mexico, killing seventeen additional American citizens. Hearst's Babacora ranch was one of the foreign concessions raided by Villa's bands in 1915.

The Hearst papers were among the first to demand American intervention in Mexico. Jingoistic editorials by Brisbane were supplemented by fake news stories and photographs. Max Sherover in his "Fakes in American Journalism" describes one such incident:

"On the twenty-second of December, 1913, the *New York American* published a picture where seven children holding up their hands can be seen on the shore of the ocean. The paper said, in black type: 'As proof of an almost unbelievable state of barbarity existing in Mexico, Mr. Russell, an English traveler, fellow of the Royal Geographical Society of London, sends the photograph shown here to the *New York American.* The children were driven into the water, forced to hold their hands above their heads and shot in the back. The tide carried their bodies away. Note the terror in the face of the one child who partly faces the shore.' "

Sherover continues: "Russell was very indignant when he saw the inscription under the picture published in the *American.* He immediately sent a communication to the *New York World* in which he said in part: 'The representative of the *New York American* manifested special interest in a picture taken by me in February, 1912, and published in the *New York Tribune* of November 1, 1912. This picture, as I explained to him, showed a number of Carib children bathing. As I told him, I had asked the children to raise their hands, so that the picture would afford a view of their remarkably fine physical equipment." The pictures, according to Mr. Russell, were not even taken in Mexico, but in the British Honduras.

Similar tactics were used by Brisbane and Hearst with reference to the peace conference arranged between Mexico and the United States which took place at Niagara Falls in the summer of 1914. One of the Hearst's ace reporters, Roscoe Conklin Mitchell, was sent to cover the proceedings. Mitchell, known for his accuracy, wrote a report, accurate but optimistic in tone, covering the initial proceedings. Not a word of his dispatch was published the next day in the Hearst press. Instead there appeared a wholly fictitious report which intimated that President Wilson was yielding in the most humiliating way to the Mexican demands. A few days later, the Hearst papers carried a sensational story—a fantastic message from President Carranza to the Mexican negotiators. This message was a fake from beginning to end. Mitchell, who had once before threatened to quit his job, now resigned. His employer wired him: "Why resign without cause? We should greatly regret it. Please be good soldier and good boy.—Bradford Merrill." But Mitchell refused to be conciliated. He left the Hearst press in disgust. A few days after the fake message had appeared in the Hearst press, the actual message from President Carranza was released for general publication. It was friendly and conciliatory.

Brisbane meanwhile kept up a running fire of attack against the Mexican government. Even after the United States had entered the World War, this continued. "Instead of lending a hundred millions to Carranza to use in Mexico," wrote Brisbane on July 14, 1917, "the United States ought to put about one half that money into the hands of judicious individuals, let them go down to Mexico, buy Carranza, Villa and the entire crowd, and extend the admirable Government of Woodrow Wilson down to the Panama Canal."

The following year he remarked: "Is it not important to think about pacifying, organizing, quieting, and if necessary absorbing Mexico?"

Major political issues in the year immediately preceeding the World War were Prohibition and Woman Suffrage.

Like his father before him, Arthur Brisbane was at all times a consistant champion of the voting privilege for women. It was one of the few reforms on which he didn't back-track through the years. He once remarked that the only real good that came to the United States out of the World War was the amendment to the Constitution granting suffrage to the women of America. Mrs. Pankhurst, the militant suffragette leader in England, he considered "about ten times as big as Joan of Arc—or a thousand times." But the comparison, flattering as it seems on first reading, loses some of its lustre when we consider his opinion of the Maid of Orleans. "Joan of Arc had no education, and therefore she knew nothing, therefore she could not do very much

. . . Joan of Arc, I suppose, was really 'the mascot' of the French Army. The things that she did were probably as important as the things that are done by the mascot of a baseball team, or the goat kept on a battleship as a mascot."

Public sentiment, which a few years earlier had been bitterly anti-Trust, found new interests. Brisbane, who knew, perhaps, better than any other editor of his day how to veer and tack with the changing winds of public opinion, let the Trust issue become a matter of secondary importance in his publications. The only exception to this rule was Standard Oil and its founder. John D. Rockefeller was "good copy" at any time, and the most hated man in the whole country. Hence, Brisbane frequently wrote about him. At times these editorials were hostile and sarcastic; at other times, friendly and apologetic.

In 1914, Brisbane had declared: "If you are ever inclined to join with Upton Sinclair and worry about the Rockefeller fortune, say to yourself, 'It does not matter to me who owns the Atlantic ocean as long as I can sail on it.' " Why worry about Mr. Rockerfeller's one hundred twenty million dollars a year income? "The people of the United States gave the oil of the United States and many railroad industries of the United States to John D. Rockefeller. And he in return, like a sort of benevolent financial providence, is giving to the people health, for the millions in oil they gave him."

On June 15, 1916, he discussed: JOHN D. ROCKEFELLER AS A MODERN ROBIN HOOD. The whole editorial was a defense and praise of the great oil magnate. "John D. (Robin Hood) Rockefeller has certainly given to the poor, whatever he might have done to oil well owners and motor car owners."

Just four months previously, on February 18th, Brisbane had demanded: IF THE PEOPLE HAVE THE POWER TO REGULATE THE PRICE OF GAS, WHY NOT THE PRICE OF GASOLINE? How

Long Will A Few Conspicuous 'Philanthropists' Continue Their Shameful Extortion? This time the readers were told: "It is bad enough to be robbed secretly by the pickpocket who escapes with your purse, but to be robbed by a national pickpocket who posts on the highways the amount that he proposes to steal today and posts tomorrow his desire to extort a still greater amount, is unworthy of men who imagine they live in a republic." In this editorial he agitated for GOVERNMENT REGULATION OF PRICES OF MONOPOLIZED NECESSITIES INCLUDING GASOLINE.

Those who in recent years have read Brisbane's frequent eulogistic accounts of the motion picture industry, its products and its leaders, will be amazed to learn that at one time he despised them. He wouldn't go to see a motion picture. Nor was he interested in film censorship. Perhaps this was due to his unfortunate experiences in trying to tie up editorials and advertising for the Broadway shows a few years earlier. Perhaps he believed motion pictures would never become large sources of lucrative advertisement for his employer's newspapers. Perhaps . . . but whatever the cause, Arthur Brisbane certainly gave a decided jolt to the film magnates of New York, and drew down upon himself a heap of abuse.

It all happened at the Motion Picture Board of Trade dinner, protesting against movie censorship, held at the Hotel Astor, March 12, 1916. The dinner, as planned by the prominent motion picture magnates, was to be a combination movie and newspaper function. The film men said that if the censorship continued unimpeded in their business, it would next attack the newspapers. To lend the greatest possible weight to their dinner of protest, they asked Arthur Brisbane to be the chief speaker.

Mr. Brisbane was introduced amid fervent applause as "The master of short expression—the greatest editor in the world."

"As for your own business," said Mr. Brisbane, "I'll say that I know very little. I am one of the few living men who have never seen Mary Pickford or Charles Chaplin or Theda Bara, or Miss Clarke. All I have seen is the Durbar, Scott's North Pole pictures and 'Carmen,' which I couldn't escape because it was given in Mr. Hearst's house and I happened to be a guest there . . ."

"I have great respect for the men who are developing the financial value and the real genius of those people, but I don't think that I should be bothered about it. As to the censorship I do not think that I can become very much excited about it. (No applause) The moving picture, so far as it is merely a melodrama, a story, a tragedy or a comedy, is only a money-making proposition, and whether it is censored or not I don't in the least care. (Silence)

The balance of the speech, with interpolations as reported by the *New York Sun*, continues:

"That part of the work is only in its infancy, and, as I say, I don't care in the least as to whether it is censored or not. (Probable mental comment such as, 'Oh, we got you the first time.')

"All the moving picture amounts to today, at least the modern moving picture, is that it is an amusement. Its success is based upon the stupidity and lack of intellectual development of the human race." (Raucous laughter from the newspaper section of the diners only.)

"The moving picture man," continued Mr. Brisbane, again going into the wails of the movie men about censorship, "has no more claim for sympathy than has the man putting up a public building who is told that the building is to be a certain number of stories high. No liberty is interfered with. Based for its success on stupidity and the lack of intellectual development of the human race, a man who will not read Shakespeare now sits for an hour and a half in front of a screen ruining his eyes.

"But if we have been using speech for only about one hundred thousand years we have used our eyes for one hundred million years. Lobsters with their eyes on the ends of sticks were our grandfathers back in remote ages. We use our eyes to select our wives and husbands, our pictures, and dress and therefore we now look at Mary Pickford in 'Rags' and there is no necessity for mental effort.

"As for the movies and decency, there is more money in running a Childs' restaurant than in running a Haymarket (theatre). So I'm sorry I can't be more enthusiastic about motion picture censorship. Censorship will not hurt the good among you and if it harms the evil they deserve it. (Tremendous silence).

"One question I should like to ask is, 'Why have you not run anything great?' There is no trouble in making a list of sixty or a hundred great works in the various art forms, but when I asked the gentleman over there, a Colonel, I believe he is, (Mr. Brisbane indicated the wholly unenthusiastic face of Commodore J. Stewart Blackton) and the other gentlemen at this table tonight what were the six greatest motion pictures they agreed fairly well that 'The Birth of a Nation,' 'Carmen,' and 'The Battle Cry of Peace' were among the six, but they couldn't agree on the three others. In an industry where hundreds of millions have been invested, if you cannot list six or even sixty great works you haven't gone far." (Prolonged gloom)

Having uttered these words of wisdom, Mr. Brisbane excused himself for hurrying away to catch his train.

The storm of criticism against the "master of short expression" which arose within the ranks of the motion picture magnates was indescribable. By word of mouth, by telephone, by letter, and by telegrams, Hearst officials from city editor to "the chief" himself were informed as to the harmful nature of Mr. Brisbane's remarks. There were even implied threats of a boycott of the Hearst press.

Brisbane quickly realized that he had spoken out of turn and must make amends without delay. His opportunity came on the ninth of April at a dinner for Marcus Loew, celebrating his tenth anniversary in the theatrical business.

"The moving picture will give immortality to the genius and the grace of the great actors," shouted the repenting sinner to his beaming listeners. "The moving picture within two or three years and perhaps this year will be the greatest weapon in political fights," he continued. Praise without end was heaped upon the motion picture. It was, he exclaimed, "one of the greatest mediums of all times for educating and developing the human mind." Brisbane did not speak extemporaneously. This time (the first prepared speech he had ever delivered, so he said) he read it from manuscript. But he concluded with an extemporaneous burst: "To atone for what I did, if the matter can be mended, I wish to say that I am going to see all three of them alive and photographed as soon as possible. I am going to see Mr. Chaplin wiggle his feet, Miss Pickford cry; and Miss Bara look fierce. I have seen their photographs and I know that is what they are famous for."

During the vaudeville which followed the speech-making, Will Rogers drawled, "This isn't a benefit except in a few ways. It gave Arthur Brisbane a chance to renege."

Mr. Brisbane did as he promised. He became interested in the movies. So did his employer—but for different reasons.

David Wark Griffith, then America's outstanding film director, had spent a fortune in screening a tender, sentimental narrative of the French Revolution, featuring Lillian and Dorothy Gish, in "Orphans of the Storm." It was a fine film but somehow the public didn't respond enthusiastically at the box office. Brisbane, ever on the look-out for new advertising sources for his paper, and determined to make good with the motion picture industry, offered his assistance. He told Griffith his advertising was poor and wasted. Instead, he proposed twelve solid pages of advertising, once a week, at a dollar a line, in the *New York American* and the *Evening Journal.* Griffith was appalled at the cost and declared the plan impossible. Brisbane countered with the suggestion that Mr. Griffith average the last month's receipts; that he authorize the advertisements and he, Brisbane, would accept in payment therefor half of the increased intake. Brisbane said he himself would write the copy. Griffith finally agreed to take the space.

The editor, with his uncanny ability to sense public reaction and sensation, prepared an entirely new type of advertising. Emphasis was no longer placed upon the romantic glamour of the history of the film nor upon the wistfulness of the leading lady. New and aggressive and novel methods were tried. One huge advertisement pictured Billy Sunday, the renowned revivalist (who had never seen a motion picture) in a leaping gesture indicating that if he ever went to a movie, it would be to see "The Orphans of the Storm;" and he told why. Churchmen, editors, explorers, historians, politicians, the names of all the great at the time were enlisted to indicate why they preferred "Orphans of the Storm."

The box office effect was instantaneous. The picture became a huge success. David Wark Griffith, who at the last noment had decided to pay the straight rate for the adver-ising, instead of dividing profits, was more than glad that e failed to agree to Brisbane's original proposal.

After Mr. Hearst himself became a patron of Hollywood, motion picture producer with his star—Marion Davies—, risbane naturally boosted the industry and above all, the ictures of Hearst's Cosmopolitian Productions. For a period f ten years or more, Mr. Hearst was associated with the Aetro-Goldwyn-Mayer Corporation. Naturally, the Hearst apers and Mr. Brisbane gave undue emphasis to all matters ppertaining to their output or their stars. When Mr. Hearst nd Miss Davies shifted from Metro-Goldwyn-Mayer to the Varner Brothers lot, Mr. Brisbane's enthusiasm for MGM vaned. Thereafter Warner pictures received the best break.

In spite of his varied activities, Brisbane continued to vatch his health and figure. He was a good amateur wrestler nd boxer but his favorite diversion remained horsemanship.

For many years, newspapermen had speculated on the uestion of whether Brisbane would ever marry. It was at ist answered in the affirmative. He had been a lady's man vhen young. Even the worries of later years had not pre-ented him from enjoying the company of women, but he ad fought shy of matrimony.

Mr. and Mrs. Seward Cary, who came from upstate New 'ork, were among his closest friends. Mrs. Cary was Ar-hur Brisbane's cousin. He spent much of his spare time at heir estate. The Carys had a little daughter, Phoebe. The vorld-renowned editor soon became her fast friend and rdent admirer. Hand in hand they would stroll through he woods. Together they played games, and Phoebe told rthur her secret ambitions, her hopes and desires. Arthur, turn, confided in her. When she asked him why he didn't

have a wife, as other grown up men did, he told her th
he was waiting for her to grow up. Then, if she'd have hin
he'd marry her.

Phoebe grew to womanhood. Cousin Arthur remaine true to his promise, made years earlier. On July 30, 1912 the were married. Mrs. Brisbane became a devoted wife. Sh never tried to interfere with the business activities of he famous husband. Their first child, Seward, was born withi the first year of their marriage. Soon five other children we born to them: Sarah, Emily, Hugo (who died in 1932 Alice, and Elinor, in the order named. Brisbane often re marked that he wanted at least ten children! He also de clared himself an advocate of late marriage.

Once when his old friend Charles Edward Russell aske him why he was so money-mad, Arthur Brisbane replied "I want to leave a comfortable income to my wife and fan ily. I don't want to see my children forced to go out int the world in poverty, as I was compelled to do."

9

TWO MISUNDERSTOOD PATRIOTS!

THE EVENTS which followed in the wake of Serajevo were as unexpected to Arthur Brisbane as to the man on the street. Ever since the conclusion of the Spanish-American War Brisbane had written thousands of editorials in which he had proved that mankind was growing wiser, better, kinder—that wars, while a necessary heritage of our past, would soon be done away with completely. To be sure, he didn't expect all warfare to end at once. But neither did he anticipate a general conflagration enveloping the whole of Europe and eventually almost the entire world. He dismissed the crisis as a mere bluff on the part of the major powers. They couldn't or wouldn't enter into actual conflict. But they did! When the armies began to march and battle, the optimistic editor explained with certainty that such a war could last only a few weeks at most.

The sentiment for peace, already a potent factor in the United States prior to 1914, gained greater momentum during the first few months of the conflict. Brisbane and Hearst decided to capitalize on it. They became, momentarily, ardent pacifists and swung their batteries of printing presses, paper pulp and ink into action.

The drive was inaugurated from Chicago by Andy Lawrence, Heart's publisher of the *Examiner*. The following exchange of letters reveals one of the methods utilized to rally nation-wide support behind the self appointed saviors of the peace movement:

August 13, 1914.

Chester M. Wright,
Managing Editor,
New York Call,
New York.

Dear Sir:

As publisher of the Chicago Examiner, I am presenting to you a matter of the highest importance.

I believe that peace in Europe will be restored only after the strongest and most persistent pressure is brought to bear by the civilized nations of the world, and that the earlier these efforts are made the quicker will results follow.

The Chicago Examiner has invited the rulers of non-combatant foreign powers and leaders of thought throughout the United States to join in a great International Peace Movement.

The replies already received have been numerous and sympathetic. They come from heads of foreign powers, ambassadors, United States Senators, Governors of States, men prominent in finance and in commercial life generally.

Your paper is invited to join in this great movement for peace. I am not requesting any mention of the fact that this movement was inaugurated by the Chicago Examiner, but that you, through your influential paper, pitch in and help.

You will find on the press sheet enclosed herewith copies of the replies which the Chicago Examiner has now received and which were published in the Chicago Examiner August seventh, eighth and ninth. You are at perfect liberty to make such use of these as you desire and in any way that will best suit your purposes.

If the press of the United States will lend its wonderful influence to bring about peace in the world, it will be reward enough.

I shall be pleased to hear from you personally regarding your ideas about this peace movement and also to receive any issues of your paper in which you may make mention of it either editorially or as news matter.

It is our purpose to publish a symposium of reviews of the leading newspapers of the country.

Respectfully,

A. M. LAWRENCE

For almost two score years, Brisbane had been parading as a "near socialist," a "sane socialist," or a "radical." Unnumbered thousands groping their way toward a new social philosophy fell under his influence. The Socialist party had at last recognized in Brisbane and Hearst two dangerous demagogues. So the managing editor of *The Call* replied to the plea for peace:

Mr. Andrew Lawrence,
Chicago American,
Chicago, Illinois.
Dear Sir:

Your invitation to the New York Call to join with the Chicago Examiner in what you term 'a great International Peace Movement' is highly interesting.

It is not long since the Hearst newspapers were lashing themselves into a frenzy of 'patriotism' in an effort to embroil the United States and Mexico in war.

Every person who follows newspapers closely remembers the pro-war attitude of the Hearst newspapers in connection with the California anti-alien Land Law.

The Hearst newspapers have left no line of type unset that might drive the United States into war with Mexico and Japan . . . and now you ask the New York Call to assist you in leading the kings abroad and the representatives of Big Business at home in an international peace movement.

Permit me to suggest that you showed far more acumen in the case of the well remembered Chicago newspaper strike than you are showing now. In that great strike you stood out as one of the most intense antagonists of the working people. As publisher of the Chicago Examiner you did your share in breaking up homes and filling the hospitals—you and your colleagues on the Chicago American and on the allied Big Business newspapers of Chicago.

It cannot be that you have so soon forgotten the work of Ed. Barrett and his crew. It cannot be that you have forgotten the assaults and the murders of those eventful months. There was a war in which you stood for war.

And now you talk of peace. Mr. Lawrence, your plea for peace it too ridiculous. It is too obviously what is known as a "Hearst play" for circulation. It is one of those situations in which you can prattle to your heart's content to the working class, knowing while you do it that you run no risk of injuring any of those interests that Hearst papers never injure.

You will have to omit the New York Call from the list of papers you are trying to enlist in this cause. The New York Call and the great Socialist movement for which it stands have fought too long for peace not to be able to continue the fight without the aid of unclean hands.

When the war clouds began to roll up over Europe there were in all that great continent none who made felt their opposition as did the Socialists. Their stand for peace was genuine. Their earnestness and sincerity as the first and most powerful force for peace is admitted by all—even by your own chain of newspapers, as pointed out editorially by them at the beginning of the conflict. We stand with the working class . . .

The New York Call
CHESTER M. WRIGHT, *Managing Editor*

The policy of the Hearst press at this time, as formulated and developed by Brisbane, was first, to clamor for peace at all costs; second, to adopt a generally anti-British attitude with reference to war news and aspirations; third, to print fake interviews, stories, pictures, and the like; and fourth, to use one type of appeal for its German-reading audiences and another for the English-reading section. A final point was to develop anew the Japanese war scare.

In conformity with this plan, the *New York American*, September 9, 1914, printed a picture of British troops with the caption: "This Is The Type of English Soldier Who Is Doing Such Tremendous Work on the Battle-front in France." On the same day, the same picture was published in Hearst's German paper but the descriptive matter had been changed somewhat: "British Troops That Run So Fast That It Is Not Possible For The Germans To Capture Them."

Stories appeared during the last few days of September telling of a peace interview with "highly placed representatives of the British Government." These were denounced by the *London Times* as entirely false. It investigated the matter and discovered there was "not even a vestige of foundation for such an interview."

War news was faked from the start. It was announced that the International News Service maintained "the greatest news gathering organization the world has ever seen . . . with representatives in every first-class city in Europe, on every battlefield . . . with more than eighty correspondents, many of them of world-wide fame."

The editors of *Harper's Weekly* investigated these well known correspondents only to discover that many of them were purely fictional characters. Letters sent to several of them came back marked: "No Party" or "Not Found."

Brisbane hurled denunciations against Wilson for his dismissal of Bryan as Secretary of State. He opposed the original Anglo-French loan and called upon President Wilson to forbid it. He called for an embargo upon all munitions to the warring nations. But the sinking of the *Lusitania*, which aroused most newspapers to a frenzy, was excused by both Hearst and Brisbane. Hearst wrote: "Whether the *Lusitania* was armed or not, it was properly a spoil of war, subject to attack and destruction under the accepted rules of civilized warfare . . . The *Lusitania* incident is, of course, no cause for a declaration of war."

Brisbane maintained the United States had no right to insist that Germany refrain from submarine warfare.

Nation after nation was drawn into the maelstrom of the conflict. Soon it became obvious that America's isolation policy was doomed to defeat. The war spirit surged throughout the country. Militant patriotism became the order of the day. Pacifists were denounced as weaklings, and cowards, and pro-Germans. American newspapers generally were taken in by the concoctions of the Allied propaganda machines. But for each story they printed about victories by the British or French, or atrocities committed by the "Huns," Brisbane filled the *New York Journal* with much that was just the opposite. He burst many a propaganda bubble of France or England by telling the truth. On the other hand, the dispatches coming to the Hearst papers from their Berlin correspondent had an obvious pro-German taint. This became understandable later when it was learned that their correspondent, William Bayard Hale, was also secretly employed by the German Embassy.

When the British Admiralty denied that a German submarine had torpedoed and sunk one of its battleships, H. M. S. *Vindictive*, Hearst was able to publish an actual photograph of the incident. Actions such as this caused the British and French Governments to refuse Hearst correspondents access to the first line trenches or the use of their trans-Atlantic cables.

Brisbane countered by devoting increased space to attacks on British censorship and British interference with American commerce. He likewise defended the Irish Insurrectionist movement, then growing rapidly, and in conjunction with his publisher gave open support to the American Truth Society, an organization composed almost exclusively of Irish-Americans and German-Americans. The action of the British Government in October, 1916, in denying further use of mails to Hearst's International News Service, followed on the 29th with similar actions from the French Government, as well as the debarring of all Hearst papers from the Dominion of Canada, augmented the fury at home against both Hearst and Brisbane.

For once the wily editor failed to sense the changing drift of public opinion. Even after he and Hearst did recognize it, they still believed themselves sufficiently strong to stem the tide. Again they were mistaken. For this double blunder, they were soon to become the victims of the mob spirit, and the emotional hysteria which they had so frequently whipped up against others. Their papers were boycotted. Copies were destroyed and burned in public. Newsdealers refused to handle them. These two "friends of the common people," were denounced in the press, the pulpit, and the street as traitors to their country.

Hearst belatedly tried to meet the situation by printing the title of his papers in red, white, and blue, and by running stanzas of the "Star Spangled Banner" at the top of the editorial page. The maneuver came too late. Circulation fell. Both Brisbane and Hearst were hanged in effigy. In desperation, Hearst, then at Palm Beach, wired his publisher, Carvalho: "Why not run the red, white, and blue title that we had for last edition through all editions for a few days during these troublous times? I think it will meet popular sentiment. Also please run little American flags to the right and left of date lines on inside pages, like *Chicago Herald.*"

A few days later he wired: "If situation quiets down please remove colored flags from first page and little flags from inside pages, reserving these for special occasions of a war-like or patriotic kind." He added as a footnote: "I think they have been good for this week, giving us a very American character and probably helping sell papers, but to continue effective, they should be reserved for occasions."

Winsor McKay was Arthur Brisbane's chief cartoonist, and supplied many of the ideas around which the Brisbane editorials were developed. They made a good team. Hearst, desirous of warding off attacks upon himself, tried to get the American public thinking in terms of other problems. Again he wired Carvalho: "McKay could make strong eight-column cartoon, occupying in depth two-thirds editorial page, showing smaller figures Uncle Sam and Germany shaking their fists at each other on left side page and on right side big head and shoulders of Japan, with knife in hand, leaning over into picture and evidently watching chance to strike Uncle Sam in back. Title of picture to be: 'Watchful Waiting.'—Look Out, Uncle Sam, Your Neighbor Japan is Eagerly Awaiting An Opportunity to Strike You in the Back."

Although the war brought about a decided drop in Mr. Brisbane's prestige, this was compensated for in part by the fact that it also enabled him to become a newspaper publisher in his own right. Thirty-four long years he had labored for others. His remuneration, financially speaking, had been of the best. But he remained to all intents and purposes a salaried employee. There had been opportunities in earlier days to acquire ownership of newspapers or magazines. None had appealed to him; he preferred real estate investments.

In 1917, he bought not one but three papers, and admitted having tried to buy another—the *Newark Star-Eagle*. Those he purchased were the *Evening Wisconsin* and *The Press* in Milwaukee (which he merged under the name of *Wisconsin News*) and the *Washington D. C. Times*, which he purchased from Frank Munsey. In taking over the responsibility of ownership for these papers he did not leave Mr. Hearst's employ, did not suffer a reduction in salary, nor did his syndicated output for Mr. Hearst diminish. On the contrary, it was increased, since it was at this time he began writing his "Today" column.

The fifty-three-year-old Brisbane shifted his office from the old *Journal* building in Manhattan to Washington. There, in the shadow of the nation's capitol, he carried on his double job of editing his own papers and those of Mr. Hearst. He was in constant conference with Congressmen, Senators, and other high government officials. Every string he could pull was used to build a barrier against the roars of "traitor"—"pro-German"—"slacker," that greeted him wherever he went. Such remarks were undignified, unjust, un-American, thought Brisbane. Once the United States entered the War, he joined the parade. He whooped it up for Uncle Sam in bigger and blacker type than all his competitors.

Even the frenzied activities of wartime did not cause him to lose touch with more commonplace problems. War was war, to be sure, but everyday issues had to be given due consideration. To his good friend, Mabel Dodge, he gave much advice on how to write her articles on love, motherhood, and related subjects. "In your article, 'The Growth of Love,' " he scribbled in a postscript, "I have changed the word 'pervert' to 'dreadful failures.' The word 'pervert' by the crowd is understood in one vile way, and represents a thought which I do not want to put into the minds of millions of people even for the sake of truth . . . Anything worth printing can be told in the kind of language that you would use talking to a girl twelve years of age."

On one occasion, he suggested that Mabel Dodge tell why women like to be married "pulling against the stake, like a little goat tied with a string.'" On another, he wanted her to write on "why every woman wants to find a master, why it is that women long to be bossed." Not content with the suggestion, he went on to give the reasons, in his own pithy style:

"Of course it dates back to the days when they were knocked senseless and dragged into the cave by some gentleman who had previously killed the other gentleman. That is shown in Patagonia where the marriage ceremony consists in standing the woman up against a tree, and knocking out her two upper front teeth.

"In real life things are different. Every woman thinks that she wants to find a master. And every man imagines that he wants to find a slave. And when the dust settles, the woman is nearly always the master and the man nearly always the slave. You might write this."

Brisbane knew he was a patriot—a misunderstood patriot. But because he was ardently pro-United States, it didn't necessarily mean that he had to be pro-French, pro-British, and pro-Japanese. Nor was he, as the following extracts from his editorials clearly indicate:

"How many millions do we want to spend?" he wrote August 14, 1917, "How many men do we want to kill, in order to get not only the peace that would satisfy us, but would satisfy England and the other Allies?

"Which is the dominating voice in the peace-making question? Is it the voice of America, which is now paying the bill, supplying the food, and asking nothing but an end of murder? Is it the voice of England, not always renowned for her unselfishness?"

On August 21 he remarks: "We must learn what England wants besides the German colonies in Africa and Bagdad and 'moral concessions for little peoples.'

"We shall probably have to continue drilling and issuing bonds until England gets what she wants—although she MIGHT be persuaded to throw off some of the 'moral concessions.'"

Three days later, he suggests: "It is one thing to make the world safe for democracy. It is a different thing to make the German colonies in Africa safe for England and the Pacific Islands of Germany safe for Japan.'"

On September 8, he asks: "How do the English do it—once more we ask? Wheat cheaper in England than in America! Flour cheaper in England than in America! And we are sending them the wheat and the flour and lending them the money to buy it!" Discussing this same issue a few days later, he launches into a series of attacks against Herbert Hoover, who is accused of being an American working for purely English ends.

"Dear old England learns quite slowly," the misunderstood patriot writes, ironically. "England takes our dollars—quite a few of them without close scrutiny—takes our word for them that they are good. England takes anything she can from us—except our word as to the character of

Americans that we send abroad to help in the War. 'Can I send over in my army American-born men of German parentage to fight for you?' asks our old uncle.

"'Ah, yes, you may do that,' replies John Bull. Americans of German descent are good enough to fight for Englishmen, good enough to buy Liberty Bonds, to provide cash for Englishmen, good enough to give money to the Red Cross, but not quite good enough to nurse a wounded Englishman, don't you know; they might put poison in his tea."

When it was not Britain, it was the Japanese who were accused of getting rich at our expense. "And they are NOT spending any of this money, millions at a time, to help their dear Allies in Europe. The dear Allies that want money must come to the United States for it.

"We are glad to give it to them and ought to be glad. But we must not forget our dear and clever friend and ally, Japan.

"While we are getting poorer—thousands of millions at a time—she is getting richer. We must save a little something, so that we may be able in case of necessity to demonstrate our friendship for her.

"Building up a good army and navy will help. But WE MUSTN'T LET OUR CASH SUPPLY RUN TOO LOW WHILE JAPANESE CASH IS PILING UP."

Another editorial says: "Can you imagine that smile on the faces of the elder statesmen of Japan as they read of our sixteen billions to be spent in the first year of war, and that we are handing out our money in little lots of one hundred millions to a thousand millions to any ally that will borrow it?" A little later he adds, "As the white races bleed year after year, the yellow races of Asia remain intact and watch. Not a pleasant thought."

This suspicion of the Japanese and of Asiatics develops

into a constant feature in Brisbane's column. At one time he says: "If China is in a state of anarchy, with no possibility of interior control, somebody will have to restore order. And our polite little Ally, Japan, living right next door to China will be found deliciously ready to take care of China, regulate her, develop her resources and earn an honest yen in the process."

At another time he adds: "Japan, if she chose, could walk into Russia, . . . and help dear old England wonderfully. But when dear old England made a bargain with Japan to be good friends forever, she bargained with somebody just a little bit smarter than herself—about the only nation on earth with that quality."

Interspersed among these editorials of Brisbane's in 1917 and 1918 were comments on the Germans. On July 2, 1917, his readers were told: "The courage of the Germans is marvelous. This applies to the men in the trenches holding off the whole of Europe. It applies equally to the German women at home, enduring starvation for the cause THEY, however mistakenly, believe to be right.

"You can't defeat a German by putting a bullet in him, unless you kill him. You can't make him give up by injuring his body . . .

"You can't defeat a German by injuring his BODY. But

You can defeat him or any other man by worrying his MIND."

Although at the time the idea seemed ridiculous, we now know the effects of propaganda were as great as, perhaps even greater than Brisbane realized. But his method of presenting the problem at the time caused both ridicule and laughter. At one time he suggested that American air fighters force an overwhelming desire for peace on the Germans, "not by butchering them, not by ripping them with shrapnel or choking them with gas, but by MENTAL WORRY."

The *New York Tribune*, during September, 1918, featured a series of articles by Kenneth McGowan, entitled "Hears-s-s-st: Coiled in the Flag." McGowan contended that since the United States had entered the War, the Hearst papers had printed: seventy-four attacks on the Allies, seventeen items in defense or praise of Germany, and sixty-three pieces of anti-war propaganda, and one deletion from a Presidential proclamation, "While America has been engaged in the life and death struggle with civilization's enemy."

Five of these articles carried the heading: "Bris-s-s-s-bane: What Hears-s-s-s-st's Editor Did With The Washington Newspaper German-American Brewers Bought For Him."

It is obvious today that McGowan himself was under the influence of war-time hysteria. But he did document his material very carefully and he leveled eleven specific charges against Brisbane—charges of methods used by him to obstruct America's effective participation in the war or to bring about a premature peace:

1. Brisbane attacked England bitterly.
2. Brisbane posed Japan as threatening American welfare and as growing stronger through a war which was weakening our own country.
3. Brisbane pictured Mexico as a danger to the United States and advocated its conquest.
4. Brisbane constantly emphasized the horror of warfare and wrote of "international murder."
5. Brisbane tried to prevent the shipment of food to the Allies on the plea that American children were starving.
6. Brisbane constantly emphasized the large size of the loans made by the United States to the Allies and the

still larger amounts being sent by the Government, expatiating on the work of social welfare they might do if they were not to be used for "wholesale murder."

7. Brisbane first pictured Germany as about to be rent and defeated by revolution.
8. Brisbane next expressed the view that if peace were made, the German people would then revolt and dispose of the Hohenzollerns.
9. Brisbane hailed *Hearst* as "the most powerful and effective peace worker in this country," and called for an immediate peace.
10. Of immediate war measures, Brisbane gave enthusiastic support only to the building of a huge aerial fleet—a prospect that has since developed grave difficulties.
11. While camouflaging his anti-war utterances in the typical Hearstian manner, Brisbane filled his columns with a confusion of reasoning and propaganda which left one single clear impression—doubt and criticism of our Allies and the War.

Brisbane's chance to explain his war time activities came n the summer of 1919, when a subcommittee of the United tates Senate held hearings on "Brewing and Liquor Intersts and German and Bolshevik Propaganda." This investiation grew out of a speech made on September 14, 1918, y A. Mitchell Palmer, alien property custodian, at Harrisurg, Pennsylvania. Palmer declared: "Let me say to you s an illustration of the length to which these interests will o, the facts will soon appear which will conclusively show hat twelve or fifteen German brewers of America, in association with the United States Brewers Association, furnished the money, amounting to several hundred thousand dollars, to buy a great newspaper in one of the chief cities of the nation; and its publisher, without disclosing whose money had bought that organ of public opinion, in the very capital of the nation, in the shadow of the Capitol itself, has been fighting the battle of the liquor traffic. That money was placed there under methods and by contrivances cleverly designed to keep secret forever who it was that put the money into that great newspaper and the purposes for which it was there."

The day following Palmer's speech, *The Washington Herald*, published by C. T. Brainard, called upon Mr. Palmer to give the name of the paper to which he referred. It was generally known that the only paper "under the shadow of the dome of the Capitol," which had recently changed hands was the *Washington Times*, purchased by Arthur Brisbane from Frank A. Munsey a little more than a year previously.

Brisbane decided it was time to talk. He came back with an editorial in *The Times* which admitted he had purchased the paper from Mr. Munsey with funds ($375,000) borrowed through C. W. Feigenspan, a New Jersey brewer. Attempting to turn the wrath from himself, he addressed his editorial to "Mr. C. T. Brainard, Manager, *Harper and Brothers*, for J. Pierpont Morgan, the owner:" who he said "manages and edits the *Washington Herald* with a brilliancy and success punctuated during the past year and a half by unsuccessful efforts to sell the paper to me.

"Mr. Brainard's *Washington Herald* expresses interest in the ownership of the *Washington Times* and wants to know if it is owned by brewers.

"Mr. Brainard will not resent the frank statement that a question coming from him would ordinarily deserve little attention. But his question may interest others. Here are the facts: The *Washington Times* is one hundred per cent my property. It was purchased from Frank A. Munsey for $500,-000 of which sum, as has been previously stated in this column—$250,000 is still due Mr. Munsey. And he holds in his possession the entire stock for the payment of the balance of purchase money due him. To buy the *Times* and put a losing property on a paying basis, I required approximately half a million dollars.

"Mr. C. W. Feigenspan, President of the Federal Trust Company of Newark, New Jersey is a friend of mine and a brewer. As every newspaper editor in the country knows, I have for more than twenty years advocated as a temperance measure the suppression of whiskey traffic and the encouragement of light wine and light beer.

"At my request, Mr. Feigenspan arranged for me a loan of $500,000. It turned out that I required a less amount—$375,-000 was sufficient for the expenses involved in putting the *Washington Times* on a paying basis.

"This amount I borrowed from Mr. Feigenspan between June, 1917, and November 1917. And the money, in due course, will be repaid with interest.

"If I have any further reply to make to Mr. Brainard, I will make it to Mr. Morgan who owns Mr. Brainard, or to Mr. H. T. Davison, who manages Mr. Morgan."

Two days later, the *Washington Herald* printed in display type the following telegram received from New York:

C. T. Brainard, *The Washington Herald.*
Washington, D. C.

I notice Mr. Brisbane's statement that he will make further answers either to "Mr. Morgan who owns Mr. Brainard, or to Mr. Davison who manages Mr. Morgan."

I regret that I do not own you as I should think you would be an excellent property. But in order to prevent any embarrassment on the part of Mr. Brisbane, I hereby specifically empower you to receive for me any answers he may wish to give me.

Mr. Davison having at the request of the President given up his job of managing me in order to manage the American Red Cross, which he seems to be doing to the satisfaction of everyone, is at the moment abroad. But I have power to act for him; under that power I hereby authorize you to receive any communications from Mr. Brisbane for him also.

J. P. Morgan.

The Senate Committee which conducted the investigation consisted of Senator Lee S. Overman, chairman, and Senators William H. King, Josiah O. Wolcott, Knute Nelson, and Thomas Sterling.

Testimony against Hearst and Brisbane was submitted by Captain George D. Lester of the United States Secret Service, Bruce Bielaski of the United States Department of Justice, Major E. Lowry Humes of the War Department, Alfred O. Becker, Deputy attorney-general of the state of New York and others. Brisbane appeared in his own defense. Hearst was not called upon to testify.

Bielaski testified and submitted documents showing that the representatives of the German Government had arranged shortly after the declaration of war in 1914 to buy the support of Jewish, German, Irish, and other groups on behalf of Germany. The preliminary work of propaganda proved unsatisfactory so Mr. William Bayard Hale was asked to take charge. Said Mr. Bielaski: "Mr. William Bayard Hale had had considerable experience in newspaper and journalistic work, had interviewed the Kaiser in 1908, his wife was German born, he had written a life of President Wilson, which had been used in the campaign, and he was ent as special agent for the President in Mexico. The Germans employed him not only to secure his services as a propagandist but in the hopes that through him they might get some approach to the President.

"Hale, as head and advisor of the German information bureau from December, 1914, to December, 1915, received a salary of $15,000 per year."

Bielaski then presented to the committee a copy of a adiogram sent by Ambassador Bernstorff through Buenos Aires and Stockholm to the German Foreign Office, June 2, 916: "In conformity with your Excellency's wish I suggest hat the present is a favorable time to get Hearst to send a irst-rate journalist to Berlin. The man selected, W. B. Hale, has been, as your Excellency knows, since the beginning of he war a confidential agent of the Embassy, and as such he has been bound by contract until June 23, 1918 . . . I request that full confidence may be accorded to Hale, who will bring with him a letter of recommendation from me o Dr. Hamman. Hearst is not aware that Hale is our agent, but knows him only as a Germanophile journalist who has ontributed lead articles to his paper."

Another radiogram, sent by Bernstorff, June 5, 1916: "As Hale tells me and Hearst confirms, the latter is rather hurt hat on Wiegand's account the *World* gets all the important nterviews. I recommend that under suitable circumstances Hale should for obvious reasons be given preference, as Hearst organs have during the course of war always placed hemselves outspokenly on our side."

Arthur Brisbane's chance to clear his record came on Wednesday, December 4, 1918. He who for years had been aying down the law to his millions of readers, to politicians, teachers, and scientists, was obviously nervous and ill at ease when he took the stand. He tried to make himself out a much misunderstood man, a patriot if there ever was one, a violent hater of all that Germany represented, and, to top it off, an ardent advocate of temperance who never would do or write anything which might encourage the consumption of strong drinks.

He asked for only five minutes to reply to the charges against him. He took up an entire afternoon. "My business is writing for newspapers, and the esteem of the public is, of course, very important to a man who writes, especially if he expresses editorial opinions, and so on.

"The newspapers of the country, all of them, practically have carried either the direct statement or the implication that I have been in some way retained in the interest of Germany; that I was, in other words, pro-German, and disloyal citizen.

"A great many thousands of articles have been printed and they were printed and made privileged, that is to say practically exempt from the bringing of libel suits, if that had been desired, (although I think a newspaper man wh brings a libel suit is rather ridiculous) and I wanted, if you would kindly give me the opportunity to reply publicly i the only place where I thought I could reply adequately I see that you are very indulgent listeners, and if you wi give me five minutes, I shall be very glad to answer what think are the charges that have been made to the publi prints."

Senator Overman: "We shall be very glad to hear you Mr. Brisbane."

Mr. Brisbane: "First, the question of pro-Germanism which, to me, is the only important thing. The other thin is how I bought the *Washington Times*. Assuming that I bo rowed the money from men who were of age and had the money, and who were willing to lend it to me, I presume that is a matter which is my affair and the affair of the men who loaned me the money, unless it be shown that there were some evil intentions, or dishonest transactions involved in it."

At this point, Brisbane digressed to discuss Palmer's charges against him. He said he called on Palmer and Palmer said to him: "Mr. Brisbane, I have made no charges against you. I have read your editorials for twenty years, and I have been educated by them. I make no charge whatever against you. Don't you want to buy another newspaper?"

To which Brisbane added: "And he tried to sell to me the *Evening Mail* of New York, which he holds as public custodian; and I take it for granted that he would not have offered to sell me the New York *Evening Mail* and thereby increase my possibilities of reaching the public and influencing the public if he had any thought or any evidence to indicate or imply that I would use it disloyally."

The charges of pro-Germanism worried Brisbane. So he set out to prove how untrue and how false these charges were.

"When the war broke out, I went to Atlanta, Georgia. Shortly after, I was there in a hospital. I was extremely ill and not expected to recover. I had, in fact, ten doctors, so that it is rather remarkable that I did recover."

The editor would fix his gaze first on one, then another of his inquisitors. Words poured out of his mouth, rolling over each other in their mad rush to convince and overwhelm the Senators.

"I want to say that when I was a boy, I went to school in France for four years. My father lived in Paris in 1828. That is a long time ago; ninety years ago. He had lived there, off and on, ever since, until his death. I have a great many friends in France. I felt very strongly on the question of the war. I was not able, at any time, to maintain the neutrality which the President recommended; and until we entered the war, I wrote very little on the subject of the war—practically nothing except very strong—I think—editorials urging the construction of flying machines, long before our war began, saying that the only way to make the Germans stop this war was to drop dynamite on Berlin. I wrote these editorials repeatedly.

"While I was in the hospital at Atlanta, I cabled Lord Northcliffe. I got to thinking over the war, and although I was very ill and not able to move, I wanted to be of service, and I telegraphed Lord Northcliffe, who is a friend of mine, that I believed the hydraulic mining machinery used in the West against mountains to wash down the gravel beds, would be of value in attacking the German trenches."

Senator Sterling: "When was this?"

Mr. Brisbane: "In 1914, shortly after the war began, when I was in the hospital at Atlanta.

"I took up the matter of the hydraulic mining machinery by telegraph with California. I got in touch with the Joshua Henley Iron Works who manufacture these machines, which are called 'giants,' and that, under terrific pressure, aim streams of water against solid embankments, and would wash down cavalry or infantry like ants before a garden hose. And I sent by express, at my own expense, to Lord Northcliffe, a sample of every kind of hydraulic engine made. The express bill alone amounted to some thousands of dollars. And the cost of the machinery, of course, was very great. I cabled Lord Northcliffe and he said that I could send it, and he would take it up with the government.

"I merely mention this to show you what my feeling was

at that time; that is, even before America had become very much aroused about the War."

Brisbane's military genius was evidently not apparent to the British command. The hydraulic machines which he had obtained for them at so much trouble and expense were not used. Brisbane then offered to turn his idea and the machinery over to the United States Government without charge. Once more his plan and gift were rejected. "I simply mention that to show my feeling in the matter. A man cannot prove his loyalty by words alone."

Here was no dollar-a-year patriot, who made millions by profiteering. He cited the case of his 6,000 acre estate in New Jersey. "I got word that the government would like to have one thousand acres of it, and I was asked what my charge would be for the one thousand acres. I wrote to the man who asked me, that I had nothing to sell to the government, but that I should be very glad to have them take the property and use it. I urged its acceptance on the Secretary of War, and he wrote me kindly about it. I said I would be glad to have it used without charge during the War, and if the government spent any money on it which would improve its value that I would be glad to turn it over to the government for one dollar, to be used for public purposes."

Brisbane told the committee that his loyalty to the United States was only half the story. He was as ardent in his support of England and the Allies as he was filled with hatred and bitterness toward Germany. "From the day I owned the *Times* I wrote as vigorously, as savagely and as earnestly on the subject of the war against the German side and in favor of America as I have ever done on any subject in my life. If any member of the committee or the representative of the Government will read my editorials I am sure that he will see that they are written with sincerity and effectively."

Senator Sterling: "What was your attitude toward England, as shown by these editorials?"

Brisbane: "My attitude toward England is that I was delighted to have England in the war, of course." Then, somewhat hesitantly he added, "I have in regard to England, some doubt as to whether, when the war ends, we shall not have our difficulties and discussions, as we may have with France and other countries."

"Did you not think your editorials manifested an intense opposition to England?"

"I do not think so, Senator."

"Soon after you acquired the *Washington Times?*" inquired Senator Sterling.

"I do not think so."

"Were not your editorials calculated to stir up enmity in this country against England?"

"They were not intended to, and I do not think they were calculated to.

"I may add that Lord Northcliffe was visiting in this country at the time. He was in Washington, and I was in Washington, and he repeatedly invited me to go to England and visit England and go to the front with him. I should think a good judge of that matter, perhaps, would be Lord Northcliffe, who is a very strong English journalist, and who was in this country, and who read those editorials, and with whom I discussed these questions. He may have said, 'I do not agree with you about this. I do not think you are right about this.' But he knew what my feeling was, and he invited me to go to England as his guest and that of the British government—not once or twice, but repeatedly; and when he was in France he cabled me a number of times to do so."

Brisbane was anti-German. Of that he was certain. From the day the war began in 1914, he assured his somewhat sceptical hearers, he had had no other feeling beyond that of favoring anything which would destroy the German Empire. "Frankly, the only thing I have to reproach myself with about what I wrote is that sometimes I wrote so bitterly that I think it was calculated to stir up dangerous ill feeling in this country among people of German names who were loyal."

Bitterly he resented the false charges made against him. Unlike others who had done nothing constructive, he had offered his land, bought machinery, and given of his editorial time and talent to win the war. He was a much maligned man, and only his staunch patriotism had kept him from telling the truth about himself prior to this time. He said he had been thanked for his support of the war and the government by the President himself. "I believe if he were questioned, he would say that no newspaper in the United States has supported the War more strongly than I have. I have the same statement from Mr. Daniels, and from Mr. Burleson who is the man responsible directly for the attitude newspapers take."

The questions next shifted to Brisbane's attitude on prohibition and his relation to the German brewers. He was, he modestly assured the Senators, the outstanding advocate of temperance in America. "I have presented these opinions as mine in hundreds of editorials that I have written on this subject, beginning in 1898, before I ever saw any brewer."

He told of his pledge to himself not to drink wine or any other liquor, until the *Journal* passed the *World* in circulation. "It worked so well that I kept it up for three years. I went to bed at half past eight and got up at half past four and went to work at five fifteen, and it took less than two months to accomplish what I was after. And when I got through, the *Journal* had a bigger circulation than the *World*.

That was my experience with total abstinence. And in the course of that experience, my weight went from one hundred ninety to one hundred fifty-three, and I found that it did not agree with me. I was working too hard. I do not believe it would agree with working men under similar conditions."

"You do not mean to argue that total abstinence reduced your weight," queried Senator Wolcott, "do you?"

"No. But it worked so well that I thought I would keep it up forever; but one morning in the house in the country where I went to sleep, and from which I came back to the office to work, I woke up lying flat on my back, with a lamp in my hand, which fortunately had gone out. I was looking for water, which, apparently, was not my natural beverage. I had this attack of heart failure, and my doctor said, 'It is extremely foolish. Go back and take your claret tomorrow.' "

Brisbane related how he urged a convention of brewers ten or twelve years previously to advocate temperance and fight whiskey. "You have got to stop it or the government will stop you."

Senator Overman asked slyly: "Are these the reasons why you bought the *Times* and got these men to lend you the money?"

Brisbane did not answer that question directly. Instead, he discoursed on why money is needed to buy a paper and make it function. Rather than go to some man like Rockefeller "who I understand is in favor of prohibition," he went to Mr. Feigenspan and said: "I want to borrow this money I shall pay it back and pay you interest. I cannot borrow from a bank." Feigenspan agreed at once to let Brisbane have $500,000 which he would raise among his friends. Asked if he knew the other men who went in on the loan, Brisbane said "No." He did not even know their names, until they were made public by Mr. Palmer.

The Senators were a bit puzzled at the ease with which this large sum was obtained.

"You gave no collateral?" asked Senator Overman.

"No, Senator, for this reason. I asked Mr. Feigenspan to take a mortgage on my real estate, and he declined, because, he said, 'I do not want to go on record as trying to influence the press.' He said, 'We are glad to lend it to you, but we do not want it known.' I said, 'Very well. It does not make any difference to me.' "

The interrogation by the Senators continued.

Senator Overman: "Their purpose in lending you the money was to have that sort of a paper here in Washington?"

Mr. Brisbane: "They would have been very glad to have me have a paper anywhere, Senator. They knew how I felt on the question of prohibition, and what I wrote about it, and they would have been glad to have me have a paper in Chicago or anywhere else."

Senator Wolcott: "Do you regard that transaction as a loan, strictly, Mr. Brisbane, or does it not come pretty close to being a gift?"

Mr. Brisbane: "It is absolutely a loan, Senator. Those men I believe would, if I had asked them, considering what I have done or endeavor to do, first by the advice that I gave them as to what was going to happen to their industry because of selling whiskey, and secondly, because of my attitude always on the subject of prohibition—if I had asked them to give me one thousand or five thousand or fifty thousand dollars, they might have done it."

Senator Wolcott: "But from their point of view it is tantamount to a gift? That is to say, they cannot *collect it?*"

Mr. Brisbane: "Yes, they can; because Mr. Feigenspan has my note at the present time."

Senator Wolcott: "But the terms of that note, as I recall, briefly stated, are about as follows: You are given an unlimited time in which to repay the loan."

Senator Nelson: "Without interest."

Senator Wolcott: "And there is no interest. You are to repay the loan only out of the profits that the paper makes; and then it is left entirely in your discretion as to how much of these profits, and when, out of these profits, you shall make payment?"

Mr. Brisbane: "Yes. That was the idea; that while I ran the newspaper, using my influence as I always have done, on their side, these men would be well repaid, and in the end, of course, they would get their money with interest.

"I could not say, 'I will borrow this money and pay it back at a certain time.' I could not tell within a year, or five years, how long it would take to put the *Times* on a paying basis. As a matter of fact, I did it in six months. It might easily have taken, however, two or three or several years, and I did not want to be compelled at any definite time to repay the money. I should have been glad to say to them at any time, 'If you are in a hurry for your money, you can take the paper.' They could have had the paper any time if they had chosen. But I paid them their highest . . ."

Senator Wolcott: "But you were not under obligation though, to do that?"

Mr. Brisbane: "No, I preferred to do it, and I expected to do it, and was able to do it, and so I did."

Senator Wolcott: "But I say, from the viewpoint of the lenders of the money, it really was a gift; that is to say, the money had gone out of their reach and they could not force you to repay."

Brisbane admitted that the brewers had absolutely no lien on the paper, but that since he was a man of honor he intended to pay them in full in the course of two years. They would also get interest in the meantime. Bragging just a bit, he continued: "While that amount of money, $375,000 seems large for a newspaper man to borrow, it is not a large amount in my case. I have a large income. If the *Times* had not paid, I could have paid these gentlemen. I have one salary, as editorial writer, of over one hundred thousand dollars a year, which would enable me to pay a debt of that size. I borrowed last year a million dollars from S. W. Strauss and Company, bankers in New York, for building.

"I am able to make newspapers pay, and I knew that after I had had this newspaper for a short time its borrowing value would enable me to carry it on successfully."

How was Brisbane able to conduct his many activities? Above all, how was it possible for him to be an editor and draw pay from Mr. Hearst, at the same time publishing his own papers in Washington and Milwaukee? Wasn't he under contract with Mr. Hearst calling for his exclusive services for five years?

"I bought the paper *(The Washington Times)* and then told Mr. Hearst that I had bought it. He objected, very strenuously. He was paying me a salary of one hundred four thousand dollars a year—two thousand dollars a week. He said: 'I am paying you to look after my papers. Now you will look after your own and neglect mine.' I said: 'I think I will not; because what I write for your papers will be in my own, and as it goes in my paper, I shall be interested in making it good. However, if you feel that my ownership of the paper would probably interfere with your work, I will agree that you can take the paper at any time you like for what it cost me.' "

Hadn't Hearst objected to Brisbane's use of material written for the Hearst papers? Brisbane replied, "Not the slightest. One reason why I wanted the paper was that he allowed me to use everything that he prepared for his own newspapers, very generously, in my own newspaper, which makes it possible to make the papers successful very quickly." However, the editor wanted it understood that he owned no shares in his employer's many newspapers.

"Have you anything to do with the policy of the papers?" asked Senator Overman, naively.

"Nothing whatever," responded the editor, "except that Mr. Hearst, I think, would listen to my advice, probably; but he very rarely asks for advice."

"Are you given a free hand to write what you please?"

"No. My understanding is that I write what I please and he publishes it if he pleases; but if Mr. Hearst has a campaign, for instance, I do not write what I do not please . . . Mr. Hearst does not wish to be told anybody's views—at least not mine. He rules his papers absolutely, and trusts to me, (as I know about what his line of thought is) not to go outside of that." At this point, Brisbane evidently recalled instances when he had gone "outside of that" for he added as a last minute reflection, "Occasionally, if he sees something in the paper that he does not like, he throws it out, naturally. The papers are his property."

Among those who had suffered heavily from the war hysteria, were the American Socialists, especially those of German birth. Victor Berger, the leader of Wisconsin's Social Democracy, elected to Congress, was thrown out during the war, and his paper, *The Milwaukee Leader,* fell under the ban of the Post Office department. Berger, himself, with other leading Socialists, was indicted for violations of the Espionage Act.

Arthur Brisbane

Arthur Brisbane and Victor Berger had been friends for many years. In fact, back in the crusading days against the Trusts, Brisbane had tried to persuade Berger to write Sunday feature editorials for the Hearst press at a salary of $15,000 a year. Berger turned down the offer.

The headquarters of Milwaukee Socialism was Brisbane Hall, built in 1910, and named after Arthur's father, Albert Brisbane. Arthur had invested money in the stock of the building as well as in Berger's Socialist *Milwaukee Leader*. When this fact became public property, Brisbane was attacked with even greater severity by the opposition press. This, too, he explained to the Senatorial committee. Berger had told him they were short of money. Wouldn't he take some stock in the building, as they had named it the Brisbane Building? The editor was flattered and bought $5,000 worth.

"Subsequently Mr. Berger was going to start a daily paper, and I advised him strongly against it, as I thought he could not possibly make it pay. However, he was going to start it, and I loaned him, I think, eight thousand dollars. Then he said he did not have control of the paper. He said he was anxious to have control and wanted to know if I would take stock instead of this money which I had loaned, which I did not get back, or the interest, and I said, 'Very well.' And I took stock in the paper."

When Victor Berger was accused of disloyalty to the Government, Brisbane wrote an editorial in his defense, which he sent to President Wilson. He also talked to Postmaster General Burleson and others about the case—but to no avail. Those who a few years earlier would have rushed to do his bidding now treated him will ill-concealed contempt, and suggested he mend his own ways instead of defending men of an alien birth and alien philosophy. In vain he pleaded:

"The merchants of Milwaukee say that Berger is a law-abiding man and defends nothing illegal. They do not agree with his theories, perhaps not any more than I do, . . . I do not believe he would suggest or do anything opposed to the law or constitution of the country; and if he is put out of his position as a leader, it would be to substitute for him as leader, some dangerous individual of a totally different character."

Every thought he had uttered, every editorial he had written had been executed upon the highest plane of morals and patriotism. Of course he had made mistakes. This he admitted. Who wouldn't, working under pressure such as he did! "You must consider that I write an editorial every day of my life, seven days a week, for an evening paper, and I write an article every morning, seven days a week, for a morning newspaper, and, in addition, I run newspapers in different places; and I write under pressure. I dictate to the phonograph, or to a rapid stenographer, and *my difficulty is to read the stuff after I have written it.* If I have a good stenographer, I frequently do without reading it. Just as I talk very rapidly now, I write under pressure, and it would be difficult for me to write every day for thirty years, and to write throughout this war, without having done things which might be condemned or which might be susceptible of a false interpretation."

Hearst and Brisbane were in a jam. Friends, associates, and employees were drawn in to prove their loyalty. They tabulated reports to show that their papers had devoted more space to stimulating support for the Liberty Loans, the Red Cross, the Young Men's Christian Association, the Knights of Columbus, and other groups, than had any other newspapers. They quoted letters from Joseph Tumulty, Secretary to President Wilson, and William G. McAdoo, Secretary of the Treasury, to prove their point. Even Mr. Samuel Insull, the Chicago utility magnate, and at that time looked upon by many as Illinois's greatest gift to the nation since Abraham Lincoln, testified on their behalf. "As Chairman of the State Council of Defense, I had occasion to watch the Hearst papers and I know that they gave my committee full and complete support, and I know them to have been very truly American and very patriotic."

The Senatorial investigation made first class copy for papers opposing Brisbane and Hearst; but no action was ever taken by the government. The report was soon forgotten in the excitement over greater post-war problems.

The two revolutions staged in Russia, March and November, 1917, added complications to the World War. Neither Brisbane nor Hearst knew what to make of it. At first they rejoiced in the fall of Czardom. When the strange crew assembled under Lenin and Trotsky began to overshadow the Kerensky forces, they became frightened. Here was no gentleman's revolution! The whole social and economic structure was being shaken to its foundations.

Brisbane's editorial ardor for the Russian experiment cooled. Soon he was thundering about the Bolshevik menace. In the summer of 1918, he suggested to his readers, and through them to the Allies, how to solve the Russian problem. "What do you think will come out of the anarchy in China and the anarchy in Russia? Read on for a possible solution.

"Japan rules China—Germany rules Russia . . .

"Anarchy rules in Russia, somebody must do something.

"The natural somebody is Germany, right next door to Russia, as Japan is next door to China.

"When the dust settles, this war is over, and part of the bitter hatred gone, *the civilization of western Europe may be very grateful to Germany if the war finds Germany with enough strength left to undertake the policing and maintaining of order in Russia—developing the resources there and making a few billions of rubles in the process.*"

In December he raised the problem once more and asked: "What will be done about Russia? How does this suggestion impress you?

"When the time comes to end this war IN THE ALLIES' WAY, say to Germany, 'You want to expand—go ahead and expand into Russia. You want more territory—HELP YOURSELF.'"

No matter how many suggestions Brisbane made for winning the war or destroying the Bolsheviks; no matter how many American flags Hearst carried on the front pages of his papers—their influence reached a new low. Even within the ranks of the Democratic party of the state of New York their names were anathema.

Hearst, suffering from a bad dose of inflated egotism and political myopia, thought he might capture the governorship nomination in the summer of 1918. Every effort was made to line up loyal supporters.

Samuel Seabury, former judge of the Court of Appeals, who, a few years previously, had been on the Hearst bandwagon, led the movement to prevent the nomination of Hearst. He submitted a resolution to the Convention which read:

"Resolved, that this conference of Democrats of the state of New York do renew to the President of the United States their wholehearted support and confidence in his magnificent struggle to make the world free for democracy, and, as an earnest of their loyalty, repudiate every truckler with our country's enemies who strives or has striven to extenuate or excuse such crimes against humanity as the rape of Belgium, the sinking of the Lusitania, and the German policy of assassination by submarines; who seeks or has sought to sow dissention among our allies or now seeks to capitalize by election to public office the latent treason whose total annihilation is the most pressing need of the hour."

It was adopted without a dissenting vote. Hearst and Brisbane, who had so often sowed the seed of hatred, were now themselves reaping the whirlwind. The *New York Times* of July 24, 1918, reports: "Late tonight it was rumored that Hearst's name might not be presented to the conference at all, the reason being that he can find no backer prepared to face the storm that mention of his name is bound to arouse."

Hearst's name was not mentioned. His leading supporters slipped quietly out of town and the nomination went instead to Alfred E. Smith.

The frenzied opposition to Hearst and Brisbane made itself felt in more ways than one. Friends vanished; acquaintances no longer cared to speak to them. Their wealth and power helped little against such social ostracism. How far Hearst was affected by all this, we do not know. But in Arthur Brisbane it brought back again vividly—all too vividly—the memories of his father, himself a social outcast for so long.

Arthur Brisbane was no longer a great popular leader; he was not even one of the crowd. For the first time in many years, the editor was able to view sympathetically the lot of the man who fights for social justice.

As the year 1918 drew to a close, the misunderstood millionaire patriot wrote an editorial entitled: SOME CHRISTMAS DAY THOUGHTS ABOUT THE TEACHINGS OF JESUS, in which he squeezed out his last few drops of idealism. It was the final flash of the candle before it went out, written with the fire and zeal of the young men who had made up Brook Farm:

"If those higher intelligences, not clogged by our fetters of flesh, look down upon this spinning ball on whose wrinkled skin we human ants run about on our little errands of brief life, what a spectacle is spread before their curious gaze this Christmas day.

"Nineteen hundred years of Christianity, education, invention and political and social experiments have resulted in an insanity of slaughter and destruction, in maniacal hatred, in sentiments, that would shock many savages, in monstrous lying and monstrous credulity, in a carnival of unreason, suspicion, intolerance and fanaticism.

"The masses have seen many of the greatest governments of the world wasting billions of wealth and millions of lives in a brutal and savage struggle to extend their own trade and territories and to diminish the trade and territories of others. The masses have seen the intellectual forces they so much respected—the professors in the universities, the writers of books, the press in all its forms—all applauding, cheering on and stimulating the bloody work of slaughter, the frightful orgy of the sword and the torch.

"And now that the ruin has been wrought, now that Hell's maw is filled full, now that the awful conflagration has burned up so much and such incalculable treasure, now that the smoke is filled with thick blood and carrion flesh—now, standing amid the wreck and ashes, the masses ask of one another why this ruin was wrought and of what value are these institutions of government and religion and industrial relations which have resulted in such a horror as this?

"There never was a time when so many hundreds of millions of men were challanging governments and hierarchies and all the customs, laws, and traditions of the established order to justify themselves before the judgment bar of the world's conscience as upon this very Christmas day.

"The Bolsheviki do not all speak Russian.

"That mighty movement of protest and revolt is not confined to the vast territory over which the White Czar once stretched the sceptre of dominion.

"Its influence is everywhere at work.

"And everywhere it demands that the established order of things give an accounting for the wreck it has made of the world.

"And upon this birthday of Jesus, this accuser and inquisitor must be faced and answered one way or the other . . .

"First of all, Jesus was what the writers of our established order would call 'class-conscious.' He took a whip to the bankers, He derided the lawyers, He denounced the clergy, He promised damnation to the rich, He had only pity, kindness, succor, and future mansions and authority in heaven for the poor.

"His eyes and ears would certainly be astonished if He went into some churches and heard some preaching today. Jesus was not only class-conscious, but He was a pacifist.

"He did, indeed, say that His teachings would bring war and set men against each other, but He did not say that in justification of war, as certain preachers have been known sometimes to distort His meaning.

"He was simply forecasting a fact, because He had foresight enough to perceive that His system of social equality and communism of property would cause the privileged and militaristic classes to try to exterminate it with the sword—which is exactly what happened . . . We think we could do worse with part of this Christmas day than to spend it in thinking about the political and social teachings of Jesus as well as His religious teachings.

"These political and social teachings involved matters of

no less importance than theology, because they deal with this very material world in which we live, the only lives that we actually know anything about and which are certainly important things for us to consider and to make happy while we do live them.

"Jesus was a very human man. He associated with the lower classes entirely. He did not approve of a social system which created upper and lower classes. He was a passionate lover of justice, fraternity, equality and liberty.

"If Jesus was right, then the social system of this day was wrong and the social system of our day is wrong—because our social system is an exact likeness of the social system of Jesus' day.

"As for us, we believe all that Jesus taught was right and we believe that human society would be very happy and charming if the teachings of Jesus were universally practiced, instead of being professed by so many and practiced by so few.

"Of one thing we are quite sure—no Christmas morning would ever again dawn upon such a horrid spectacle of woe and waste as this Christmas morning sees, if all men were to practice henceforth the social precepts of that wonderful Teacher whose birth we are celebrating this day."

10

THE BOUNTIFUL TWENTIES

THE PROVERBIAL silver lining appeared on the horizon a few months after the World War officially ended. The boom days that followed in the wake of that world disaster were comparable only to the decade immediately following the Civil War. In spite of Mr. Brisbane's many dark editorial forebodings, the United States emerged from the conflict the richest and most powerful nation on the earth.

Internal markets had expanded beyond one's fondest dream. Europe was bankrupt. Not only did it have to arrange for loans from America in order to buy much needed American supplies—machinery and foodstuffs—but the confusions of the first few years gave to American manufacturers and producers a distinct advantage over markets formerly monopolized by Great Britain, Germany or France.

The lessons learned from war profiteering were extended to the days of peace. Trust-busting gave way to the demand for bigger trusts. New York, Chicago, Boston, and other metropolitan centers attained new levels in political corruption. Paralleling the Grant Administration, corruption extended once more directly into the President's cabinet, culminating in the exposure of the Teapot Dome Scandal of the Harding-Coolidge administration. The reformers and radicals of former years grew silent and cynical or hopped on the bandwagon of post-war exploitation and speculation.

Arthur Brisbane and his publisher boarded the prosperity "special" too. They whooped it up for one hundred per cent

Americanism. They campaigned against the League of Nations and the World Court. They demanded American isolation at all times and at any cost. They joined in the cry for a bigger army, a bigger navy; bigger buildings, bigger cities, and bigger profits.

Sentiment for prohibition swept over the country. The Volstead Act was passed and the Eighteenth Amendment was jammed through Congress and the state legislatures. Arthur Brisbane's long fight had finally brought results. Jubilantly he wrote on January 17, 1919: "One hundred per cent efficiency has been added at one stroke to the people of America . . . half of the misery of half of the people has been abolished. Three hundred thousand saloons have been eliminated, three hundred thousand traps have been closed into which a considerable portion of the youth of the country fell every year . . . strong drink has destroyed much more each year than the World War destroyed . . . The suppression of the drink traffic is an expression of the higher morality upon which we are entering."

Fortunately for Brisbane, the public has a short memory. War time hatreds were soon forgotten in the era of good feeling and prosperity which characterized the nineteen-twenties. Once again Hearst saw newspaper circulation booming. In rapid succession he acquired several additional papers, among them the *Washington Times* and the *Milwaukee Wisconsin News.* The publisher purchased these papers in 1919, shortly after the Senate investigations, at a time when their owner, Mr. Brisbane, was most happy to be released from further responsibility of them.

The syndicated column "Today", instituted in 1917 at the time Brisbane purchased the *Washington Times,* was an outstanding success from its inception. People clamored for it. Soon it was being sold to many papers outside the Hearst chain. As a result, Brisbane's salary was increased by $50,000 a year. His readers mounted into millions. By 1923, his influence probably attained the highest point in his long career. His rapid fire comments on persons and problems of the day continued to be interspersed with the proper moral precepts. He attained a prestige so overwhelming that his nearest competitors, Dr. Frank Crane and Edgar Guest, were completely overshadowed. Brisbane had become in truth the sage of the crossroads store and the Demosthenes of American barber shops.

Unlike his employer, Mr. Hearst, who had once remarked at the conclusion of a conference with reference to a truth-in-advertising campaign, "I have observed that principles are the impediments of small men," Brisbane continued to hurl principles at his readers, even though he seldom followed his own precepts. His defense of sensational journalism was on the same high moral plane that it had been twenty years earlier.

Sensationalism, he remarked, is also the method of heaven. The rays of the sun are yellow, and the gold for which all men strive is of the same color. The first page of the *New York American*, said Heywood Broun, "reminded Brisbane of the sky. He compared the screaming headlines of red to the lightning; he saw type in thunder clouds and comic sections in sunbeams. But he neglected to state where the star-gazers should look for the coupons . . . "As a matter of fact," continued Broun, "it seems to us that Mr. Brisbane is mistaken. We find practically no similarity between the methods of heaven and those of the *New York American*. None of the noisy things in nature, like thunder, amount to much. Most of the potent forces of the world proceed quietly without capitals or black type. O. Henry pointed out in one of his stories that one of the least boisterous events in the Bible was the creation of the world. It does not begin to be as noisy as the building of the tower of Babel, which came to nothing."

Big, bold face type, leg art, sensational news, scandals, divorces, murders and sex stories continued to dominate the pages of the papers which Brisbane edited. The jazz age wanted no introspection. It craved action, spice and pep. The Hearst-Brisbane combination was ideal for this. "Newspapers are not dull, they are simply more or less accurate reflectors," said Brisbane "People are dull, life is dull, crime, races, politics, divorces—all these are dull when seen by dull brains."

Brisbane's private views did not always coincide with those expressed in his editorials or his speeches. He once told his friend, Whidden Graham, that "a paper, according to my idea, would have no big headlines, no fight stories and no pictures. It would be much like the *New York Post* used to be. But such a paper would bring me an income of only five thousand dollars per year or so. Now I get over one hundred thousand, which is much more pleasant."

The renewed public interest in popular science gave Brisbane a chance to pass judgment and issue edicts on the problems of the world, which seemed to qualify him to be looked upon as one of America's leading sciosophists. Sciosophy is a word coined by the late eminent biologist and educator, David Starr Jordan, who described it as "systematized ignorance, the most delightful science in the world because it is acquired without labor or pain and keeps the mind from melancholy."

Paul Mickelson, a New York sports writer, has told a story that illustrates how well Brisbane fitted Dr. Jordan's definition.

Brisbane had long been irked by the inability of handicappers to pick more winners for their public. One day he called in Hugh Fullerton, an expert sports writer for the Hearst chain. "Hugh," he said, "this handicapping of race horses is all wrong. The boys don't go at it in the right way. Science! That's it! Come on, we'll show them!"

Fullerton wondered whether heat or old age was affecting his employer, but Brisbane went on with his plan of action. He ordered Fullerton to get an x-ray expert, to take him to the race tracks and x-ray the hearts and lungs of every horse nominated to run in the big race.

"Get the pictures from every possible angle on each horse," ordered Brisbane, "and bring the plates to me. We'll show those fellows! Why, it's simple. You can tell a winner by his heart."

Fullerton knew that the owners of the race horses wouldn't permit an x-ray machine to come anywhere near them. But orders were orders. An old friend of Fullerton's, to whom he explained his predicament, came to his rescue. He had an old broken down horse and told Fullerton to take all the x-ray pictures he wanted.

Fullerton brought the x-ray technician out to the stable where he shot pictures of the broken down horse's heart and lungs from all angles. This was done so cleverly that each picture looked different. Fullerton chuckled at the hoax as he listed the name of a Derby starter on each plate.

These were then brought to the great editor. Brisbane rubbed his hands in glee, "Now, Hugh," he said, "we'll show 'em something," as he studied each plate intently. Finally he picked one. "Here's your winner," he beamed proudly.

The following day Brisbane used two whole paragraphs to describe his new "scientific" method of picking race horse winners. He named the horse that the x-ray picture revealed had the largest and most heart. "That horse," wrote Brisbane, "was a cinch."

"I laughed till I cried," said Fullerton, "But what do you think happened? The horse he picked won the race!"

On Hearst's 350,000 acre ranch at San Simeon, California, Brisbane had once noticed a new born calf "full of scientific interest." It galloped down the steep hill on its shaky little legs rejoicing in its freedom. Then it started to gallop up again to its mother. "It is amazed," Brisbane wrote, "at the difficult return. You cannot explain to him that an eternal law of gravitation makes it easy to go down, hard to go up. He will die in about two years without knowing that . . . But, as to the ultimate cosmic truths, causation, and purpose, that new born calf knows as much as Einstein. *And he has Dr. Einstein's beautiful innocent expression.*"

Brisbane's "Today" column, which was neither directly news nor editorial, became the outstanding column in American journalism during the nineteen-twenties. For six days a week it appeared in the left hand column of the first page of the many Hearst morning papers. Two hundred other daily papers reprinted it. Rewritten under the title "This Week," it appeared in over eight hundred country weeklies. Nearly one third of the population of the United States read it and discussed it.

This column, so widely read, was prepared and revised each day in from forty-five minutes to an hour. The Brisbane procedure when he was in New York astonished most of his colleagues in journalism. The late afternoon papers would reach his desk at four o'clock in the afternoon. The editor, surrounded by newspapers, books, letters, drawings, and memoranda, piled high on all sides of him, would glance over the news items. When anything of interest struck his eye, he would begin dictating into the machine in short, staccato sentences. He would occasionally interrupt the process of dictating this rapid-fire comment on the news of the day to answer telephone calls, bark out orders to his secretaries, scribble notations on newly submitted cartoons, and occasionally conclude a real estate transaction.

Promptly at four forty-five, he would leave his office, take a cab and reach the ferry in time to catch the five o'clock train for Lakewood, New Jersey. If the column had not been completed by the time he left his office, he would continue the work in his car on the way to the ferry, for in it was installed a dictaphone.

Secretaries would type out the material as rapidly as the cylinders were filled. Usually, he had a typewritten copy by the time he got on the ferry or the train. His copy was then corrected, turned over to one of the secretaries ever at his beck and call, and rushed back to the composing room to be set up and wired across the country.

Although Brisbane traveled a great deal, the daily column was never neglected. His recording machine and his faithful secretaries followed him wherever he went and his editorial material would be sent back by wire or by phone to the New York office, from which, in turn, it was relayed to all other papers.

Mr. Eugene Hudgins, New York correspondent of Mr. Hearst's western newspapers and superintendent of the typographic department in New York, has described the typical Brisbane methods of working: "He used to leave for Buffalo on the New York Central and write continuously until he reached his destination. By a pre-arrangement, I would have the station masters at Poughkeepsie, Albany, Utica, Syracuse, and Rochester pick up his copy and wire it in to the New York office. By a chart system and a code he and I worked out, it was easy for me to mark up the type spaces and push his stuff right through the composing room with publication dates all indicated just as if he had done this work from his private office in the old Tribune Building."

Brisbane was always on the watch for first class men to add to the staff of the Hearst papers. Men who were or had been radicals were preferred. They knew how to talk to the man in the street. Many succumbed to the fat contracts offered them. A few refused. Among the latter was Oscar Ameringer, sometimes called the Mark Twain of the radical labor movement. Moses Annenberg, who, together with his brother, Max, had built up the strong arm squad for Hearst's Chicago papers, moved to Milwaukee to function in the same capacity for Brisbane's journalistic venture. Annenberg watched the news stand sales of the various Milwaukee papers very carefully. He noticed that people who purchased the *Milwaukee Leader* almost invariably read Ameringer's column on the front page first. Even Annenberg's wife said she invariably read the Ameringer column first.

So in 1920, when Oscar Ameringer was editing the *Oklahoma Leader*, he received a wire signed by both Annenberg and Brisbane requesting that he come to New York to see them. They had an attractive proposition to make. Ameringer went. Brisbane then told him: "We want you on our staff. I've looked over your stuff. You use too much humor and irony which is over the heads of our readers, but outside of that, your stuff is very good." The attractive proposition was a job at one thousand dollars a month.

When Ameringer asked: "But what shall I do about my baby, *The Oklahoma Leader?*" Brisbane and Annenberg had a solution. Mr. Hearst would buy it from him but would publish it merely as the Sunday paper in Oklahoma. Then

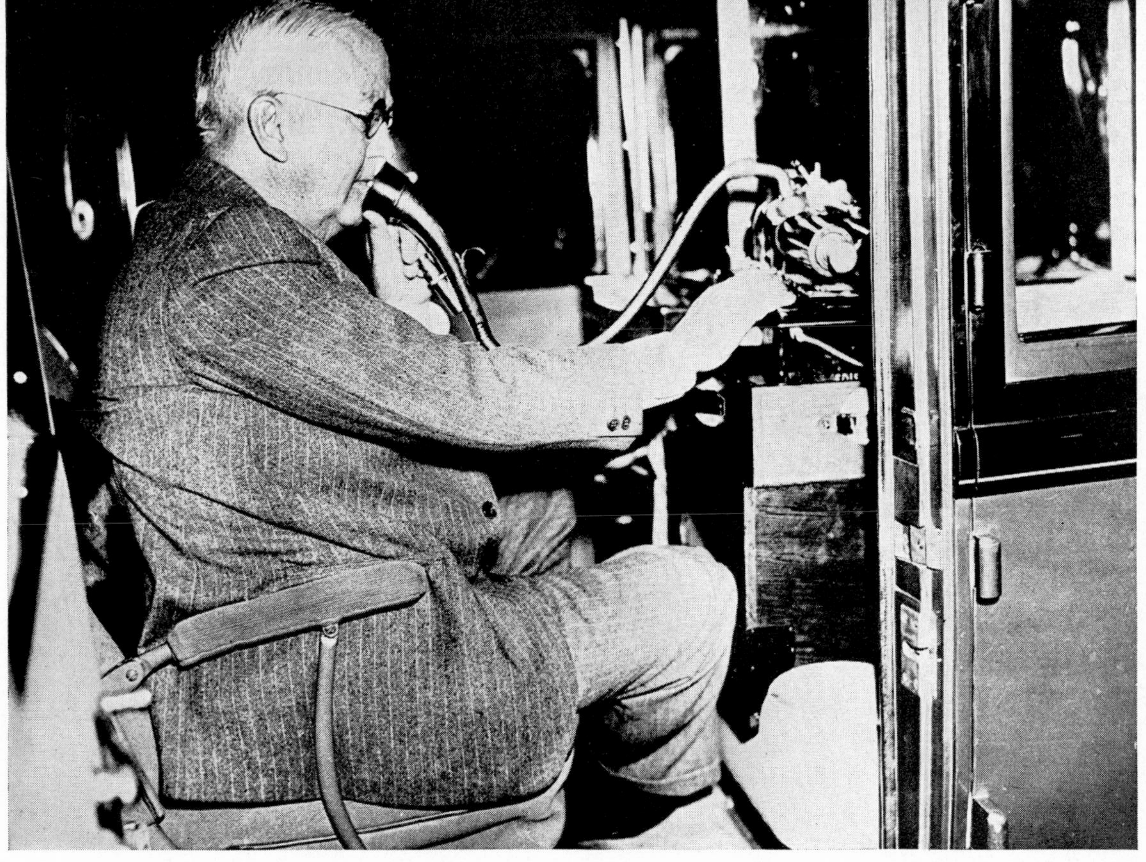

Arthur Brisbane dictated columns and editorials even while he travelled in his automobile.

Ameringer remarked that he would not like to work in such a dirty place as the South Water Street Building where the *Journal* offices were located in New York. Brisbane met this objection by assuring him he could do his writing anywhere in the United States so long as he could reach a Hearst wire with his material.

"I told them I'd want to think it over for a day before arriving at a decision. I was told to come back the next day and lunch with the leading Hearst executives.

"Upon returning to Mr. Brisbane's office the next day, I found him bent down over his waste basket feverishly tossing about him the odds and ends of the heavily filled container. He was breathing hard and swearing under his breath. I was reminded of a dog trying desperately to dig out a rabbit from a hole. When Brisbane finally looked up, I asked him, 'What's wrong—did you lose some important clipping or part of one of your editorials?' 'It's worse than that,' said Brisbane, 'I clipped a twenty dollar coupon off of one of my bonds a little while ago and I've lost it.'"

Brisbane, Annenberg, Ameringer and a few Hearst executives went to lunch. "The food and the drinks were good," said Ameringer, "But I was amazed to watch these high priced writers and executives gulping down their food as though they were at some lunch counter. Hardly waiting to finish, they pushed the dishes aside and began a dice game. The minimum stake for each person was five dollars a shake and the gusto which they should have bestowed upon the food was given instead to the crap game.

"After our return to the office, I told Annenberg and Brisbane I couldn't take the job. Annenberg said, 'Ameringer, I thought you were a smart guy, but you're a damn fool to turn down twelve thousand dollars per year to continue editing a lousy sheet out in Oklahoma. Why, within six months you may get fifteen, twenty, or twenty-five thousand dollars a year. Look at Arthur here, he gets two hundred fifty thousand dollars, and in my opinion, you write a damn sight better column than he does.'"

When Ameringer offered some other reason for not being able to take the job, Annenberg retorted: "We want you, and we're ready to give you the pick of our papers. If you think twelve thousand dollars isn't a lot of money let me tell you that we can get just about the best newspaper men in the world for that price. Think it over. We want you and we'll pay you well if you'll join us."

Ameringer admitted later that he had been seriously tempted by the offer, but decided against it.

The election campaigns of the nineteen-twenties found Brisbane invariably on the side of conservatism. In the guise of general news reporting, he managed to make a "below the belt" hit at the Democratic candidate, Mr. Cox, by remarking in his column on the eve of the election, November 2, 1920: "The last feature of the campaign is unpleasant and ought to cost Mr. Cox many votes, especially in the South. Democrats spent large sums of money circulating printed matter carrying the false statement that Senator Harding, several generations back, had African blood in his family. The statement is false and is proved to be false.

"How many Americans will vote for a man, Mr. Cox, in whose behalf those working for him circulated a most shameful and libelous attack on women?

"It happens, and there is no reason for concealing what is court record, that *Mr. Cox is a divorced man* . . .

"Mr. Cox is a divorced man. That fact used through the campaign would have cost him hundreds of thousands of women's votes, and as all readers can testify, the subject was ignored by Mr. Harding and every man working for him."

Praise of President Harding replaced the abuse that had been poured upon Wilson. Harding's death was considered a national calamity. But Calvin Coolidge was hailed as a worthy successor. Brisbane remarked in his column on the eve of the 1924 election: "Whoever is elected (Davis or Coolidge) we shall have an honest man in the White House. I had better say nothing as to who I think will get it, but I am going to vote for Coolidge."

No other President ever found his entire administration so consistently in the good graces of Hearst and Brisbane as did Coolidge. It seemed so unreal that H. L. Mencken in the May, 1927, issue of the *American Mercury* exclaimed: "For two years past they have been lathering the grotesque Mr. Coolidge, with frequent sweeps of the brush toward Judge Gary, and even John D. Rockefeller. If Mark Hanna were still alive, would they be anointing him too? It seems very probable. But by the same token it is also irrational, monstrous, and against God. Hearst genuflecting before such bladders is somehow quite as shocking as Nietzsche in a baptismal tank . . . Now Hearst repudiates the philosophy of a life-time, and led by the platitudinous Brisbane, sets up as a Babbitt in his declining years. All the characteristic cautiousness of a Babbitt seems to have got into him. Bishop Manning begins to show signs of forgiving him. He will be cheered, on some near tomorrow, at a session of the Iron and Steel Institute. It is a sad story."

Revival of the Ku Klux Klan in 1923 and 1924 with its nightshirts and "invisible government" became for a time a major political issue. Brisbane pleaded for a neutral attitude on this threat to democracy while Klansmen were beating up, killing, and kidnapping their opponents.

Just prior to the 1924 elections, a young man was shot and killed by the Klan in Niles, Ohio. People everywhere demanded some word from the President, but Coolidge remained silent. Brisbane, rushing to his defense, declared: "The Duty of the President of the United States is to keep out of the discussions and denunciations and NOT TO USE HIS OFFICIAL POSITION *for propaganda along the line of his own personal views, whatever they may be.*"

Between Calvin Coolidge, the Republican candidate, and John W. Davis, the Democratic candidate, there was little difference. "Fighting Bob" LaFollette, of Wisconsin, ran on a Third Party ticket which called for an end to political corruption, advocated government ownership of the great public utilities, and condemned America's policy of Dollar Diplomacy. Brisbane, who for more than a score of years had advocated most of the planks in the LaFollette platform, not only failed to support that candidate, but did his best to undermine him. When LaFollette charged that "world-wide exploiters are undermining the nation," Brisbane retorted: "This nation NEEDS world-wide exploiters—men with ability to reach out for business all around the world."

Another potent political figure against whom Brisbane tilted his editorial lance during the nineteen twenties was Alfred E. Smith, who had worked himself up from lowly ward heeler to the governorship of the state of New York. Smith had refused to heed the orders of Hearst, so the feud was on. Al Smith swore he would drive Hearst and Brisbane out of politics in New York State. For a time, at least, he very largely succeeded.

During the milk famine of 1919 in New York City, Brisbane had charged Smith with being a tool of the milk truck barons. When this failed to mobilize opinion against Smith, Brisbane's paper featured a whole series of illustrations supposedly representing pitiful groups of tenement house children pleading with the stony-hearted governor for a drop of milk before they died.

This was too much for Al Smith. He challenged Hearst to a public debate in Carnegie Hall. Hearst, of course, did not accept the challenge. At the mass meeting, Al Smith delved into the record of Mr. Hearst, and his chief editor: "If the Hearst newspapers were the text book for the children of our schools," roared Al Smith, "they would have to spell out of every line that no man can be trusted in this country after he is put into public office; and no man thinks enough of real Christian character to do the thing right; no man that ever held great public office had enough of respect and regard for his mother and his wife and his children and his friends to be right in office . . . About that there can be no question, because no man in this state, from Grover Cleveland right down to today, has ever escaped this fellow. We all know that. The children in the street know it."

Mayor Hylan, a tool in the hands of the Hearst machine, was used by Hearst and Brisbane to fight the nomination of Al Smith in the 1924 Democratic Convention. Again, in 1926, they tried to defeat Smith for reelection by supporting Ogden Mills, multimillionaire financier. The bitterness of the struggle against Smith reached its apex at the 1928 convention. Thirty years' accumulation of journalistic trickery and political skullduggery were hurled into the battle to stem the forces of Smith. But Smith was victorious.

There was a good chance that Al Smith might be elected President. Hearst and Brisbane beat a hasty retreat. They could not afford to be left completely on the outside. So, though they did not campaign on his behalf, Hearst issued a statement which read, in part: "Smith's record as Governor has been notable, and his record, plus his popularity, has transformed the state of New York from a state which was almost surely Republican, into a state which can now be considered safely Democratic . . . If Governor Smith is nominated, he should have the united and whole-hearted support of his party."

While Hearst tried to make his peace with Smith, Brisbane was under instructions to campaign for the Republican candidate, Herbert Hoover. This he did, with the same enthusiasm he had used to malign him during the days of the World War: "Herbert Hoover as social engineer is the right leader appearing at the right time . . . In this age of engineering, in the event of Hoover's election, the world will note with interest that he is the first engineer elected president of the United States since the election of George Washington." Editorially he underscored the statement of Andrew Mellon: "If the people are satisfied with the kind and quality of government they have had, they should insure a continuance of its benefits by retaining the service of those who made good."

To the end of his days, Arthur Brisbane loved to refer to himself as a reporter. Actually, he did very little reporting after his early days with Pulitzer. His news and views were almost wholly second-hand in character—a re-write of what others had seen or heard or said or done. However, he did cover certain important events, notably the great national political conventions, and the major prize fights.

All the world knows the story of how, in one of his descriptions of two prize fighters, he concluded his remarks with: "And a gorilla could have whipped both of them." He had followed the prize fighting game since the eighteen eighties, and was personally acquainted with almost every boxer of note. The great John L. Sullivan had been one of his close friends. Once when Sullivan was to box before the then Prince of Wales, the royal equerries tried to bar

Brisbane from the scene. Sullivan heard of it and roared: "If my pal can't come in, they won't be no boxin' "—Brisbane was permitted to witness the bout and he obtained an exclusive story of it.

Damon Runyon, a sports writer for the Hearst press, thinks that though Brisbane professed a keen dislike for professional fighting, he covered almost every big bout during the past twenty years and had a startling knowledge of the finer points of the game. He recalls that Brisbane "walked to Boyle's Thirty Acres, the afternoon of the Dempsey-Carpentier fight, arrived a little late, wrote 7,500 words in long hand—and a great story it was—grabbed his hat before the bout that followed the main event was over, and left muttering, 'John L. Sullivan could have licked them both.' " Runyan says that Brisbane also admired Gene Tunney, "especially after he learned that he knew his Shakespeare."

The writer of "Today" was in constant demand as an after-dinner speaker during the twenties. Most of these talks were given to advertising clubs, Chambers of Commerce groups and the like. Advertising, propaganda, the value of newspapers and the need for THINKING were the general topics he discussed. Speaking to a group of Harvard professors, he compared the water in the Boston Bay to the books in the public library. "God Almighty, who understands, takes the water out of the ocean and drops it one drop at a time, and things grow. There are minds that need irrigation. You have books that weigh four pounds. If you drop such a book on a man's head, he gets nothing. The newspapers make it their business to take serious information and distribute it, like drops of water, over the country in such a manner that it is easily absorbed."

One of his most popular topics was an analysis of the elements which make a newspaper successful. He listed these in their order of importance as follows: first, news; second, comics; third, sports; fourth, fiction; and editorials, "if they are written so that men and women will read them, come after the other things. However, the editorial is something like the backbone in the human body; you don't see it, perhaps you don't think much of it, but it holds the body up. And a newspaper that lacks a consistent, sincere, editorial policy will lack consistent and permanent success."

Legitimate publicity he defined as "the spreading of truthful information, or facts, about any cause or condition which is of interest or importance to people generally, and not for the pecuniary or other advantage of the persons spreading it." Propaganda, on the other hand, was defined as "the giving out (or hiring) of opinions, arguments, or pleas, to induce people generally to believe what some individual, groups of individuals, or organizations want them to believe, for the pecuniary or other advantages of the individual, group, or organization, giving out (or hiring) the propaganda."

To see no difference between these two—publicity and propaganda—he said, "is to see no difference between nutritious food and insidious poison." Carping critics have been known to suggest that it was unfortunate that the readers of Mr. Brisbane's editorials failed to appreciate and act on the basis of this definition.

Brisbane understood the art of flattery. In 1922, he told the representatives of the Brooklyn Chamber of Commerce that Brooklyn would soon be the biggest city in America, possibly in the entire world. The same speech, in all essentials, was delivered to gatherings at Chicago, Los Angeles, Detroit, Cleveland, St. Louis, Milwaukee, San Francisco. Every state in the union through which Brisbane traveled was likewise given its share of flattering words in his column. Swamplands, plains, and mountainous country—all received unstinted praise. "There is interest in every mile of travel across our glorious country," he would declare at the slightest provocation. Once, on the way to Omaha, Nebraska, and almost in the heart of what has since become the great American dust-bowl, he wrote, "This train is rushing through a mine of wealth that will never be exhausted, increasing in value, and productive power as the mines of agriculture develop."

His boost for Southern California deserved top rating. "Paradise itself," he exclaimed ecstatically, "could be no more beautiful than Los Angeles and its environs." This continuous praise in his widely read column caused much anguish in at least two quarters: Florida and San Francisco. The California Hotel association, on the other hand, recognized the good work done by Brisbane. Its executive secretary wrote: "I was directed by unanimous vote of the Association at its annual meeting to give expression to the appreciation of the hotel industry for the many kind things you have said and are saying in your 'Today' column and in the columns of the Hearst publications concerning California, and to express to you the view of the hotel men of this state that your writings have resulted in a largely increased travel to the Pacific coast and in its permanent development and that you have thus rendered a public service to the people of California."

His response was immediate: "I am glad indeed to know that the California Hotel Association feels that the articles that I have written for Mr. Hearst's newspapers have been of value. You know, doubtless, that it is Mr. Hearst's wish, recently expressed, that all of his newspapers throughout the nation be used in every possible way to benefit his native state, California, and the interests of California's citizens."

At the Fort Worth, Texas, Centennial Celebration in November, 1923, Brisbane was the honored guest and chief speaker. The editor was amazed at the reception given him and the vehicle in which he was driven from the railroad station to his hotel. The cavalcade was made up of Texans dressed in the garb of early pioneers. Brisbane was seated on a wooden-runnered sled, a one seater, with a canopy thatched with hay. Derringers hung from each of the canopy uprights and across his knees was laid a flint-lock musket. On the side and back of the vehicle were hung pots, pans, axes, firewood and other pioneer equipment. And a black hound dog, roped fast, trotted on behind. Mr. Brisbane in his sledge was dragged up Main Street by a large black mule which, in turn, was piloted by a small burro.

The Brisbane of the nineteen-twenties hobnobbed with financiers, merchants, industrialists, astute politicians, and clever manipulators of public opinion. He worshiped bigness and success and gave fulsome praise to the side of the largest cannon or the noisiest claque. The Jeffersonianism which both he and his employer had so long professed was quietly put away like a garment out of style.

One of his close friends was Henry Ford, the auto magnate, whose weekly publication, *The Dearborn Independent*, became during the years 1923-1926 the leading organ of anti-semitism in America. All the trumped up charges against Jews the world over were rehashed and served up to the American audience by Mr. Ford's editor and with Mr. Ford's knowledge and consent. American Jewry, as well as progressive minded citizens generally, protested vigorously against these articles. Finally a million dollar suit was brought against Ford. The auto magnate became convinced he was in a bad spot, and backtracked. It was through Arthur Brisbane and the Hearst press on July 8, 1927, that Mr. Ford's retraction was first made public. The statement was a major newspaper scoop in every sense of the word. Ford said:

"In the multitude of my activities, it has been impossible for me to devote personal attention to their management or to keep informed as to their content. It has therefore inevitably followed that the conduct and policies of these publications had to be delegated to men whom I place in charge of them and upon whom I rely implicitly.

"To my great regret I have learned that Jews generally, and particularly those of this country, not only resent these publications as promoting anti-semitism, but regard me as their enemy. Trusted friends with whom I have conferred recently have assured me in all sincerity that in their opinion the character of the charges and insinuations made against the Jews, both individually and collectively, contained in many of the articles which have been circulated periodically in the *Dearborn Independent* and have been reprinted in the pamphlets mentioned, justifies the righteous indignation entertained by Jews everywhere toward me because of the mental anguish occasioned by the unprovoked reflections made upon them.

"This has led me to direct my personal attention to this subject, in order to ascertain the exact nature of these articles. As a result of this survey I confess that I am deeply mortified that this journal, which is intended to be constructive and not destructive, has been made the medium for resurrecting exploded fictions, for giving currency to the so-called Protocols of the Wise Men of Zion which have been demonstrated, as I learned, to be gross forgeries, and for contending that the Jews have been engaged in a conspiracy to control the capital and the industries of the world, besides laying at their door many offenses against decencies, public order, and good morals.

"Had I appreciated even the general nature, to say nothing of the details, of these utterances, I would have forbidden their circulation without a moment's hesitation, because I am fully aware of the virtues of the Jewish people as a whole, of what they and their ancestors have done for civilization and for mankind toward the development of commerce and industry, of their sobriety and diligence, their benevolence and their unselfish interests in the public welfare.

"Of course there are black sheep in every flock, as there are among men of all races, creeds, and nationality who are at times evil doers. It is wrong however to judge a people by a few individuals, and I therefore join in condemning unreservedly all wholesale denunciations and attacks . . .

"I deem it to be my duty as an honorable man, to make amends for the wrong done to the Jews as fellow men and brothers, by asking their forgiveness for the harm I have unintentionally committed, by retracting so far as lies within my power the offensive charges laid at their door by these publications, and by giving them the unqualified assurance that henceforth they may look to me for friendship and good will."

Brisbane came immediately to the defense of his friend, Mr. Ford. He said Henry Ford had requested him, Brisbane, to make public the retraction at such a time and in such a way as he thought proper. There were many who believed Brisbane had helped Ford in preparing the statement. This Brisbane denied. He told his readers, "Mr. Ford, who knows little about newspapers, probably sent the statement to me because I have known him personally for many years, and because he knew that daily articles written by me appear in all of Mr. Hearst's newspapers and in many others to which they are sent by one of Mr. Hearst's syndicates . . .

"I had nothing to do with preparing Mr. Ford's statement and did not know it had been written until Mr. Ford sent it to me two days before I published it . . .

"I have for several years talked to Mr. Ford on this subject as have many others. I am absolutely certain that Mr. Ford did not realize the full effect of the articles that had been published with his name back of them. *He had probably not read one of them.*"

William J. Cameron, the editor of the *Dearborn Independent*, expressed great surprise at the announcement. Mr. Ford had told him nothing about it. Although Cameron was held responsible for the material appearing in the *Dearborn Independent*, by Henry Ford in his retraction, Cameron did not lose his job. He has remained in the Ford organization ever since and at this writing is the spokesman for Ford on the weekly Ford radio hour.

As the year 1927 drew to a close, there occurred the most sensational episode in Hearst's long career as yellow journalist. This was centered around the case of the famous Mexican Documents which ran from November 14 to December 10, 1927, under headlines reminiscent of the Spanish-American War days. The documents, declared Mr. Hearst in a signed statement, "are the originals in every case and they bear the recognized and attested signatures of the President and the leading representatives of the Mexican Government." Here was an obvious attempt to draw the United States into war with Mexico. That government was accused of financing Chinese radicals, aiding the revolt in Nicaragua; making secret deals with Japan; attempting to bribe the American press; donating money to the Russian Soviets; and bribing four United States Senators.

These stories were a sensation. Ernest Gruening, then of the staff of the *Nation*, brought suit against the New York *American*, William Randolph Hearst, Arthur Brisbane, and others, for statements accusing him of 'communist activities' on behalf of Mexico. On December ninth, the United States Senate appointed a special committee to investigate the charges that Senator Borah had received $500,000, Senators Norris and Heflin each $300,000, and Senator La Follette, $15,000.

Although the *Journal* featured the Mexican documents, to the same extent as was done by the *New York American*, Brisbane himself made only one reference to them. This came on December 9, 1927, when he said: "Documents from the archives of the Mexican government show that one million two hundred thousand dollars was set aside for the three members of the United States Senate, whose names, of course, are not published, although they appear in the Mexican documents. An investigation will doubtless show how much of these appropriations went to middlemen, how much was kept by those that ordered the payments and perhaps used conspicuous names to hide their own stealing."

There was not the slightest intimation on the part of Brisbane that these documents might be forgeries. Quite to the contrary, his readers were left with the impression that they were undoubtedly genuine. The story of the investigation has been told in detail in "Hearst: Lord of San Simeon." * Experts employed by the committee who examined the documents found them to be palpable forgeries. Hearst himself, and Brisbane too, were forced to admit as much. They beat a hasty retreat and covered up their action by screaming headlines on the Parker-Hickman kidnap murder case, which happened opportunely at this time.

"The record which you have made in this matter," wrote Senator George W. Norris from his sickbed, "is sufficient

* *Hearst: Lord of San Simeon*, by Oliver Carlson and Ernest Sutherland Bates.

to place your publications in disrepute in the minds of all honest men, and it demonstrates that the Hearst system of newspapers, spreading like a venomous web to all parts of the country, constitute the sewer-system of American journalism."

Brisbane, having conveniently forgotten the Mexican forgeries, went on to tell his readers the purpose of a good newspaper which "tells the old truths with sincerity and earnestness that makes them new," which "expresses the thought, wishes, troubles, aspirations and just complaints of the public," which feels towards its readers—the great body of them, not the chosen few who can repay favors—as an honest lawyer feels toward the client that retains him."

Samuel Crowther, who interviewed Brisbane for *Collier's* in the middle of the twenties, said of him: "His real job—the job that holds him—is that of an educator."

"On the side," added Crowther, "Mr. Brisbane is what might be called a real estate operator. He has thousands of acres in New Jersey and on Long Island, and in New York right now he is putting up one forty-two-story apartment hotel building, another thirty-story apartment hotel building, a theatre and two twenty-story office buildings, in addition to some safety garages. These operations run into the millions . . . He went into real estate only because, as he told me, 'it is such an easy way to make money.'"

If one were to judge by the newspaper items in the *New York Times* real estate section during the nineteen twenties, Mr. Brisbane must have worked very hard at his avocation. Many of his purchases centered in the Madison Avenue, Park Avenue, Fifty-seventh, and Fifty-ninth street sections of Manhattan.

Early in 1920, he purchased the properties at 33 and 43

East Fifty-seventh Street, and also at 103 and 105 East Fifty-seventh Street, whose gross rentals amounted to $50,000 a year. In May, he purchased the apartment house at 513-15 Madison Avenue adjoining the other estate. In August, the firm of Lane Bryant Inc. took a long term lease on Mr. Brisbane's property at 26 West Thirty-ninth Street, which was next door to the sixteen story building Mr. Brisbane had erected for that firm a few years previously and leased to them. During 1921, he purchased two additional properties on Madison Avenue and Fifty-third Street; and further purchases were made on Thirty-ninth Street and Madison Avenue during 1922. The following year he bought the home of Mrs. O. H. T. Belmont (formerly Mrs. William K. Vanderbilt) at the corner of Fifty-first Street and Madison Avenue for an estimated price of $500,000. The Belmont mansion was for many years one of the great show places of New York and the scene of many of Manhattan's most brilliant social festivities. Shortly thereafter, the S. W. Strauss and Company announced it had underwritten a first mortgage to the extent of $1,400,000 on five pieces of Mr. Brisbane's property. The loan was to be used for rebuilding and modernizing several of the properties. A number of additional properties were purchased during 1923 and 1924. In the latter year, he also purchased the New Rochelle home of Nell Brinkley, the newspaper artist who worked under him for many years.

Another loan, this time for four million dollars, was obtained from the S. W. Strauss Company in November, 1924 to finance the erection of a thirty-story apartment house at the northeast corner of Park Avenue and Fifty-seventh Street. This building, known as the Ritz Tower Building, was leased, upon completion, to the Ritz-Carlton Hotel interests at a rental of $1,000 a day.

Together with Will Hays, then Postmaster General and Chairman of the National Republican Committee; Dr. Albert Shaw, editor of the *Review of Reviews;* Charles H. Christie, of Christie Comedies; and John H. Perry, of the American Press Association, Brisbane purchased the old pirate stronghold of Innerarity Island near Pensacola, Florida.

Brisbane had long owned a huge alfalfa ranch near Hodge, California. His boosting for that state had caused some of the Florida papers to omit too obvious references to the Golden State. Florida railroad and real estate interests were very anxious to have Brisbane realize the beauties and wonders of their state. At last they succeeded. On April 1, 1926, it was announced that Brisbane had purchased a large tract of Florida land. Mr. F. Davies Warfield, president of the Seaboard Airline Railway, announced the sale of the ten thousand acres at eighty dollars an acre. The news was broadcast throughout the nation. Florida real estate men felt sure that no longer would discrimination be shown against their state in Mr. Brisbane's column.

The statement of Mr. Warfield declared: "Two years ago, Mr. Brisbane spent two days automobiling with me over Florida land. He was impressed with what he saw and expressed the desire to purchase sufficient land to demonstrate in a comprehensive public way, the advantages of Florida as a home for agriculturists because of the extraordinary fertility of its soil and its superior climate. This sale is the consummation of Mr. Brisbane's wish and the desire to have Mr. Brisbane, known throughout the United States for his daily writings in hundreds of newspapers, interested in Florida's development."

Population pressure, augmented by advertising ballyhoo, skyrocketed real estate prices everywhere. Brisbane's purchases were usually in the path of new developments such as railroads, highways, bridges or subways. As a consequence, his earnings mounted rapidly. He loved to tell about his own shrewd investments. "Ten years ago," he told a group of Queensborough real estate men in 1931, "I paid fifteen thousand dollars for a piece of property in Jersey City. I lease that property to the Schulte interests for sixty-three years; sixty thousand dollars a year net for the first twenty-one years, eighty thousand for the second twenty-one years, and one hundred thousand for the last twenty-one years."

Frequently he used his editorial column to turn public attention in the direction of his or Mr. Hearst's realty holdings. In the early twenties, he agitated for the erection of an elevated station at Thirty-eighth Street and Sixth Avenue. It was unfair, he asserted, to make people walk all the way back to Thirty-fourth Street or up to Forty-Second Street if they worked in the Thirty-Eighth Street area. He made no mention of the fact that he was a heavy holder of properties there and would benefit by the new station.

Hearst had great confidence in the business ability of his chief editor, but was himself on various occasions the victim of it. As he remarked to a friend, "Arthur comes to me all the time with some wonderful plan to make money, but when I examine it, I find the profits are to be divided ninety per cent to Arthur, ten per cent for me."

It was Brisbane who persuaded Hearst to purchase his property on South Water Street and build the new *Journal and American* building there. The purchase was made without an inspection by Hearst, and a big price was paid for it. After the building had been erected, Hearst decided to visit his new plant. Much to his amazement, he was driven through slums, fish markets, and narrow streets. When he finally reached his building, he was so disgusted he refused to enter it and said he never would do so. Brisbane was roundly unbraided for this action, but he assured his employer that he would so arrange matters that the property would eventually become one of great value. He was as good as his word, and campaigned for an East River elevated highway.

The S. W. Strauss Company offered the public another bond issue on Hearst-Brisbane properties in June, 1925. The offering this time amounted to $7,000,000. In the prospectus, Brisbane was described as "President of the Borrowing Corporation . . . While probably best known to the public as editor of the Hearst papers, Mr. Brisbane is a most succesful real estate investor. His holdings of income producing real estate in New York City alone, total over nine million dollars and he has a very large income from this source. We have had many satisfactory dealings, aggregating millions of dollars, with Mr. Brisbane, covering a period of ten years."

New Yorkers, on the morning of August 5, 1926, were amazed by the sight of a full page advertisement appearing in every important paper. It was in the form of an open letter, in huge bold-face type, addressed:

TO ARTHUR BRISBANE

"Because I know your belief in the value of sound realty investment, I am respectfully asking you to consider what I believe to be one of the greatest investment opportunities ever offered in greater New York.

"Vast multitudes have been inspired by you to give heed to investments in real property.

"You have advised, out of your own wisdom, your judgment, and your strong common sense, that the soundest investment and the largest returns come from real estate."

Brisbane was praised for several more paragraphs but regret was expressed that he had never made a definite statement on the value of ocean or waterfront property. The Lido Corporation, the advertisement announced, had such property for sale within easy motoring distance of Manhattan. Mr. Brisbane was asked to make a public statement on such property. The advertisement was signed by William H. Reynolds.

Five days later, August 10, 1926, the *New York Journal* contained a full page reply, also in bold face type, headed:

ARTHUR BRISBANE TO SENATOR REYNOLDS

He began with a statement that life began in or at the ocean. Then followed a discussion of the place of salt water in relation to the evolution of man. Following this scientific diatribe, he concluded: "That ocean real estate, well placed, possesses value that will increase as the pressure of populations increase is evident . . . In buying near the ocean's edge, a man buys more than a piece of land with a prospect of future profit. He buys health, happiness for children, a place to which friends from the crowded cities like to come, especially if it is within easy motoring distance . . . I recommend matrimony and the wise purchase of real estate . . ."

Arthur Brisbane

A postscript declared: "I reply to your open letter because you spent a large sum advertising extensively in the newspapers. I hope your enterprise will be profitable to you and useful to the public."

The acquisition of real estate continued unabated. Together with Bernard Gimbel, New York department store owner, Max D. Steuer, famous attorney, and Louis J. Gorwitz, Brisbane purchased a large plot of land in Long Island

City near the Queensborough Bridge Plaza and the Long Island Railroad yards. He already owned several blocks of property along Queens Boulevard. His interests there naturally led to a good many boosts for that region in his columns. He was also a heavy investor in Jersey City real estate property in partnership with Mayor Frank Hague, the unofficial boss of New Jersey.

Brisbane was alternately the delight and the despair of New York real estate experts. Some regarded him as a shrewd operator. Others considered him as haphazard—he seemed to buy on hunches. But all of them admitted that he was courteous, friendly, and careful to see that they were protected in the trades they made on his behalf. Mr. Peter Grimm, president of William A. White and Sons, New York real estate brokers, relates his initial experience with Brisbane. It was at the close of the war and Grimm was just getting started on his own as a real estate broker. Looking through some records, he noted that two brown stone houses on east Fifty-Seventh Street, in one ownership, adjoined a house owned by Arthur Brisbane. He thought it logical to suppose that the editor might wish to buy the property. Grimm fixed a price on it—about $250,000, and finally gathered up enough courage to call on Brisbane. To his great surprise, when he stated his object to Brisbane's secretary, he was ushered in to see him at once. Somewhat hesitantly, he told the great editor about the property and mentioned the price. "That's rather expensive, isn't it?" asked Brisbane. Grimm said he thought the price not excessive. It was valuable property. To his amazement, Brisbane replied: "Very well, I'll buy it."

A few days later, Grimm was informed by Brisbane that another real estate broker who handled most of Brisbane's real estate deals, had suggested the same deal on the following day. "I told him," said Brisbane, "that you came to see me first and you were entitled to the business."

Although Grimm represented Brisbane on many other deals in later years, never again was he able to see Brisbane so easily nor was he able to consummate a deal so quickly with him.

The affluence of Arthur Brisbane was evident in the type of editorials he now wrote. Calvin Coolidge was proclaimed a great President; Andrew Mellon a great Secretary of the Treasury; John D. Rockefeller was now a philanthropist, and Judge Gary, head of United States Steel Corporation, was lauded as one whose object was "to make competitors grow and thrive rather than to extinguish them. The Judge has promoted a spirit of friendship in place of the former hostility."

Everyone, so ran the tone of dozens of his editorials, was a real or potential capitalist in America. Radicals, reformers, and cranks had no business here.

Brisbane was a millionaire. Success and prosperity combined to dull the edge of his editorial sword. In 1904 he had accurately pictured the degeneration of the radical journalist. As the nineteen-twenties drew to a close, that picture had become a true likeness of himself:

"Everybody knows that in America especially, a man is what he owns . . .

"Journalistic success brings money. The editor has become a money man, and he thinks and works as a money man. 'Where your treasure is, there will your heart be also.' When the treasure has been accumulated, it is in Wall Street or that neighborhood and there the editor's heart is also.

"The editor, with his heart in Wall Street, ceases to be yellow. He takes on a superior, dull, golden hue and that is reflected in the changed tone of his newspaper . . .

"The thin, keen, editorial bird, of real convictions, and a desire to help other thin birds, changes into a morally fat and sleepy bird when prosperity comes. He then thinks, acts, and looks as the other fat birds do . . .

"That editor was the sincere friend of other thin men when he was one of the thin. He is the sincere friend of other fat prosperous men now that he has become fat. He conscientiously adapts himself to the needs of his new class."

11

YOU CAN'T SELL AMERICA TOO HIGH

TO THE casual observer, Herbert Hoover took his oath of office as President of the United States in March, 1929 under sky unruffled by any economic or political disorder. We were entering upon a new stage of civilization, declared Professor Thomas Nixon Carver. Classes were almost completely obliterated. Everyone was, so to speak, a capitalist.

Real estate values continued to mount and there was no stopping the upward trend of stocks. Wall Street was no longer the octopus, sucking blood from the mass of the people. Instead, it had become a great pump pouring out wealth and affluence to all who played the market. It was an era of easy money. Our great American sport was to watch the daily stock quotations. Club women and socialites, janitors, school teachers, butcher boys, doctors, lawyers, housewives, so the story went, joined in the mad scramble.

Prices were rising, but who cared? The golden age had truly begun. The government, which for many years had fought the encroachment of the trusts, had now become an active aid in the development of new super-trusts. Consolidations and mergers were the order of the day; and corporation lawyers worked out a new device, the holding company, which, for the time being at least, netted fabulous fortunes to the insiders.

Banks established subsidiaries to engage in speculation. And the Federal Reserve bank system, instead of attempting to curb this action on the part of its member banks, permitted and encouraged it. By the close of 1929, there had taken place 217 mergers affecting 2,621 companies with securities whose market value totaled $21,655,068,000.

Credit buying had been developed to a degree hitherto unknown. Radios, automobiles, washing machines, vacuum cleaners, furniture, homes—all could be bought on credit. The high-pressure salesmanship methods of the twenties had filled the homes of American citizens with both necessary and useless gadgets—all bought on the installment plan.

Even the Communists were worried. Their membership was dropping off rapidly. William Z. Foster and Earl Browder referred with alarm to the "bourgeoisification of the working class." Labor unions speculated as wildly as the common man. They built banks; they invested in businesses. One union bought a coal mine. When the John L. Lewis organization proposed to unionize its miners, the unions owning the mine objected. The mine, its officers heatedly argued, was a business venture. To permit unionization of its employees would reduce the profits.

There was another side to the picture which was not so rosy. A crisis in American agriculture had begun immediately at the close of the World War. It continued to grow steadily worse with each year. Farm income dwindled while taxes mounted and prices for manufactured goods continued in their upward trend. Farm tenantry, which in 1900 had been confined almost entirely to the tier of states below the Mason-Dixon line, now spread rapidly into the north central states. Farms were abandoned, as the trek to urban centers grew apace. Michigan alone reported nearly 50,000 abandoned farmsteads by 1929. The plea for help on the part of the agricultural population of the American Farm belt was largely ignored or pooh-poohed by the solons in Washington. Local representatives of these farmers were referred to by Senator Moses, of New Hampshire, as "sons of the wild jackass." Such bits of farm relief legislation as were proposed and enacted between 1920 and 1930 merely scratched the surface of the problem.

Farmers themselves, in most instances, couldn't understand what was happening. Their credit was good, so they continued to buy on credit the thousand and one commodities needed or unneeded, hoping against hope that next year they could pay. In many cases, disaster was temporarily forestalled by sons and daughters of the farmers who trekked to the city and were able to send home portions of their earnings. Untold thousands of farmers within close range of the great industrial centers would, themselves, go to the city after the harvest each fall, to work in the industrial establishments until spring.

In this way, American agriculture was being subsidized, so to speak, for a period of years before the crash. Nevertheless, the downward trend continued, steadily but inevitably. Neither Wall Street in New York nor LaSalle Street in Chicago was able to reflect accurately the crisis in American agriculture, which sooner or later was bound to draw American industry along with it. For it must be borne in mind that the American industrial plant up to the time of the World War at least had been definitely harnessed to America's agricultural population and its needs.

The expansion of American trade to Europe in the postwar period had been achieved through American loans to finance these purchases. When the time came for the repayment of Europe's short-term loans, these could not be met. The only way to solve the problem and to keep the wheels turning was to make new loans, greater loans. By 1929, American investors held billions of dollars of foreign securities.

The industrial employment peak had been reached in the fall of 1927. The drag of unemployment had had eighteen months to accelerate its pace by the time Mr. Hoover became President. The vast shrinkage of the farmers' dollar, the slower, but nevertheless steady shrinkage of the industrial worker's dollar, augmented by the fact that Europe was unable to repay its debts, were stage settings for a financial and economic debacle the like of which America had never seen before. Those who issued warnings against the possible snap back from undue credit inflation were howled down as calamity prophets.

Arthur Brisbane, as we have noted, did not lead, but merely followed the current stream of thought. "Prosperity," he wrote, "real prosperity, had just begun.

"Uncle Sam continues to prosper, in spite of increasing expenses," he wrote in his "Today" column, October 4, 1929. "It is a big rich country, with one single city spending in a year as much as the United States used to spend before the war . . .

"Business and buying generally throughout the country, continue active . . . The automobile industry also is cheerful . . . stock gamblers may be worried, but the people at large feel cheerful."

The only issue of importance before the people, thought Brisbane, was that of prohibition. By this time it was highly unpopular. The "higher morality" which prohibition was to bring to America was now discovered to be un-American. "After four more years of shooting, spying, keyhole-peeking and interference with fundamental rights and liberties by fanatics and professional busybodies, the country will be ripe for a revolution against un-American conditions of this oppressive and offensive kind," wrote Hearst. And his chief editorial writer began attacking the temperance groups.

The Arthur Brisbane of 1929 was busier than ever before in his life. A dozen times a year he would travel to California or Florida or make the circuit of the United States. His own business interests covered much ground and he had to attend to his employer's interests as well. His salary was $250,000 a year, which placed him far in the lead of other newspapermen.

He was slightly paunchy now, but his movements were abrupt, sharp, and staccato. His voice had become colder and harder, but the rapid flow of words continued as in earlier years. The skin stretched tightly over his face made sharp lines that ran down from the corners of "a small querulous mouth" to the square chin. The brow was bomb-shaped. From behind a pair of tortoise shell glasses, Brisbane would view his callers with a comprehensive sweep of his cold blue eyes. The glasses were constantly flopping down on his short nose, but the alternate twitching of the muscles of the nose and a contraction of the muscles of the face would work them back into place again.

His office was barricaded by heaps of books and newspapers. And on his desk were the accumulated layers of newspapers, books, letters, drawings, and memoranda. Those on top were new and fresh; those at the bottom already yellowing with age. There in that jumble of hodgepodge, seated behind a bewildering clutter of papers Brisbane would use some small cleared surface of his desk for his writing. There, America's champion of reading, writing and real estate carried on his work, wrote his columns, issued his orders, and "on the side" conducted his private business ventures.

Brisbane knew he was a great man, but he wanted his subordinates to realize it, too. One of his associates during that period said to him: "During my ten years or so with the

Hearst organization, I frequently heard men talk affectionately about Mr. Hearst, but I fail to recall a single instance where anyone used affectionate terms about Brisbane. Perhaps it was his niggardliness, as compared with Mr. Hearst's reputed generosity. Perhaps it was the ruthlessness and disloyalty that he frequently showed to men who had picked their own brains in his service. I heard him threaten to fire Steinheuser (Brisbane's private secretary) over some trivial bit of office politics among his secretariat. That secretariat, by the way, was probably the most cowed and fear-ridden group of individuals in the office. One of them would sometimes sit mouse-like for hours in one corner of Brisbane's office ready to jump at the slightest nod of the master."

Brisbane, in editorial command, meant Schrecklichkeit. He was fond of using a quotation to the effect that to obtain efficiency and obedience men must be ruled by fear, and this policy he followed. Woe to the faltering worker. He was subject to immediate dismissal, irrespective of how many years he had spent in the organization. "Big George", as he had been nicknamed by "Tad" Dorgan, never permitted any of his subordinates to develop a swelled head. Artists or feature writers frequently had their products thrown back at them with a disapproving growl, to be followed almost immediately by his barking into his dictaphone the latest inspirational message on the value of Courtesy and the Humane Heart.

During October, 1929, trading was feverish on the stock exchange; the prices of securities were based on the assumed earnings of years to come. But the possibilities of these earnings began to fade very rapidly during those last few days of October. Credit expansion had reached its limit and was already beginning to snap back. For two or three years past, farmers had been unable to pay their bills. Industrial workers, up to their necks in weekly or monthly payments, were unable to meet them as the cost of living mounted more rapidly than wages. Bankruptcies among smaller stores and business institutions increased rapidly. Wholesalers were forced to cut their credits to retailers because manufacturers were closing out the wholesalers; and the banks were closing in on the manufacturer. The vicious circle had been completed. Only Wall Street seemed oblivious to it all – Wall Street and America's economists and newspaper editors.

Mr. Brisbane's comments in his daily column during those days immediately preceding and after the crash reveal his wish-thinking and superficial grasp of the economic situation. On October 16, to allay any fears, he had quoted Thomas Lamont, who "says business is good and will continue good. Gerard Swope, president of General Electric, says, 'Amen' and means it. Orders received by his company for the three months ending September 30, 1929, were $116,688,014 as against $90,348,666 in the same period last year. That increase of twenty-nine per cent has prevailed throughout the year."

The next day Brisbane remarks: "Samuel Insull Junior, following in his father's industrial dinosaur tracks, as president of the Midland United Company of Chicago, tells the American Gas Association that to boom the gas industry and increase sales, they must cut prices, and use 'persuasive advertising and proper salesmanship.'

"If young Mr. Insull follows out those ideas, he, too, will be a big industrial dinosaur some day."

On the 20th, Brisbane's chief concern is the Philippines and the Russians. About the first he says, "If we free those poor Filipinos they won't be able to send sugar to the United States without paying a high duty.

"So our sugar men say: 'How can you bear to hold those poor Filipinos in bondage?'

"On the other hand, the intelligent Filipinos say: 'We don't WANT to be free. We want to belong to our dear Uncle Sam if freedom is going to cost us money.' "

With respect to the Russian situation, he reports: "Clemente Voroshilov, Russian War Commissar, says war must surely come between capitalism and the proletariat.

"Therefore, Russia is engaged on a five-year program which Voroshilov thinks will make capitalism behave, or conquer it, if necessary. The proletariat, which means the mass of the Russian workers, has, of course, little to say about war and peace. Their business is to cheer all official decisions.

"In that, they are like the proletariat in other countries."

Rumblings of the impending disaster were heard on the 22d. But they didn't affect Brisbane and he was sure they didn't affect the country. He laughed at the "little lambs" who had been taken in by the wise guys of Wall Street. He reports: "Sad news from Wall Street. Many earnest little lambs when the tickers stopped, might have been mistaken for hairless Mexican dogs, shaved off.

"Some stocks, selling at twice their value, (no need to name them) went part way toward the right price.

"Good stocks, that in a few years will go three hundred per cent above their present prices, dropped heavily. Foolish speculators usually sell good stocks to protect bad ones, partly because there is a market for good ones, none for bad."

The next day, the 23d, Brisbane comments: "Charles E. Mitchell, head of New York's National City Bank, told the world yesterday that economic conditions are fundamentally sound, and backed his opinion in Wall Street in ways that big bankers understand.

"Market prices jumped with fierce energy, one as much as thirty dollars per share, 'Big Steel' leading.

"That will interest, but won't help little lambs, whose fleece, white as snow, has been neatly removed during the past few days."

On the 24th came the deluge. Twelve million nine hundred thousand shares were traded that day. Tens of thousands who had been trading on margins were wiped out. Many large brokerage concerns went under. Wall Street was stunned and so, too, were 120,000,000 Americans.

Brisbane rushed in to stop the gap. "Those that foolishly talk about a national panic will please remember that the income of this nation is $100,000,000,000 a year." The statement sounded reassuring. The fact that Brisbane erred to the extent of seventeen billion dollars in his statement was of minor significance. Our national income for 1928 was eighty and one half billion dollars, for 1929, (the highest ever) it was eighty-three billion dollars.

The shock which the nation experienced from the crash on October 24th gave Brisbane a chance to moralize the following day: "Recently Will Rogers told readers of the *Seattle Post Intelligencer:* 'There never was a time when so many fools were making money.' Today he can tell them there never was a time when so many fools were losing money so rapidly.

"One solemn New York banker thinks that the drop in stocks 'will send back to work many people who have been sitting around brokerage offices, on the trail of easy money.'

"Time wasted watching tickers or blackboards will doubtless be spent more usefully hereafter.

"But usurious money lenders who have been charging stock gamblers eighty to twenty per cent interest are not the men to rebuke the gamblers.

"You will hear perhaps today: 'Big bankers have stepped in and stopped the decline.'

"That happens after little people have been shaken out and stocks have dropped to a fine investment basis.

"Millions today sorrowfully realize that it does not pay to gamble."

To Brisbane, the whole affair appeared to be a conspiracy of a group of gamblers who had forced down the price of stocks in order to make a clean-up. The slight rally which began on the twenty-sixth (and lasted for the next few days before the avalanche began sliding again) renewed hope that all was well. Brisbane himself, on the twenty-sixth, said: "The question is not what has happened to those that gambled in spite of warning; but what, if anything, has happened to the nation, and its general prosperity." He quoted with obvious approval the statement of James Simpson, head of Chicago's Marshall Field and Company: "I am a firm believer in the doctrine which you (Brisbane) preach. Don't buy on margin and don't sell America short. The present liquidation in the stock market is not due to nor does it reflect general business conditions throughout the country. In the long run prices of securities must be determined by their yield and earnings on an investment basis. I believe basic business conditions sound and the production and consumption of goods in most lines have been fairly well balanced. Beyond this there appears to be no evidence of speculation in commodities such as that which occurred in 1920. The present liquidation in the stock market was inevitable and unless it goes too far and becomes too drastic I'm inclined to think it will be helpful to the business situation rather than hurtful."

To this statement Brisbane adds: "No buildings were burned down, no industries have died, no mines, railroads, fields have vanished. Paper profits have been reduced to scraps of ticker tape. That's all!"

On the 27th, he informs his twenty-five million readers that "Wall Street's big stock market opened quietly yesterday. There was a slight dizziness, as of one that has come from a shock while sleeping. The prices were better.

"President Hoover's assertion of the soundness of national prosperity, reassures many.

"The President, as he proved when in charge of the Department of Commerce, understands business as few men do in the United States.

"His mind, thoroughly trained, is not deceived by appearances or hopes.

"When he says: 'The fundamental business of the country is on a sound and prosperous basis,' the people may rely on it that he knows."

To prove his own point and that made by the President, Brisbane asserts there is "a tendency of wages to increase, and the output per worker in many industries again shows an increase, all of which shows a healthy condition." He cites the statement of Frederick H. Ecker, President of the Metropolitan Life Insurance Company, who shows that the wage earners of the United States get more than $60,000,000,000 annually out of the $100,000,000,000 national income. Brisbane adds, "They (the wage earners of America) need forty billions for the cost of living, leaving twenty billions for investments, savings, and the pleasures and luxuries of life.

"Stock gamblers may worry, but there is nothing the matter with national prosperity."

Brisbane's Sunday editorial of October 27th carries the caption: RUSHING TOWARD THE MIRAGE. The cartoon pictures a man, labeled "Millions of Us," running over a rock labeled "Real Opportunity." He is running toward a mirage, sketched in the background, consisting of sacks labeled with dollar signs, palaces, a man having breakfast served to him in bed, an automobile, a steamship and a sailboat.

"This picture," says Brisbane, "seen in Sunday newspapers by at least twenty-five millions of Americans, ought to do some good in this period of gambling, politely called speculation. Thousands have risked money that they will never see again, money that might have been used as a cornerstone of real success . . . The vision of 'easy money' is only a mirage, a false hope, 'fool's gold' that vanishes as we rush toward it. THERE IS OPPORTUNITY NEAR AT HAND AND IN YOUR BRAIN AND WILL POWER THERE IS POWER TO CHANGE OPPORTUNITY INTO SUCCESS." He concludes with a quotation from Proudhon, the French anarchist: "Monarchies are destroyed by poverty, Republics by wealth."

Day after day, Brisbane tried to instil courage in his panicky readers. He reassured them that all was well with the country; only fools and speculators had lost out. But the decline continued. The President issued a demand that wages be kept at the same high level. Mr. Ford stole the show by announcing wage increases for his employees. Hearst announced that wages must be kept where they were, and then put through an immediate wage cut to his employees.

On November sixteenth, Brisbane declared: "The writer is able to state positively that throughout the whole 'cyclone' only two big banks in New York borrowed from the Federal Reserve, and they were not among the biggest . . . There should be some way of reaching and silencing financial scandal mongers, as vicious and harmful in a period of financial stress as the wreckers of old days that killed passengers and stole their goods as they came ashore from a sinking ship . . .

"This is written by one who did not sell a share of anything in the hubbub, as he took his own advice—'Don't gamble.' "

Brisbane, had, no doubt, forgotten that November 2, 1928 he had written an editorial entitled "Get Aboard," in which he said, "The important thing is to know when to *get aboard*. In buying real estate or stocks, in joining others in any undertaking, make up your mind and then GET ABOARD. If you are in doubt, keep away. If you can't afford the undertaking in hand, let it alone. But if you are able, and think you ought to do it, GET ABOARD."

Will Rogers, the popular comedian, whose short syndicated column was then almost as widely read as Mr. Brisbane's "Today," remarked in one of them that "there is only one rule that works in every calamity—be it pestilence, war, or famine;—the rich get richer, and the poor get poorer. The poor even help to arrange it. But it is just as Mr. Brisbane and I have been telling you: 'Don't gamble.' Take all your savings and buy some good stock, and hold it until it goes up—and then sell it.

"If it don't go up, don't buy it."

Soup kitchens and bread lines spread rapidly during 1930 and 1931. Inspirational messages failed to stop the economic decline. At least once a week, Brisbane would amplify any news item which would give hope and courage to his readers. Thus, when Sinclair, the oil magnate, announced that he had seventy-two and a half million dollars ready to lend, Brisbane asked: "Does that sound like we're poor?"

He added: "What's the matter with us? Is there ANYTHING the matter with us, except lack of courage and the fact that some backbones that were made of granite in September, 1929, were suddenly changed to mush in September,

1930?" What was needed, he kept repeating, was backbone, courage, a real fighting spirit—the spirit of the pioneers who had made America. "Let's all get back to work again forgetting our dreams of easy money."

To the business interests of America he recommended more advertising. There was plenty of money in the country but people were jittery. There was an unconscious buyer's strike so the thing to do was to spend more money in crying one's wares. Meanwhile the Hearst press proposed to bring back prosperity by means of a "Buy Now" campaign.

Brisbane made a personal canvass of the great department store executives and made more speeches to Chambers of Commerce and special trades groups. Advertising, he told them, is to business what speech is to the human race. He considered it one of the most important modern ecomonic forces and listed it as one of the greatest inventions of all times. "It enables a man to do with his business, his book, his new ideas, more in a three months' good advertising campaign, than could have been done by old methods in three years or in a whole lifetime."

When asked what he considered the best advertisement he had ever seen, Brisbane replied: "The rainbow in the sky. It is one of the few advertisements that are written for all time. It advertises the fact that the world is not to be wiped out by flood again, and that's an important advertisement. It has excellent position, it has its entire advertising medium, the sky, all to itself, and it is done in color. Everybody sees it and everybody knows what it means."

The writing on the walls in Rome, telling about what happened in the Senate, he also considered a fine piece of advertising. This he credited to Caesar, "who had brains enough to know that the way to get on in the world is to let the people know what you are trying to do."

To one advertiser who complained about lack of results, Brisbane snapped back, "You advertise the way my cat walks into the room. If I don't see her by accident, I don't know she is there. An advertiser must command attention."

Futile advertising, like futile talk, Brisbane used to say, is that which PRODUCES NO RESULTS. "One kind of futile advertising is the advertisement written to please the man who pays for the advertisement instead of being written to make money for him." His theory of advertising was that it must have five qualities. First, it must be SEEN, Second, it must be READ; third, it must be UNDERSTOOD; fourth, it must be BELIEVED; and fifth, it must cause the reader to WANT the thing advertised. Effective advertising, he maintained, must be very simple and at the same time spectacular. And to advertising executives, he would repeat Tom Watson's formula for his own success as a public figure: "Always remember that it is impossible to exaggerate the stupidity of the public."

Although Brisbane beat the drum for advertising in general, what he always had in mind was advertising for his papers. He didn't like direct mail advertising (though this was used by the Hearst papers themselves) and he campaigned against it. As a result, he was flooded with letters of protest from advertising concerns and the Direct Mail Advertising Association of America protesting at his discriminatory remarks.

During the late summer of 1930 Hearst readers were permitted to forget domestic affairs for problems of international relations. France for a few months replaced Great Britain as our hereditary enemy. Mr. Hearst, Miss Marion Davies, and their company left for London, then Paris, followed by a month's tour at Bad Nauheim, Germany. On his return to France, Hearst gave an interview to the *Frank-*

furter Zeitung in which he denounced the Versailles Treaty for having put a yoke around the neck of the German people. When he arrived in France, he was notified that he had four days in which to leave the country. He left precipitately. Immediately upon his arrival in England, September 3, 1930, he told his side of the story, which made banner headlines in British and American journals: "I have no complaint to make. The French officials were extremely polite. They said I was an enemy of France, and a danger in their midst. They made me feel quite important. They said I could stay in France a while longer, if I desired, and they would take a chance on nothing disastrous happening to the Republic.

"But I told them I did not want to take the responsibility of endangering the great French nation; that America had saved it once during the War, and I would save it again by leaving it . . .

"The reason for the strained relations—to use the proper diplomatic term—was the publication of a secret Anglo-French treaty two years ago by the Hearst papers, which upset an international 'apple-cart' but informed the American people, and of course that being the reason, the French Government was entirely right in leveling its attack at me."

Hearst gloried in his martyrdom. The greatest and most powerful nation on the European continent was his private enemy. The Hearst organization at home and abroad, from Brisbane to the lowliest office boy, was mobilized in a campaign to picture Hearst as a great patriot. And as Hearst rushed homeward on the steamship *Europa*, public receptions were arranged for him in New York, Chicago, San Francisco, Los Angeles.

These "spontaneous" demonstrations made more good newspaper copy. The depression in the United States, Hearst told his audiences, was due in large part to the greediness of the European powers. They had taken freely of our wealth in gold and goods and man-power, but now they refused to repay. The depression could be ended quickly if only they would pay up their honest debts.

The Hearstian ardor for the great engineer, President Hoover, was already growing cold, and he took this occasion to let it be known. In a nationwide broadcast Hearst said: "Some of you will say to me, 'Why did you not sue the French Government?' and I say, 'First, because I did not want to magnify the incident, and, second, because I had the simplicity to believe, fellow citizens, that somewhere among our paid servants at Washington there might be found some public official with backbone enough and American spirit enough to defend the right of law-abiding citizens abroad.'" He ventured to hope that "American spirit and American independence and American loyalty to the rights and liberties which we inherited from our fathers had not really perished with Grover Cleveland and Theodore Roosevelt."

Quite mysteriously "Hearst for President" buttons began appearing at these meetings. Hearst expressed great surprise . . . But the attempted political boom died aborning. Somewhat petulantly he remarked at the end of his tour: "Now, I am going to board a train and go down to my ranch and find my little hideaway on my little hilltop at San Simeon."

Brisbane loyally had done his best during the whole episode to whip up a journalistic furore, but he had refrained from mentioning it in his "Today" column, and wisely so. Instead he gave his approval to another great man. "You are reminded," he wrote, "that one man can change conditions throughout an entire nation, by Italy's celebration this week of the seventh anniversary of Mussolini's rise to power.

"WHAT THAT MAN HAS ACCOMPLISHED WILL REMAIN ONE OF THE MARVELS OF HISTORY, WHATEVER MAY BE THE FINAL RESULT. MOST SURPRISING IS THAT MUSSOLINI HAS BEEN SO LITTLE SPOILED BY HIS SUCCESS.

"The king still sits on his throne, and while Mussolini's word is absolute law, forms of government are carried out in the usual way. It would not have been so in the old days of Rome."

The world had changed a great deal. Not so the Hearst publications. In makeup and content they followed the formula laid down by Brisbane and Goddard thirty-five years earlier. A copy of "The American Weekly—Greatest Circulation in the World" picked at random from the issues of the nineteen-thirties is made up as follows: The front page has a colored illustration of an almost nude woman, supposedly a character from one of the Arabian Nights' tales. Then follow the feature articles: 1) "Lots of Clothing But It Doesn't Cover Them," with cuts of two American girls now dancing in Paris; 2) "Astonishing Exploits of the Marquise Casoci;" 3) "Photographed—The Lovers As They Attempted Suicide;" 4) "Prettiest Legs in Hollywood?"—with plenty pictures; 5) "Highlights From Reverend Billy Sunday's Sermon;" 6) "Little Annette, Her Snakes and Her Monkeys;" 7) "Battle with Giant Baboon on Edge of Precipice;" 8) "Incredible Record of the Ace of All England's Impostors;" 10) "Mystery of the Tourist Who Vanished in the Desert;" 11) "Romance of the Horse-Loving Heiress and the Poor Farm Hand;" 12) "D'Annunzio Bares the Secrets of His Love Affairs"—with photos; 13) "When a Pretty Girl Grows Old"—the interesting pictorial history of Lady Diana Manners; 14) "Confessions of a Fashionable Drug Addict;" 15) "Mystery and Love Stories."

Eleanor Medill Patterson, editor of Mr. Hearst's *Washington Times*, and a competent woman journalist, reported in February, 1931, that she had by chance come upon Dr. Albert Einstein in the nude at the Samuel Untermeyer estate at Palm Springs, California. She became so flustered that the interview she had planned failed to materialize. The story gave Brisbane an opportunity. "Under such circumstances, Nellie Bly, best American woman reporter, with the possible exception of Dorothy Dix, would have got a blanket, put it over Dr. Einstein and got the interview, if necessary, sitting on the blanket and Einstein to keep him from getting away."

On one occasion, in April, 1931, the editor, who was in fine prophetic mettle that day, informed Will Rogers (who was a guest at the 10,000 acre Allaire estate) that Hoover would be relected by a bigger majority than previously and that Al Smith would be or would nominate the next Democratic candidate. In the Soviet Union, continued Brisbane, everyone was working; the American people couldn't compete with them merely by passing resolutions against them. The solution to the labor problem could be solved by legislating a shorter working day and week. He ended by stating that 1937 would be the first prosperous year of America.

Will Rogers, who reported his friend's views in his own column of chatter, added: "You don't suppose I went clear down there just for the horse back ride, do you? I got horses at home, but I can't learn anything riding 'em."

Edwin Markham, the poet, asked Brisbane for advice concerning a moderate and safe investment. Brisbane advised him. Then he put that advice in bold-face type in his column of September 19, 1931. "INVEST YOUR MONEY, OR PART OF IT, IN THE COMMON STOCK OF THE HUDSON-MANHATTAN RAILROAD COMPANY . . .

"If you buy it for thirty-five dollars per share, your money earns exactly ten per cent. If you follow this advice, pay no more than thirty-five dollars a share, and if your banker or broker can't get it for you at that price, wait until he can get it."

Whether or not Brisbane informed Mr. Markham, we do not know, but certainly he failed to inform his millions of readers who might rush to invest in Hudson-Manhattan Railroad stock that the author of the recommendation to buy that stock was at the time a director of that corporation.

This case is paralleled by his continual boosting of the new East River Drive project in Manhattan. In addition to numerous editorials pointing out its many benefits to the city, he also ran a series of maps in the *Journal* further to emphasize the fact. This project, now under way, had been planned during 1928 and 1929 but was known to only a few Tammany insiders. It ran past the South Street properties of William Randolph Hearst as well as an entire block of property at East River and Eighth Street, which Brisbane purchased from the Long Island Railroad in 1929 for $315,000.

The famous Tennessee "monkey trial," at which William Jennings Bryan and Clarence Darrow locked horns on the question of revealed religion versus evolution, gave Brisbane material for abundant copy. It also gave him a grand opportunity to ridicule the old "Commoner," to inform his readers of the essential unity between science and religion, and to discuss star-dust, nebulae, geological formations, early forms of animal and vegetable life, the age of the dinosaur, the upward struggle of man from savagery to civilization, and to reiterate that the "two things most important in man are, first, and above all, the BRAINS with which he imagines and plans; second, HIS THUMB, giving his hand its usefulness . . . We have our brains for thinking, our hands with two able thumbs for doing. The trouble with most of us is that we THINK and DO even more vaguely, or not at all."

Strained American diplomatic relations with Japan during late 1931 and early 1932 gave Brisbane the opportunity once more to tell his readers about the cunning and the avarice of "our little yellow brothers." Fortunately, the Japanese crisis passed in the excitement over the kidnapping of the Lindbergh baby.

The horror of this deed was deeply felt by every American. Brisbane exploited the event to moralize on crime, burglary, kidnapping, education, and allied subjects. His editors were ordered to print stories of kidnappings and murders of other days, thus fanning the flame of public indignation.

As the days passed and the child was not found, Government agents, local authorities, and amateur detectives joined in the frantic search. But it remained for Arthur Brisbane to conceive and execute the most disgraceful piece of journalism connected with the whole tragic affair. He scooped the country in interviewing Chicago's notorious gangland chief and racketeer, "Scarface" Al Capone, in Cook County jail about the kidnapping. The tragedy of the Lindbergh baby turned out to be a springboard for the eulogizing of Al Capone and the sensational interview was calculated to boost the circulation of the Hearst papers. From coast to coast the story of the scoop was printed under screaming eight column heads:

CAPONE ASKS FOR RELEASE TO HUNT LINDY BABY; TELLS BRISBANE HE WILL SEEK NO REWARD

Gang Chief Offers Young Brother As Hostage

'ANY BOND'

Editor Interviews Scarface Al in Prison

With startling sympathy Brisbane explained that the gangster chief was as much excited about the kidnapping as anyone else. He was a married man and had a small son whose picture hung on the cell wall. He wanted to help: "'IF THEY LET ME OUT OF HERE I WILL GIVE ANY BOND THEY REQUIRE IF THEY ARE INTERESTED IN THE CHILD . . . I would put my young brother here in my place to wait here until I come back . . . I don't ask any favors, don't want any gratitude or anything else in case I can be of any use. I can imagine how Col. Lindbergh feels . . . It would be hard for any man that found the man that stole that baby not to take a crack at him.'" Capone would do his best, and if he failed, he would return to jail, "'take my brother's place, and let justice go on with her racket.'"

"Scarface" also assured Brisbane that he was deeply concerned with the problem of the unemployed. "'I have given work to the unemployed. At least three hundred young men, thanks to me, are getting from one hundred fifty to two hundred dollars a week, and are making it in a harmless beer racket, which is better than their jobs before. I have given work that has taken many a man out of the hold-up and bank robbery business and others worse. Suppose they put me out of business permanently, and all of my men lose their jobs. They're making a good living now, they have little families, and little houses. They couldn't get thirty dollars a week in any legitimate racket now. What do you think they would do? Go on the streets and beg? No!'"

Brisbane concluded his story by urging Chicago citizens interested in Capone's appearance of unusual power to take a look at the equestrian statue of Colleoni by Veroccio, "finest equestrian statue in the world" at the Chicago Art Museum.

"Colleoni, greatest of Italy's condottieri, had powerful

shoulders like Capone, with a neck and head like his. If Colleoni and Capone had changed places in history, Capone might be riding a bronze horse in Venice today and Colleoni, who fought for and against this city and that, and finally left his great fortune to Venice, might be sitting now in the jail on the west side . . .

"We have a civilization built up under prohibition, a civilization of bootlegging, gangster rule, kidnapping, gigantic financing of crime and rackets of a thousand kinds.

"No wonder Capone says, 'If I am a bootlegger, so are they all.'"

The interview was a typical Brisbane exploit, shrewd, bold, and precisely on the borderline of journalistic integrity. For it, the Hearst press was unmercifully flayed by other large papers and news syndicates. United Press informed its clients that it had "approximately the same interview" with Capone several days earlier, but had killed it because "we feel that our service should not be used for the glorification of criminals." The *New York World-Telegram* refused "to believe that American justice had sunk so low that it must go begging and bargaining for such help."

Three years later when Bruno Hauptmann was captured and brought to trial in New Jersey, Brisbane reported the case personally. The *New York Journal* and other Hearst papers did their best to make it appear that Hauptmann was an innocent man. When the trial was over, it was said to be the constant hounding of Mr. and Mrs. Lindbergh by Hearst photographers and reporters which finally compelled them to leave the land of their birth and flee to England for quiet and privacy.

Shortly following his sensational interview with Capone, Brisbane wrote a series of boosts for Florenz Ziegfeld's new revue, "Hot-Cha," which is understandable in view of the fact that Hearst and Brisbane owned the theatre and wanted the production to be a success. Brisbane also used it to indicate that the depression wasn't so bad as it might be. "Somebody seems to have money," he wrote March 9, 1932. "Last night, when Florenz Ziegfeld's new show, bearing the deep and mystifying title, 'Hot-Cha,' opened, eighteen thousand people were not there that wanted to be there. They were unable to secure tickets, for the theatre was 'sold out.' And the tickets for the first night cost $15 each, plus $1.50 tax, or $16.50 each."

The following day he reviewed the performance, since "a Ziegfeld Follies first night interests thousands not interested in the Einstein theory." He reported the celebrities present—Walter Chrysler, W. Averill Harriman, Herbert B. Swope, Paul Block, William Randolph Hearst, Jr., and many others. Mr. Ziegfeld at the moment "specializes in tall girls, with bored expressions, long legs, and no more hips than a plucked canary. Lupe Velez, a Mexican, is the star of the show. Thirty 'glorified American girls' that stand behind her, and also wriggle, are, compared to Lupe Velez, like thirty plates of vanilla ice cream standing behind a red hot coal."

At a party for Marion Davies at Santa Monica in the early fall of 1931, a special edition of the *Los Angeles Examiner* was set up and distributed to guests. It was a burlesque of the whole Hearst organization. The usual motto of the paper, "A Paper For People Who Think," was replaced by "A Paper For People Who Drink." The front page was plastered with pictures of Miss Davies, together with a large cut of a group of platter-lipped Ubangi natives, captioned: "Friends Meet Famous Star At Train . . . Davies stepped off the train this morning all aglow with hives." There was also a column entitled "Doomsday" by Arthur Membrane which reported "Miss Marion Davies left New York Friday and arrived at Los Angeles Tuesday morning. It will surprise Miss Davies to learn that a thousand years from now, dozens of men now living will be able to leave New York Friday and arrive at Los Angeles Monday night. They will do this through the means of a monster Choo-choo, which now is just an idea in the minds of engineers."

Brisbane's rhapsodies about California sunshine, sky, flowers, ocean and mountains never attained the heights he reached during the Olympic Games in the summer of 1932. Florida papers, especially, were enraged when he reproduced the statement by George Young, publisher of Mr. Hearst's *Los Angeles Examiner:* "There is nothing remarkable about the fact that so many Olympic and world records have been beaten at this Olympiad. IT IS ALL DUE TO THE STIMULATING EFFECTS OF CALIFORNIA'S WONDERFUL SUMMER CLIMATE. It is time the world knew that California is the world's most marvelous summer resort, in addition to having its most superwonderful winter climate." As Brisbane's enthusiasm for Los Angeles grew with each succeeding day, the editor of the *Miami Herald* tossed out the whole column in disgust.

Brisbane had indicated on many occasions that he was certain Hoover would succeed himself as President, As the election year of 1932 approached he declared "there is only one, real live issue before the people and that is prohibition."

Mr. Hearst, meanwhile, began to sing the praises of his old friend, Jack Garner of Texas, as potential party nominee of the Democrats. Mr. Garner he described as a "loyal American citizen, a plain man of the plain people, a sound and sincere Democrat; in fact, another Champ Clark." The slogan of the day, according to Hearst, must be "America

First." With that keynote, Brisbane launched forth. "We haven't lost land, mines, men, or our intelligence. Nothing tangible has been lost in this country. Our only loss has been that of courage—of confidence in ourselves." The difference between 1929 and 1932, he said, was the difference between a live man and a dead one. Both had similar organs, but in the dead man the circulation of blood had stopped. "Money, the blood of industry and business, is not circulating."

Mr. Brisbane's zeal and influence led the publishers of the Wichita, Kansas *Beacon*, Max and Lewis Levand, to telegraph the columnist June 18, 1932 urging him "as the world's most famous editorial writer, thinker, student, one of this country's most successful business men—a man of unwavering honesty" to run for President. They had been prompted in this suggestion by the large number of returns for Brisbane on a straw vote conducted by their paper. "Mr. Brisbane," they added, "is the best qualified man in the United States to lead the country back to the high level of prosperity that was enjoyed in 1928."

Brisbane was flattered. For a day of two, he toyed with the idea. Perhaps he was the right man to lead the country back to prosperity! Therefore, instead of immediately rejecting the proposal, he wired, "I am so overwhelmed by this complimentary nomination that I find it difficult to express my appreciation of the good wishes of my friends who would like to see me go to Washington."

Upon further reflection he realized that if Mr. Hearst couldn't make the grade, neither could he. Two days later in his column he reported "I feel bound to support the newspaper candidacy of Will Rogers for the presidency. This is a flying age. Rogers is a good flyer, and, while I don't know what kind of a President he would make, I am sure he would be better for the job than I would be."

12

FROM NEW DEAL TO RAW DEAL

NINETEEN-THIRTY-TWO was a year of disaster.

Banks were crashing. Factories were closing their doors. Poverty and uncertainty increased. The unemployed began to organize. Rent strikes took place and anti-eviction groups were formed in every major city. Hard-working farmers, dispossessed from their land, organized to prevent foreclosure sales. The "farm holiday" movement swept across mid-western states.

Private charity organizations broke down under the new case load. The Federal Administration under Mr. Hoover, when pressed to give federal relief to the unemployed, replied that this could not be done. "The dignity of the American people would not permit them to take such relief." The only aid given was that to railroads, banks and major industries through the Reconstruction Finance Corporation. This action, though it saved some of them from bankruptcy, did not stop the downward trend.

The World War veterans clamored for the bonus to help them in their plight and to help revive business. A mass march on Washington was planned by the veterans. The President ordered his troops to disperse the bonus boys. They were attacked, driven across the borders of the District of Columbia, and their temporary homes on the mud-flats of Anacostia were destroyed and burnt up. Whatever chances Mr. Hoover might have had for reelection prior to that time were seemingly destroyed. A wave of indignation swept over America. Even Hearst was aroused. In a telegram to E. D. Coblentz, editor of the *New York American*, he ordered: "I do not care if every paper in the United States comments favorably on Hoover's action. I think it was the most outrageous piece of stupidity, if nothing worse, that has ever been perpetrated by the Government." Brisbane immediately came forth with a series of editorials denouncing Hoover for this action. He likewise flayed him for failing to support Heart's five-billion-dollar public works plan. When the demand that Europe repay its indebtedness to the United States was met, instead, by a moratorium on the Allied indebtedness by Mr. Hoover, even Brisbane, poor political prognasticator that he was, could see that Hoover's chance for reelection was out of the question.

John Nance Garner, one of the original Hearst brigade boys in 1903 and 1904, was picked by the editor and his publisher as the logical candidate of the Democratic party. There were other good men in the Democratic Party, they admitted—men like Franklin Roosevelt, Al Smith, Owen Young, Newton Baker and Governor Ritchie of Maryland—but all, unfortunately were tainted with "Wilson Internationalism."

Garner controlled the Texas Democratic delegation; William Gibbs McAdoo that of California. McAdoo, it must be remembered, had long been friendly to Hearst and was associated with Brisbane in the Hudson Manhattan Railroad Company. The Hearst machine was strongly entrenched with the Chicago Democratic Party group under the leadership of Mayor Cermak.

In spite of Arthur Brisbane's predictions made in February of 1932 that Al Smith would be the Democratic candidate or name its choice, Smith's influence was definitely on the decline. Franklin Roosevelt, successor to Al Smith in the governor's chair at Albany, was the outstanding candidate for the presidency.

John Francis Neylan, Hearst's chief legal counsel and financial adviser, soon realized that there was no chance for Garner to get the nomination. But a deal could be made with the Roosevelt forces whereby the vice-presidency would be assured Garner in return for his support. This arrangement was worked out in advance with James Farley, Roosevelt's campaign manager. A deal was also arranged whereby the Illinois and California delegation would vote together. Hearst's determination to support Roosevelt was a choice of the lesser evil. His big job, he felt, was to stop Al Smith.

When the Chicago convention went to three ballots with Roosevelt still far from the necessary two-thirds majority, Farley telephoned Neylan in San Francisco and said the hour had come. Neylan telephoned Hearst in Los Angeles: "Roosevelt must have California and Texas now." Hearst telephoned McAdoo and Garner, and the deed was done. It was an instructive example of the way in which American presidents are chosen.

No editor of an American newspaper campaigned with greater enthusiasm for Mr. Roosevelt, "Champion of the Forgotten Man," than did Brisbane, who had been cool and indifferent toward him while he was governor of New York state. The drift to Roosevelt became so pronounced that Brisbane, who had been asked by Lord Beaverbrook, owner of the *London Express*, for an opinion on the outcome of the election, sent him the following cable on November first: "Believe Republican defeat overwhelming. Doubt if Republicans can carry ten states." They carried only six. Two days after the election, Brisbane said in his column: "When Wall Street awoke yesterday and measured the height of the tidal wave, it was frightened. Prices that had gone up before the election dropped again. Strange phenomenon, for even the dullest multi-millionaire might have known what the result would be. Even this writer knew, or thought he did . . . ANYBODY MIGHT HAVE KNOWN IT."

In the same column, he reported that three baby boys born in the Brooklyn Beth-El Hospital on election night were named: Franklin Delano Mayblum, Franklin Delano Finkelstein, and Franklin Delano Ragin. "May the three infants prosper and never have cause to wonder why THEY WERE NAMED FRANKLIN DELANO."

Speaking over a nation-wide NBC hook-up on the night of November ninth, Brisbane eulogized the new chief executive. "We know he is a man of fine character, a man who has worked hard for his country, conscientious and manly . . . I believe he will make a good president, a very good president."

He looked upon the results of the election as a lesson in the art of self-government by the nation as a whole.

To Roosevelt's New Deal program he gave hearty approval. Every measure proposed was given unstinted recognition. Even the National Recovery Act was hailed by both Brisbane and Hearst as a worthwhile and essential piece of legislation. Brisbane spoke over a nation-wide radio hook-up at the request of Recovery Administrator Hugh S. Johnson in October, 1933 on behalf of the NRA. He told his listeners that the present economic situation was "an infinitely greater danger than confronted us when this nation was dragged into the war that concerned Europe and not business men. Subordinate your own ideas, and, if necessary, your immediate profits, to the national welfare and a national program." Stand behind the President, he urged, and encourage business. Promote the belief that better times are here. Enable employers to engage more men and pay out more in wages.

A Brisbane speech, like a Brisbane editorial, was incomplete unless it pointed a moral lesson. Nor did he fail to do so in the radio speech: "Good often comes from evil. From these days of depression and anxiety it is reasonable to hope that there will come permanently what the human race deserves—a shorter week; a shorter working day with better pay; leisure for the worker and undiminished profit for those that deserve profit, with machinery doing most of the hard work."

Brisbane's faith in Roosevelt continued for many months after Mr. Hearst soured on the nation's chief executive.

Harry S. Bressler, who drew more than two hundred fifty cartoons for Brisbane during his editorship of the New York *Mirror*, reports of this period: "Perhaps the happiest phase Brisbane went through was during the five or six months after he took control of the *Mirror*. He really believed in Franklin D. Roosevelt's program for the betterment of America. Roosevelt was trying to carry out a program that Brisbane had repeatedly espoused in his more beatific Sunday sermons. As one who saw him daily and occasionally two or three times during the day, I found it a real joy to work with him during this period. Practically every pro-New Deal suggestion was immediately approved, and the usually laudatory lines were dictated to go with each cartoon. Of course it was too good to last, for all the while the *American* and all the other Hearst papers were bitterly attacking the President. We knew that it would be only a matter of weeks, perhaps days, when the thunder would roll out of the west.

"Mr. Brisbane was summoned to spend a week or so at San Simeon. When he came back the change was unmistakeable. The type of New Deal cartoons which had been approved with alacrity were now taboo. Neither Packer nor myself was told to take a daily slam at the New Deal or at the President, but we knew exactly what we were supposed to do—when certain of our ideas hit the waste-basket."

In May, 1934, Mr. Hearst visited Mussolini in Italy and Hitler in Germany. He was particularly impressed with the efficiency of the Nazis, and made a deal to secure a monopoly of all American news published in the government-controlled German press. The effectiveness with which Herr Hitler had been able to crush the German labor and revolutionary movement intrigued Hearst. Perhaps some such method should be tried in America. Maybe he could become the savior of American capitalism. A drive must be made against all agitators, educators and enemy aliens. It must be backed up with the constant cry of "America for the Americans."

The new policy was inaugurated in the summer of 1934, at the time of the San Francisco longshoremen's strike. The trade unionists of the Golden Gate region became, according to the Hearst press, communists overnight. The keynote for this new policy was announced editorially: "If the small group of Communists, starting with their control of the longshore and maritime unions, extend their power over the community of the bay area—and then into the whole, or even part of the state—California would be no more fit to live in than Russia."

The red scare inaugurated on the west coast was spread to other parts of the country. In November, 1934, the "Little *Red* Schoolhouse" was attacked. Professors at Columbia University such as George S. Counts and William H. Kilpatrick were charged with being responsible for "red degeneracy" in the American school system. Syracuse University was found to be infected with Communism. Reds and pinks were found in almost every leading college—New

York University, Harvard, Yale, the University of Chicago and many others. Fake interviews, distortions, and every other method developed during forty years of Hearst journalism were used to discredit American college professors.

Brisbane was compelled to have his papers, the New York *Journal* and the New York *Mirror*, join in the witch-hunt.

American educators have been notably timid and supine. But Mr. Hearst's uncalled-for attacks caused a reaction. At the National Educational Association's meeting in February, 1935, the department of superintendents adopted resolutions favoring the formation of a nation-wide federation of teachers, clergymen, and newspaper editors to safeguard the freedom of the press, and Charles A. Beard, famous historian, was cheered when he said: "I have never found one single person whose talents and character commands the respect of the American people, who has not agreed with me that William Randolph Hearst has pandered to depraved taste and has been an enemy to everything that is noblest and best in our American tradition . . . There is not a cesspool of vice and crime which Hearst has not raked and exploited for money-making purposes . . . Unless those who represent American scholarship, science, and the right of a free people to discuss public questions freely stand together against his insidious influences, he will assassinate them individually by every method known to yellow journalism."

The elderly editor suffered no moral qualms as he instructed his reporters to shift the attack from the "red" professors to churches and religious organizations, new centers of Communist propaganda.

Laudatory articles about Hitler (and a series of especially written articles for the Hearst press by Goering) were followed by a campaign of slander against Soviet Russia. Once more the old stunts of using fake photographs, misleading headlines, and articles by discredited journalists were resorted to in order to fan the flames against the Republic.

Meanwhile the charge was made that "the whole administration, President and Congress alike, are going on a money-spending debauch." Some of the latest proposals of the government, it was charged, were "not merely for the purpose of restricting business, but for the purpose of destroying business." The administration was accused of trying to "distribute wealth by plunder," and prepare the way for "an era of crime, communism, and confiscation."

When the National Recovery Act was declared unconstitutional in May, 1935, Mr. Hearst exclaimed, "THANK GOD FOR THE SUPREME COURT!" The New Deal became the "raw deal." Roosevelt's policy—particularly his income tax bill —was called one of attempting to "soak the thrifty!—Loot Industry! and Spread Poverty!" The attacks grew in vigor. Soon readers learned that "President Roosevelt had repudiated the Constitution. He has repudiated the fundamental Democratic Doctrine of state rights."

When a Republican defeated the Democratic candidate in the first Congressional district of Rhode Island in August, 1935, the Hearst press went wild with joy. Flaming headlines announced that THE RHODE ISLAND ELECTION IS A REPUDIATION OF "RAW DEAL" SOCIALISM. And Mr. Brisbane was able to write: "It has taken the country two years to recover its face in the presence of broken promises, confiscatory taxation, the Russianization of the agrarian and business interests of the country, and the paranoiac spending, cynical contempt for the Constitution, malicious baiting of successful enterprises, the pyramiding of bureau on bureau, commission on commission, and all the rest of the crack-pot proceedings of INCOMPETENT VISIONARIES AND BRAZEN DEMAGOGUES."

Brisbane had finally swung around completely to his employer's point of view. When one of his subordinates ventured to indicate an obvious inconsistency between a cartoon that he was changing and one published only a week before, he turned upon the man and barked, "You make the picture. Let me take care of the rest!"

The former friend of the under-dog now sanctioned vigilante raids with the same vehemence that he opposed the new wave of unionism. When asked about the raiding of the Communist headquarters in San Francisco in the summer of 1934, he said, "If a Communist is trying to overthrow the government, I don't blame the government for trying to overthrow the Communists."

The development of the American Newspaper Guild became a thorn in the side of both Hearst and Brisbane. The editor said of it: "I'm against trade unionism in journalism. Of course, you might establish a moron class of newspapermen and let them remain where they began."

In the eyes of millions of his readers, Brisbane was undoubtedly "the greatest newspaperman in the world." To his employer, however, he was just another hired man, whose opinions were permitted to appear so long as they didn't conflict fundamentally with those of Mr. Hearst. We have noted instances of these conflicts earlier in the book. One such interesting episode took place in December, 1932.

On Friday, December 22, Brisbane devoted several paragraphs of his column to the case of Robert Elliot Burns, then living in New Jersey. Burns had twice escaped from a Georgia chain gang. Georgia wanted him returned to finish his sentence but Governor Moore of New Jersey refused extradition. Said Brisbane: "After his release, the crowd pushed and struggled to congratulate him. All very pretty, BUT making a hero of a criminal should not be overdone.

Those who say, 'In his hold-up he got less than five dollars' should remember that he got all his victim had. Had the victim had $5,000, he would have taken that, and, presumably would have been $4,995 worth more cheerful.

"In addition, this particular criminal, like thousands of others at large in this country, would doubtless have murdered the man he held up, had he resisted. It isn't wise to be too enthusiastic or cheerful about a young gentleman, who, after being indicted for forgery, goes out on a highway to rob, with the possibility of murder.

"It is the opinion of this writer it would be a wholesame thing to let Mr. Burns go back to Georgia, and learn that not everybody in the United States sympathizes with hold-up men, gangsters, counterfeiters, and potential murderers.

"Georgia may be annoyed by exaggerated accounts of her prison cruelties, but she has one comfort that other states haven't. HOLDUPS *in Georgia are comparatively few, and gangsters avoid that state. They don't like people that take crime seriously.*"

The next day, Brisbane continued the discussion of the Burns affair and took another crack at Governor Moore. "New Jersey's governor refuses to return to Georgia an escaped convict who has confessed to robbing an old man with the help of others and with deadly weapons.

"Governor Moore apparently doesn't approve of Georgia's prison system, which is alleged to hurt the mental and physical feelings of convicts.

"Governor Russell replies, emphatically, that he thinks Governor Moore refuses to return the convict because he only stole $4.50 from a poor man. 'In Georgia,' says Governor Russell, 'we attempt to punish highwaymen whether they rob the rich or the poor. New Jersey evidently does not think a highway robber should be convicted unless he happens to rob the wealthy and secures a large amount of money.' "

This column appeared only in the early edition. In later editions Brisbane's column was thrown out on orders from San Simeon.

The next day, Christmas Eve, the Hearst paper carried an editorial (probably written by Brisbane) taking exactly the opposite point of view from that Brisbane had expressed the previous two days. It said: "Governor Moore, of New Jersey, should not take too much to heart the few criticisms made of his action in refusing to send Robert Elliot Burns back to a Georgia chain gang.

"The Governor of Georgia is quoted as saying that the Jersey's governor's refusal was in violation of the laws of his own state and of the United States Constitution.

"In point of fact, there is ample precedent in the records of many states for Governor Moore's humane decision.

"But even more compelling than strict legalism is the moral aspect of Governor Moore's courageous deed. In effect he merely ruled that chain gangs are barbarous. Many good citizens of Georgia will confirm this opinion and thousands of citizens everywhere will insist that Governor Moore decided rightly."

And on the same day Brisbane published in his column a long telegram from San Simeon which read in part: "Dear A. B.: I cannot agree with your statement that because a man stole three dollars we should assume that he would have stolen three thousand, and that he should be punished according to this assumption.

"This contention means that there is no degree of difference between petty larceny and grand larceny—and there is a difference." Hearst went on to cite the difference between the two. The Captain Kidds of industry, he said, do not get such treatment, nor the Wall Street speculators who precipitated the panic and made millions of American citizens jobless and homeless. "Are any of these in the uncivilized chain gang? Are any of them even in civilized jails?

"Not at all. We Americans are a big, broad minded people. We have a frank and wholesome admiration for everything that is grand, including grand larceny, and a corresponding cynical contempt for anything that is petty, including petty larceny." In stinging words Hearst went on to castigate Brisbane and Governor Russell of Georgia and to give credit to Governor Moore of New Jersey, who is "exactly right in refusing to extradite Robert Elliot Burns to be murdered or maddened in the inquisition of the chain gang."

Hearst, having read Brisbane's Saturday column, wired Coblentz to throw out the whole column, and this order was repeated verbally in a transcontinental phone call. Soon another telegram from San Simeon arrived pointing out it was poor judgment to run an editorial backing Moore and also a Brisbane editorial against him. Hereafter, this telegram said, Arthur Brisbane's column didn't have to go on page one; furthermore, editors were to edit it as they saw fit so that it would agree with the paper's policy. Similar telegrams were sent to all Hearst papers using the column. One of the insiders, whose name must obviously be withheld, added: "Later, another telegram arrived saying that Hearst and Brisbane would settle the thing between them. But there was no telegram rescinding the others and, I hear, the master minds of the *New York American* believe that they may edit Arthur Brisbane's column at any time from now on."

More than once during the last few years of his life Brisbane found himself in hot water with his master. There were days on which his entire column was thrown into the waste basket and other days when whole paragraphs were deleted.

His 1934 July Fourth editorial quoting the declaration of Independence was shelved. On another occasion, his reference to Roosevelt – "He's at least trying, which is more than Hoover did." – was eliminated. Again on April 7, 1936, commemorating America's nineteenth anniversary of entry into the World War, on orders from San Simeon, the following was relegated to the waste basket: "Various parades and performances assisted by our army 'celebrated' the nineteenth anniversary of Uncle Sam's joining the big war.

"That seems like celebrating the time you fell down stairs and broke your leg. We had no business in that war which caused us to squander fifty thousand million dollars with enough extravagance plus ten thousand millions to dishonorable borrowers in Europe.

"Celebrating foolishness of that kind seems childish. For the next hundred years this country will be paying for that war in pensions, bonuses, heaven knows what. The last pensioned widow of the War of 1812 has just died and that war occurred 134 years ago.

"The man to remember and honor at this time is the dead Senator LaFollette, who made a vigorous fight against United States entrance into the War.

"High finance disguised at patriotism had its way, so we had our war, and now we have our depression."

Brisbane's references to the Popular Front Government of France and the sit-down strikes were removed on instructions from above. One of these paragraphs read, "In France at one time it was forbidden by law to eat the bodies of those who died from plague. That law is no longer needed, thanks to better government and an end of the 'Divine right of kings.' But the workers were far from satisfied and believed they should actually rule. The old fable of the feet rebelling against the head. The heads in many places have guided badly. Perhaps the world is about to see what the feet can do."

There is no record that Brisbane ever raised a serious objection to the way in which his column was edited. Once when Hearst rebuked him for his heresies, the columnist replied, "I write this column. As long as you pay me for it, you may print it or not, as you see fit."

Brisbane thoroughly enjoyed writing his daily column and convinced himself that he was serving a vital need of the nation. He would discuss anything from the size of George Washington's feet to the theory of relativity. Indicative of the range of subjects dealt with, here is a day by day list for one week in 1933:

September 16—United States Navy Plans, Apartment Houses in Germany, French Gold 'Hoarding,' Banking in the United States, Upton Sinclair, Nudists, Frank Brangwyn.

September 17—Russian Finance, Muscle Shoals, Homely Philosophical Musings on Electricity, Conditions in Iraq, The Mollisons, Adolf Hitler.

September 18—Mr. Wickersham and the NRA. W. R. Hearst, Homely Philosophical Musings on the Seasons. Crime in Africa. Sleeping Sickness.

September 19—The American Dollar. Texas Guinan, Telephones in Germany, Postmaster General James A. Farley. The Lindberghs.

September 20—The Jewish New Year, Potato Growing in California, Aimee Semple McPherson, The Chicago Exposition, Japanese Politics, Crime in Oklahoma.

September 21—Theosophy (inspired by death of Mrs. Annie Besant), The Value of the American Dollar, The British Labor Party, Gold in the Philippines, Russia, Mexico.

September 22—The Bible, Greek and Teutonic Mythology, Popular Science (sociological discussion), Pep Talk to Business Men, General Criticism of the Paris Stock Exchange.

Mr. Brisbane, as we have frequently noticed, was long the prime fixer of ailing papers. Mr. Hearst's tabloid, The New York *Mirror*, was not doing well. It was a slavish imitation of The *Daily News*, with which it competed unsuccessfully.

In 1924, at the time plans were made to start the *Mirror*, Brisbane telephoned to Hearst's managing editor in Chicago, Walter Howey, saying, "Can you start a tabloid newspaper in ten days?" To which Howley replied, "Nine days will be plenty." So Brisbane snapped out the order: "Then come on to New York, but don't move your furniture."

The *Daily Mirror* had promised that its program would be ninety percent entertainment and ten percent information, but circulation grew slowly. The only bona fide drawing card on the *Mirror* during all its years was Walter Winchell. But the *Mirror* couldn't succeed on that alone, so in November, 1934, Hearst ordered Mr. A. J. Kobler, publisher and nominal owner of the *Mirror*, to report at San Simeon and at the same time instructed Arthur Brisbane to take over editorial direction of the tabloid.

Brisbane entered upon his new job with enthusiasm. He had always liked a picture newspaper. To his reading public, he announced, "I have undertaken editorial direction and management of the New York *Daily Mirror*, and hope to contribute something to a newspaper that already has a great circulation, more than half a million daily, more than a million Sunday . . . Published within reach of twenty million population, it hopes to include among its readers a fair share of that population."

Within a few hours after Brisbane's arrival, the staff of the *Mirror* felt his presence. Unlike Kobler, who secreted himself in a palatial office two floors above the dingy city

Hearst and Brisbane in 1933.

room, Brisbane had an office for himself and his secretaries partitioned off in the midst of the clutter and action. From his sanctum he could look through the open door to observe the comings and goings of the entire staff. His subordinates decided within a week after the new editor's arrival that he did not intend to be a figure-head. He was there to stay and undoubtedly would cause many shake-ups.

Brisbane's first illustrated editorial on the *Mirror* dealt with Sir Oswald Mosley. A dotted line, drawn across the British Black Shirt's cranium, indicated that he "has too much face, too little head."

Brisbane always felt a degree of jealousy towards fellow journalists whose earnings were also large. The thousand dollars a week paid to Walter Winchell, the former vaudeville trouper, by the *Mirror* for his gossip column worried Brisbane not a little. And when he learned that Winchell was getting another two thousand dollars a week for radio broadcasting, he felt still more ill at ease. "Is Winchell really an asset to the paper?" he asked his associates. Those who had courage to speak up informed him that so far as a circulation getter was concerned, Winchell *was* the *Mirror*. "All right," growled Brisbane, "but no amount of money would make me read him."

Essentially a practical man, however, Brisbane soon realized the value of Winchell to the *Mirror* staff, so he persuaded him to write a column for the Sunday edition. Finally, Brisbane arrived at the point of praising his chief circulation-getter. He was, wrote Brisbane, comparable to Keats' "Bright star . . . hung aloft in the night."

Never had Brisbane worked so hard as he did to give body and substance to the *Mirror*. His editorials were simpler than ever. Each day they were illustrated by capable artists. New blood was added to the staff. Stanley Walker, city editor of the *New York Herald Tribune*, was brought over at a large salary with an iron-clad contract. Walker, who admitted he took the job because of "fun and money," added that "he didn't know anything about this picture paper business and it's time I learned. It's a faster game than I've ever been in and I'm going to lose a whole flock of inhibitions. If some ideas I have should work out, this will be the damnedest paper you ever saw."

The battle was unsuccessful. For the first time in his life, Brisbane failed to accomplish that which had been expected of him. Soon he was asked to leave the staff of the *Mirror*. Stanley Walker had left long before, fed up with Hearst journalism, his contract having been settled.

The trend of events in the middle thirties definitely puzzled Brisbane. One day he would remark in his column that conditions were growing worse. The next, things were better. He tried to cater to the increased liberalism of his readers. At the same time he wanted to stand in the favor of his advertisers. So he carried water on both shoulders, relying upon the short memory of his readers to overlook his many inconsistencies. He favored Social Security, but he attacked the Black-Connery Bill to limit the working week to thirty hours. "In outlawing full time employment," he charged, "the bill stands in the way of economic progress. It represents a muddle-headed and fallacious approach to diffusing leisure among the working classes." He took an obvious part, at Mr. Hearst's request, in fighting the Tugwell Bill of 1934. "Mr. Tugwell is wrong," he informed a gathering of drug and chemical men, "and business men are not all morons and do not need nurses to keep them from falling down and breaking their necks."

In an attempt to win the clergy and religious readers to his column, he began an attack against atheists. The non-believer he compared with the rhinoceros mouse, "which rejects what he cannot understand and he understands very little. The preposterous atheist rejects what he cannot understand, and HE understands very little." The article was called to the attention of eminent clergymen who were asked to comment on it. These were then reprinted in an attempt to win new readers.

Brisbane, not content with interviewing potential advertisers in person, or making suggested layouts for them, tried to build up interest in the Hearst press by announcing its effectiveness as an advertising medium through boosts in his syndicated columns.

Writing from Chicago, in January, 1935, he declared: "One entire twelve page section of today's *Chicago American,* carries a single advertisement by the Fair Department store. A similar advertisement published in the *Chicago American* a week ago produced such results that the advertisement is repeated today.

"The Fair realizes that it is not wise to whisper in a great crowd of readers when you can afford to shout." For several additional paragraphs, he explained the advantages of advertising in the Hearst papers and appended, "Major Namm, owner of a Brooklyn store, recently advertised on the same big scale in the *New York Evening Journal.*"

Perhaps his most surprising bit of boosting occurred on August 20, 1935, when he was making his first airplane flight. His column was three times as long as usual. At one point in the report, which was carried as a front page feature article in every Hearst paper, he said, "The stewardess warns passengers, 'Be careful about your fountain pen here ten thousand feet up. The vacuum makes it flow freely. Some men get ink all over their clothes.'

"Fountain pens," observed Brisbane, "have been known

that would stay dry on top of Mount Everest. For pens that flow evenly, perfectly, everywhere, at all times, *see our advertising columns*."

December 12, 1934 was a banner day in Brisbane's life. It was the occasion of his seventieth birthday anniversary and his fifty-first year as a newspaper man. Congratulatory telegrams by the thousands poured in on him. President Roosevelt himself, slyly borrowing a phrase from the editor's column, telegraphed congratulations: "This is momentous news. It is so momentous that I am moved to comment and congratulations . . .

"Your writings, in my judgment, always have been marked with merit. Not that I have agreed with you at all times, but because I have always been an admirer of things simply and clearly put. You have simplified the interpretation of news for many millions of people, and I make the statement, with little fear of contradiction, that none of these millions was ever at a loss to understand exactly what you meant when you transferred your thoughts into printed words." David Lloyd George, a frequent contributor to the Hearst press, cabled congratulations, as did General Italo Balbo and 3,000 other persons, great and near-great. Mr. Hearst wired: "Of course Mr. Brisbane is not seventy years old. That would make me a centenarian . . . We must not expect too much of a kid, but certainly expect a lot of a young man when he grows up."

The birthday party was broadcast on a coast-to-coast network. Charles M. Schwab, head of Bethlehem Steel, was one of the speakers. Among the distinguished guests were Walter Gifford, president of the American Telephone and Telegraph Company, Hiram Maxim, the inventor, Major-General Bennet Nolan and Rear-Admiral Yates Sterling.

Brisbane himself was in fine fettle. When his turn came

to speak, he feigned modesty; he did not talk about himself —that would be a sign of old age. Instead he would tell about his newspaper work. So he reiterated what every one of his constant readers had been told a dozen times: A newspaper is a mirror in which are reflected events and human beings. "Don't break the mirror." The newspaper is also the second hand on the clock of time. And it may be compared to rainfall, distributing its information in drops easily absorbed. "The first great piece of news sent out was the rainbow, put in the sky, promising that there would be no more floods . . . When the Ruler of the Universe has anything to say He piles up the black clouds, bigger and blacker than any type we can use, and if that isn't enough, He shoots red lightning through it. Then He does what we can't do unfortunately, but what we would like to do—He makes the front page thunder." A newspaperman's work, he went on, is forgotten, but so is everything else in due time. Even the earth will grow cold and old and die. "But it all offers opportunity. A man is made from nothing, does not know how he got here; does not know where he is going; does not know what he wants to amount to, but he does know that he is a small part of the entire thing. He has an opportunity to work. If he does his best and lives up to the opportunity that is given to him, he should not pity himself, but thank his Maker."

The importance of Arthur Brisbane's speech on his seventieth birthday was not so much in what he said, as what he left unsaid. The panorama of history he had watched and reported for more than fifty years was left unmentioned. At his father's knee he had been told repeatedly the story of the struggles of America's early reformers and radicals. Many of them he had seen and heard. He had known Europe of the late 1870's and early 1880's. He had seen the United

States transformed into a leading financial and industrial nation. He had met and interviewed rogues and rascals of low and high degree, reformers, inventors, politicians, religious leaders. He had served under two of America's great journalists, Dana and Pulitzer, and was still in the employ of its most notorious publisher. He had watched ten presidents enter the White House. He had helped to create the Spanish-American War; and had himself felt the pressure of war hysteria in 1917 and 1918. He had witnessed depressions and periods of prosperity.

Few men in America had had an opportunity to get such a complete and inside picture of the social, economic, and political forces at work. But Brisbane, the moralist, the man who was always drawing lessons from history, had nothing to say, no moral to point, no lesson to draw from all this on his seventieth birthday. His own writings—those endless columns and editorials of words, words, words,—millions of words had been forgotten by his readers almost as rapidly as the issues of the paper on which they were printed. He had said and written so many things on so many subjects. But the products of his fifty years of labor were slowly turning to dust on the crumbling pages of the newspaper files in public libraries or morgues of the newspapers for which he had worked.

In the main his prophecies had been as bad as his science. His zeal for reform and idealism was never more than skin deep. For forty years, at least, it had usually been hitched to the frequently perfidious plans of his employer. Brisbane had early developed a cash-register mind and of him it could be said, as it was said of Chief Justice John Marshall, "his financial interests overran state boundaries, and his political principles followed eagerly in their train, washing away all local and sectional loyalties."

13

SCIENTIST, LITERARY GUIDE, POLITICAL PROPHET

It is to be assumed that many inconsistencies would creep into the five or six hundred thousand words which Brisbane dictated every year. A collection of such errors would easily fill a large volume. Many of these misstatements or strange prophecies were made repeatedly.

We have seen how Brisbane attacked the race horse problem by x-raying the animals' heart and lungs. Even Will Rogers, who was so friendly with Brisbane, reported, "he wrote Saturday about Mr. Hearst's fifteen thousand Holstein cattle. Now, a Holstein is an old black and white spotted milk cow. She is a beverage animal entirely. She is raised for her juice, and not for her T-bones. Why, even Mr. Hearst hasn't got enough editors to milk fifteen thousand old 'bossies.' Of course, what he meant was fifteen thousand Herefords. White faces, faces made up like women.

"Now here's what we got to do with this writing business. We've got to have it divided according to talent. I'll handle the cattle end. He takes disarmament, unemployment, wars, past and future, history gone and coming, and the advantages of living in California and Florida.

"And, of course, I'll take over discussion of the foreign debts, and give him ten per cent of all I collect. But, he is to have all the dissatisfied Republicans to blame the loss of the election on."

Brisbane's palpable errors were occasionally uncovered, but most of the time the millions of readers who relied upon him for their information accepted his statements as matters of fact.

He wrote: "A gabon viper, female, in New York's Zoo, coming from hot Africa, surprises everybody by producing twenty-seven little vipers at one birth. Born alive, not from eggs, if the gabon lady acts as other vipers do, her babies, when danger comes, enter her open mouth and run down her throat for safety . . ."

The herpetologist of New York Zoological Park was dumbfounded at the statement, as were other zoologists generally.

When Henry Fry questioned his statement, he said, "I have received letters from the learned and the simple saying 'the mother viper does nothing of the kind.'

"I never saw the performance but I have been practically raised in the belief that that is exactly what the mother viper does, and I should be sorry to give up one more of life's delusions."

Bull frogs and beauty contests also interested Brisbane. "If bull frogs," he suggested, "had a beauty contest, only the legs would count, legs being all of a frog that count . . . Something more is asked of a young woman . . . In any beauty contest the forehead would count sixty, eyes twenty, mouth and figure each ten per cent."

A newspaper item to the effect that a young lady sneezed violently and dislocated her left arm at the elbow because of it, brought forth the following remark: "This incident reminds you that an inclination to sneeze should not be repressed, ordinarily, because sneezing *kills by violent shock* harmful germs that inhabit the nose and throat.

"A sneeze not merely violent enough to dislocate an arm will always kill many millions of germs. A sneeze to them is as great a cataclysm as a falling rock of Gibraltar would be to you. Sneezing and violent laughter are both good for human beings and bad for germs."

For the benefit of families who plan a summer sight-seeing trip by automobile, Brisbane had excellent advice! "When you next start on a 'seeing America first' trip, by automobile, take a good milk goat along in a sufficiently roomy box, fastened at the rear or on the left-hand mudguard.

"Camp for the night, unload and milk the goat, feed the baby, while the goat feeds herself. She will eat anything. Remember *goats do not have tuberculosis.*" He promised his readers much more information about goats. "Goats are not appreciated in America, and we need goats."

On another occasion he admonished mothers to bathe their babies in water of a temperature of 212 degrees fahrenheit, "not one degree less."

As we have noted previously, Brisbane devoted much time to describing the ravages wrought upon the human system by alcohol and hard liquors. Smoking, too, was condemned, especially for women. "Alcohol, fortunately, ruins the complexion. And for the sake of their looks, women often deny themselves and show a strength of resolution that would not be called forth by any moral appeal. Cigarettes, in short order, make the face sallow, spoil the shape of the mouth, make the eyes heavy, fill the hair with permanently unpleasant nicotine suggestions, develop a mustache —and women are cured of cigarette smoking by a look in the glass, when they could not be cured by cheerful appeals of wise philosophers." Such positive statements of the effects of cigarette smoking appeared frequently in Brisbane's editorial columns up to nineteen twenty. Thereafter, they began to disappear. It is a moot question whether increasing cigarette advertisements or Brisbane's realization that he could do nothing to stop the habit from spreading caused this defection on his part.

He denounced the folly of women trying to get thin who are told by ignorant specialists: 'Sugar will make you fat.' Brisbane adds: "Sugar will not make you fat. On the contrary it will supply heat and burn up waste tissue."

Few writers have made virtues out of their own habits as consistently as did Brisbane. He married late in life and he continued to argue that late marriages were the proper thing for men. He had a large family—six children—and large families were proper, too. He was fanatical about the virtues of wholesale motherhood. In 1935, he nominated Mme. Dionne, mother of the quintuplets, as the outstanding woman of the year. Shortly thereafter, when addressing a gathering of fashion experts in New York, he urged them to forget about clothes and fashions. Instead he told them to "go home and have six children" each.

When tight corsets were the order of the day, he advanced scientific reasons against them. But the advent of short skirts and abbreviated dresses at the close of the war was not acceptable either. He mourned the passing of women's long hair and he deplored women in shorts and slacks.

His attitude on education was likewise largely a justification of his own life. He had never gone to college. Colleges weren't much good. Frequently he told his friends: "I was going to go to Harvard when I was nineteen. Thank heaven I went on the *Sun* instead . . . . In other words, I got my chance at a time when I might have been wasting years in Harvard, after having wasted several years in schools in Europe. Had I gone to college, I am perfectly certain that I should have been a flat failure."

In his column he wrote: "The work of college is this: A half-baked boy lives surrounded by other half-baked boys, when he ought to be living among men learning to be a man. He takes himself, the other boys and their opinions seriously. An able educator says a boy needs ten years to get over the harmful influence of college life."

Then *The Varsity*, a paper published by the students of Toronto University charged that a large percentage of the undergraduates were "practical atheists" Toronto became much excited. Brisbane said this excitement was unnecessary. "Students are, mentally speaking, half-baked products, attaching unnecessary importance to what they would describe as their own ideas." On another occasion, he declared, "Schools educate of course, although unfortunately the public schools are managed chiefly with the idea of ridding mothers of the nuisance of children during their working hours." The best he was able to say for higher education was to quote a French proverb about travel: "Travel forms youth when it doesn't deform it." He added: "College does harm more often than it does good. A young man in five years or four years gains the IMPRESSION that he is educated—WHICH HE ISN'T—and that he is better than somebody else. Which he isn't."

But if education could not be obtained in the public schools or colleges of this country, how was one to get it? The answer was simple. "Two hours of study a day in five years will make an educated man." But what was to be the material used to acquire that education? First, and foremost, read Brisbane columns and Sunday editorials. Second, read the Hearst papers in toto. Third, read the books recommended by Mr. Brisbane in his editorials and his daily column. In an editorial, "The Truth Sets You Free" he said: "First you want to know what and where this earth is on which you live. Read a good, simple book on astronomy. Flammarion's "Astronomy" is good . . ."

"Then read a book on evolution, about the development of animal life on the earth, how you have gradually risen to an erect position, and learn to study the stars instead of studying ways to kill and eat your neighbor. Wallace's book on Darwinism is good.

"The history of Philosophy written by George Lewes, husband of George Eliot, is easy and pleasant to read, and sufficiently although not perfectly accurate."

Brisbane admonished his readers that no matter what other books they read, at least fifteen minutes every day should be spent in reading Shakespeare. "Other books feed different parts of the mind. Shakespeare feeds the entire brain." He recommended reading the essays of Bacon and Montaigne and the maxims of La Rochefoucauld as well as the "Spirit of Laws" by Montesquieu, which should be read slowly. "You will find in Montesquieu the history of man's struggle to attain justice. In Montaigne you will admire solid wisdom and keen satire. The brilliant duke of La Rochefoucauld will show you how to use language and with most brilliancy."

To these he added Buckle's "History of Civilization in England," Lecky's "History of European Morals," and Guizot's "History of Civilization." The fables of La Fontaine were recommended for clear expression and simple thought, Sterne's "Sentimental Journey" for the best English prose, Homer's "Odyssey" to cure one of admiration for fancy writing. Dante's "Inferno" and his "Paradise Lost" for magnificent writing. Don Quixote for wit and satire, and "Gulliver's Travels," Goethe's "Faust," and Heine's "Reisebilder." To these he suggested adding the lives of important men—Socrates, Alexander the Great, Aristotle, Caesar, Napoleon, Voltaire, Michaelangelo and Leonardo da Vinci.

"If you want to know something about education for your children's sake, read Herbert Spencer's book on education and Rousseau's "Emile." Add to these, if you are industrious, the works on education by Froebel and Pestalozzi. But Spencer and Rousseau are enough for the average parent." This completed the list.

The reader will note that the book list consisted almost exclusively of the products of eighteenth and nineteenth century writers. The books on astronomy, both admirable in their way, have been out of date for more than a third of a century. Wallace was a contemporary of Darwin, and his book, though a good summary of the picture of evolution as seen by the scientists of half a hundred years ago, is today outmoded and replete with errors.

The writing of history, too, has undergone a profound change. Buckle and Lecky were pioneers, but to recommend their books for an understanding of history is like recommending the purchase of a Model T for modern travel. Guizot's "History of Civilization" is colored throughout by his intense nationalism. Probably Brisbane had never heard of the works of such modern historians such as Breasted, Beard, or Robinson. Both Rousseau and Spencer were great men. But their contributions to the science of education were small indeed. Sociology, anthropology, psychology, seemed to have arrived too late to be included in a Brisbane list. Not one contemporary writer is included, nor any American, for that matter. Forgotten or ignored are such world renowned figures as Thomas Hardy, Bernard Shaw, Anatole France, Romain Rolland, Gorky, Dostoievsky, Walt Whitman, or Mark Twain.

In his "Haphazard Reflections on Grave Topics" Brisbane once announced that marriage was brought about on this earth by the will and wisdom of God Almighty working through primitive babyhood. He told how primitive man recognized his likeness in the child and wanted to serve its needs. Therefore, to "childhood, helpless, and beautiful, we owe marriage and all that growth of morality which is gradually making us really civilized." He discouraged any suggestion of "trial marriage." "Theoretically, this would be beautiful . . . but it wouldn't work. It would be all right for women. They are only too willing to be faithful and permanent.

"But men cannot be trusted. The animal in them, so essential long ago, when the race was struggling for a foothold, has not been obliterated. They have got to be *made* responsible and *held* responsible."

If men only learned "to realize that one half of what they eat keeps them alive and the other half kills them," he predicted they would live to reach 140 years of age.

Along with such predictions and prophecies, Brisbane inevitably interspersed a heavy supply of advice on how to succeed in life. He would advise, "The main thing is for each man to *live* earnestly, *think* earnestly, *do* the best that he can." Or, "The commonest form, one most often neglected, and the safest opportunity for the average man to seize, is *hard work*."

He was a strong advocate of thrift. "If it is possible for you to live, *it is possible for you to save*." Of course you shouldn't starve yourself but it might be more extravagant for you to spend thirty cents daily on a luncheon than it would for some other person to buy a five thousand dollar automobile. No matter how small your income, you could always practice economy. Always save and you will never suffer hunger. "If you have ten dollars a week only and are careful, you will live to be envied by the man whose big income you envy now, if that man is foolish and extravagant.

"Although the accumulation of wealth should not be the sole interest in one's life, yet it was one of the most important. "Senseless denunciation of legitimate wealth is harmful to the country as well as unjust."

In these days Brisbane admitted the highest reward that one man or a body of men can offer another is apparently a great sum of money and if this is what the able men want, concludes Brisbane, they should have it, "for the laborer is worthy of his hire, and we should be prepared in this country to pay the highest legitimate prices, not only for eight hours of manual work each day, but for eight minutes, or eight seconds of the inspired work which develops a great idea and involves, perhaps, employment for thousands."

Arthur Brisbane's religious feelings have been open to question, but he knew that the bulk of his readers were religious and he always had a good word to say for religion. "To take away faith, without supplying knowledge and strength of character, is brutality and cruelty. Millions of mothers have actually believed that they could see an angel taking their child to realms of eternal happiness, where the child will wait for the mother to come. Who would disturb a picture that consoles millions of mothers?"

On frequent occasions he announced that it was religion which freed men from brutality, superstition, hatred and cruelty. Likewise, it was religion that "freed slaves, abolished infanticide, and gave to the serf the right to own the land on which he worked."

In an editorial, "The Future of the World," he remarked that three questions occupy men's minds: 1) How and Why do we come here? 2) Where do we go, if anywhere, when we leave here? 3) What is to be the future of our race here? "Fortunately for the masses of human beings, these questions have been answered by various revealed religions.

"Answers given by religions of different kinds have been far apart, but they have all fulfilled one important purpose. They have saved harassed, worried human beings from the hardest of all work which is—THINKING."

On another occasion he remarked: "Whoever leaves the supernatural out of religion leaves out the only thing that makes religion interesting." The tendency of many modern religious groups to emphasize the ethical and humanitarian aspects of life rather than dwelling upon hell and brimstone and the wrath of Jehovah, didn't appeal to the editor. "It seems strange to talk of religion," he said, "with no mention of 'sin;' but to ignore sin is one of the peculiarities of the day."

Brisbane's economics were a strange compound. At one moment he would inform his readers that the basis of all wealth was human labor. He would advocate thrift to gain financial independence, and would follow this with a sermon on the folly of trying to become rich. "Safe Investment at Good Interest Is What the People Want," was the title of one of his editorials, with the subhead, "S. W. Strauss has provided such investment to the tune of $150,000,000. He talks of Thrift with knowledge of the subject." Brisbane admitted that savings banks were admirable institutions but they had a great overhead of expense. Not so with the men who ran the S. W. Strauss Company. "They make the man who BORROWS money pay all the cost—title insurance, investigation, overhead, and everything else—in the form of an extra commission on the loan. And those who invest their money get all the benefit, all of the interest that the borrower pays. In other words, the savings bank lends money at 5% to the borrower, and gives 3% to the man who deposits money in the bank . . . S. W. Strauss and Company lend money at 5½% to the borrower and give 5½% to the indi-

A realistic picture of Arthur Brisbane in his last years.

vidual who buys their bonds—and none of those buying the bonds has ever lost a dollar." (This was written in 1916, long before the Strauss Company crashed carrying with it untold thousands of depositors and investors who had followed the advice of Mr. Brisbane to invest in their bonds. Some of these Strauss "guaranteed" mortgages, incidentally, were on Brisbane properties.)

For more than forty years Brisbane kept telling his readers they must THINK. "Your only property," he said, "is CAPACITY TO MAKE MENTAL EFFORT." Despite his continuous pleading for this, the advance made in the United States seemed very slow. Once, in exasperation, he wrote: "In France there is done by the average citizen at least a thousand times as much earnest thinking on national politics as is done in this country." France had no Hearst and no Brisbane. The answer is perhaps to be found in another Brisbane editorial entitled, "THE POWER OF SILENCE." There he declared: "The success of the country boy is based largely on the fact that he is FORCED TO KEEP HIMSELF COMPANY and THOUGHT—if he has any brain at all—is forced upon him." The French population is still predominantly rural, which perhaps explains the previous statement. But silence alone is not enough. There are two kinds, according to Brisbane, PASSIVE AND ACTIVE. As examples of the latter, he cited Napoleon, "digging up silently, OUT OF HIS OWN DEEP MIND the solution of his world problems." And there is Newton, who "ALONE AND THINKING in the moonlight saw the apple fall which started the thought that immortalized his name." Brisbane added: "Had he been at that time in a crowd, chattering and gossiping, he might have picked up the apple to eat it—talking between bites. But he could not have done the concentrated thinking which made him ask WHY THE MOON DID NOT FALL AS THAT APPLE HAD FALLEN." Brisbane's thought-provoking editorials were almost invariably written in the midst of noise in the most populous city in the world.

Brisbane believed in the superiority of the blond and blue-eyed people. He was certain a high forehead indicated high intelligence and a square jaw, determination. But he didn't believe in palmistry. "Are you plagued with the foolish superstition that makes men and women study lines in their hands and pay cunning palm-readers?" Those lines, he informed them, "were formed in the closed hand of the unborn child, all accidental, like the wrinkling of rose petals in the rosebud." But if he didn't believe in palmistry, he was certainly interested in graphology. Miss Dorothy Sara, of New York, met Mr. Brisbane at the home of Mrs. William Randolph Hearst where she (Miss Sara) entertained the guests by handwriting analyses. Not only was Brisbane interested in graphology, but his daughter, Sarah, was also attracted by it. In a letter to the graphologist, Brisbane wrote: "My dear Miss Sara: I remember with pleasure meeting you at Mrs. Hearst's. I hope, for obvious reasons, that in my case, the handwriting is not the man, or at least all of him. *Always* tell masculine clients, 'Your writing shows inflexible will power,' and they will call again. Sincerely, Arthur Brisbane."

In *Harper's Bazaar*, a Hearst publication, in April, 1934, Miss Sara made the following analysis of Brisbane's handwriting: "Notice how disconnected the writing of Arthur Brisbane seems to be. This shows intuition, impulse, and whenever possible he escapes from boring details. He makes the same letters in different formation, such as a small 'f' and a small 'g.' These varying formations show his versatility and adaptability. He has a grand sense of humor, a simple nature and an utter distaste for superficiality of any sort. He has an insatiable curiosity and the ability to absorb knowledge from every contact he makes."

In the field of political prophecy, Brisbane failed completely. Charles Edward Russell said of him: "He never could tell how an election was coming out. He had a sort of political blindspot, guessing wrong in almost every election campaign and he never overcame this shortcoming. For example, in 1920 Brisbane, at the Chicago Convention of the Republican Party, expected a deadlock to ensue among the forces campaigning for Governor Lowden of Illinois, Senator Johnson of California, and General Leonard Wood. As a result he was absolutely convinced that the nomination would go to Hughes. Hearst was of the same opinion."

In April, 1932, Brisbane made a speech to the Rochester, New York, Chamber of Commerce in which he said, "To nominate any other democratic candidate but Alfred E. Smith in 1932, is to spell failure of that party—and Democratic nomination in opposition to the wishes of Smith will be defeated."

With reference to war and international conflict, Brisbane predicted as late as January, 1936, in Hearst's *Cosmopolitan* Magazine, that wars would soon end because "war is considered an unpleasant necessity, not a career of glory desirable in itself . . . In the ancient world great men were usually great fighters; in the present world there are few if any great fighters."

His prophecy made at the time when the Volstead Act was passed that "one hundred percent efficiency has been added at one stroke to the people of America" was modified as popular pressure began to grow against prohibition. By 1927, he was able to write, "Gradually it seems to be dawning on some of the population that bootleg whiskey which sometimes makes you blind, sometimes kills you and always poisons you, isn't such a great improvement on old whiskey."

In two instances, however, Brisbane prophesied correctly.

The first was that wars of today would be fought largely in the air. And that air transportation would soon become a major industry. This he predicted twenty-five years ago.

In the suit brought by former Ford stockholders against Henry Ford in 1926, attorneys introduced an editorial by Brisbane in which he predicted with remarkable accuracy the development of the automobile industry. On April 27, 1912 (when Ford was producing at the rate of 78,600 cars for the year and was selling his model T for $600) a Brisbane editorial published in the *New York Journal* said that some manufacturer in the not distant future would turn out one million cars a year; that his net profits would be from $25,-000,000 to $50,000,000 a year and that the price of the car might be less than four hundred dollars. Ford's earnings passed the fifty million mark by 1916. In that same year the base price of the Ford car fell from $440 to $360 and the million car per year production was reached shortly thereafter.

Arthur J. Lacy, attorney for Senator James Couzens, one of the petitioners, said: "I have never encountered a more amazing journalistic prediction. If Mr. Brisbane erred at all, it was on the side of conservatism. His vision has become fact. He forecast production, earnings, retail sales price, manufacturing methods and type of car with an accuracy that seems almost uncanny."

14

WRITTEN IN SAND

THE flow of words was to continue for another two years—as massive in quantity, as repetitious in ideas, as uniform in style.

The only shift was that made on the day after Mr. Roosevelt's re-election in November, 1936. Governor Landon, who had been "discovered" by William Randolph Hearst and Arthur Brisbane as the man to stop "raw deal socialism," went down to an overwhelming defeat and sank into an almost immediate oblivion.

The suddenness of Hearst's right-about-face as the election returns poured in left even his critics gasping with astonishment. "Perhaps I was wrong in my estimate of Mr. Roosevelt. Maybe he is a great Jacksonian democrat, after all," remarked the Lord of San Simeon.

As for Brisbane, the belated repudiation of the President in 1935 kept him in a steady movement from adulation to contempt and thence on to hatred. Without stopping to apply his emotional brakes at that point, he was easily able to sail on until his circumnavigation brought him back again, worshiping at the shrine of Franklin Delano Roosevelt. His pessimism of the year before ("the only people in the United States not wanted, are the people who created the United States, that is, business and thinking people,") was conveniently forgotten as he heralded the good times about to dawn.

He turned his back on politics to continue his admiration

of Southern California, much to the disgust of the Floridians. "After a soul has spent a thousand years in Paradise," he wrote, August 10, 1935, "it probably forgets to wonder, and no longer mentions the marvels of the place, pavements of gold, walls of jasper, strange pieces of cloth, for the red, black, white, and grey horses."

"So here in California, after one hundred visits, you take for granted that which amazes you and exhausted your adjective supply on the first few trips . . . come and see, remembering that in California, the summer season is the best season."

His dislike of the Japanese continued to the very end. As for the British, his remarks on the abdication of King Edward VIII tell the whole story: "Many would have been better pleased had the king said to Baldwin, '*I am going to marry the lady, and retain the throne*, and you are going back to raising thoroughbred pigs on your farm.'

"Had he said it, Baldwin would have gone; the pigs and the British Empire would gain thereby."

In his old age Brisbane began to view the past through rosy glasses. He was no longer a circulation-getter or an effective editorial acrobat. He was mellow. He felt that good reporters had become scarce. In the good old days, things were different. Then a reporter went out and talked with the people he was to write about, and came back and wrote his own story. He had plenty of time. He was encouraged to write into his story humor, pathos, romance or whatever quality of emotion the situation demanded. "Now we find that it is cheaper and more efficient to give our readers their daily ration of humor, pathos, love interest and whatnot in the form of syndicated features. And the news, for the most part, is cut down to mere bones, the facts gathered by legmen and telephoned in to a rewrite desk."

As 1936 was drawing to a close, King Features, a Hearst subsidiary, asked Brisbane two questions: "1) What event of 1936 contributed most to mankind's progress? and 2) What do you most hope or expect to happen in 1937 of most importance to mankind?" To the first, he replied: "The successful completion of the two hundred-inch telescopic reflector, which should increase human knowledge of the universe outside of this little quarreling, cheating, seething, superstitious murderous planet."

His answer to the second question was no answer at all, but it made interesting reading: "I think mankind will trot along about as it has been doing, following some plan mapped out far away and beyond our understanding. Man should find comfort in the fact that he has done pretty well considering the fact that he is only twelve thousand years from the Late Stone Age . . . If man has risen from the back of a tame buffalo to an airplane in twelve thousand years, what will he do in fifteen billion years still ahead of him?"

In June of 1936, Brisbane sailed with the Hearst party for a trip to Europe. Germany, France, Italy were once more visited and from each country Brisbane continued his daily output, although he confessed on various occasions that he felt tired and was not well. Petulant because he was not supplied with a private car and chauffeur as were the other members of the group, he left the Hearst party and traveled by train instead, offering, as a reason, ill health. But this snub was part of Hearst's growing habit of ignoring his formerly effective editorial miracle-man.

The daily grind continued upon Brisbane's return to the United States. Friends and associates remarked that he looked visibly older and more stooped, but the clear cold blue-grey eyes remained as keen as ever and the sharp voice poured out its never ending comments on world news. He spent less time at the office. His ill health, which grew rapidly worse through the fall of 1936, was kept a secret from all but his most intimate friends and advisors. His step-mother in California knew of his illness and told friends months before he died that he was in a critical condition and would very likely die before she did. "In more ways than one, Arthur and I are contemporaries," she said.

Henry F. Pringle, who had been commissioned to do an article on Brisbane for a leading magazine, requested an interview. This was, in due time, granted and took place just ten days before Mr. Brisbane's death, at Brisbane's Fifth Avenue home. The editor was in bed, looking old and very tired. He gave Pringle the interview but remarked: "Don't say that you saw me in bed. It might hurt the syndication of my articles." And in a letter to Pringle he declared: "I am sorry to have to advise you that I am laid up and in no shape to do much talking. Perhaps my secretary, Miss L. B. Krause, . . . could give you any suggestions you want. She knows more than I do about what I have done in the last fifteen or twenty years; . . . back of that is the paeolithic age for young people like you . . .

"I have been trying for two years to write about myself for the magazines, for the very dull reason that it would help me buy shoes for my children, but I have not the time to get at it."

A year before his death, the editor was stricken with a bronchial ailment which clung stubbornly to him. His powerful frame, torn by this illness, began to break down. Soon came a mild heart attack, followed by others, each stronger than the previous one. By November, he was compelled, under advice from his physician, to stay in bed. He continued his work without interruption. His daily column and his weekly editorials appeared unfailingly, and on time.

He wrote and answered scores of letters and telegrams each day. He issued orders about his real estate and other business ventures, and followed the stock market carefully—all the while conducting conversations with members of his family, his staff, or outsiders.

A card had been placed on the side of the door leading to Arthur Brisbane's bed room, announcing, "Please limit yourself to five minutes." However, this rule was seldom lived up to, for Brisbane himself, now that he was bed-ridden, was anxious to talk at length with anyone who reached him, and would keep his visitor, sometimes for hours, while others were left to cool their heels in his palatial drawing room.

There, in that immense gallery—for such it seemed rather than a drawing room—the waiting visitor could inspect the allegorical wall decorations, representing "Europe Through the Ages." He might contemplate the heavy handpainted beams which stretched across the ceiling, or view the many *objects d'art* which crowded the room. Or perhaps he would gaze with awe upon the many signed photographs, visible signs of the greatness of the editor. There, on a table, stood a glowering photograph of Il Duce himself. Opposite, on a highboy, was one of Cardinal Hayes. Another, of President Roosevelt, was inscribed "to my old friend, A.B." And a large, smiling photograph of the Lord of San Simeon bore the legend "W.R. to A.B. I'm glad the *Journal* is doing well." But the *piece de resistance*, occupying the main table in the room, was a photograph of the artist, Charles Dana Gibson. Framed with it was a letter from Gibson expressing pleasure that the mighty editor had asked for his picture. The artist asked for one in return—Might he have a side view, "showing your brain box?"

The room, huge, impressive, ornate, was the outward expression of all that Brisbane craved, and it reflected far more accurately than any mirror his own self-esteem and importance. He used it frequently to receive the important personalities who passed within range of his orbit, or to dazzle and entertain important advertisers as a prelude to signing contracts for space in the *Journal* or the *Mirror*.

But neither the quiet of his Fifth Avenue town house nor the best of medical specialists could keep the weakened heart of Arthur Brisbane functioning. On December 24th, Christmas Eve, he dictated his last column—the only column he failed to finish himself. His son Seward wrote the final paragraph. He began his Yule-tide message:

"Another Christmas has come, a birthday that means kindness and hope for so many millions of human beings. Nineteen hundred and thirty-six years ago a beautiful Child came into the world; a few years later, the three crosses were erected on the bare hill called Golgotha, meaning 'The Skull' . . ."

He painted a picture of a world at war, a world of cruelty, and suffering and sorrow. But true to his fifty-year old habit of giving his readers the desired happy ending, he concluded, "Progress has been steady . . . 'Peace on earth and good will toward men' will surely come."

Brisbane lay back in his bed, exhausted, to sleep his last sleep. To his son-in-law, John Reagan McCrary, he spoke his last words, a quotation from Voltaire's "Candide"—"This is the best of all possible worlds." They were appropriate words, indeed, to close the career of a "successful" man. Death came at 5:35 A. M., Christmas morning.

The death of Arthur Brisbane was front page news and vied for the place of honor with the "Wally" Simpson romance, Il Duce and Hitler's backing of the proposed four power treaty concerning Spain, and the ailment of Pope Pius. To the bereaved family came an endless flow of letters and telegrams, indicative of the prominent place the late great editor had occupied. Not a newspaper in the country failed to discuss his passing and his place in American life and letters. Extravagant praise was meted out by the Hearst papers: "His keen insight, vast knowledge, human understanding, and marvelous power of conveying thought in the simplest words, stimulated the intelligence and influenced the lives of millions of men and women.

"Like Lord Bacon, he took all learning for his province, and perhaps no man since Lord Bacon has written more understandingly or packed more meaning into fewer words.

"Philosophy, religion, science, art, literature, economics, politics—the most abstruse phases of these and all subjects he touched were transformed into words of crystal clearness which the least educated might read and comprehend."

And almost equal praise from the *Cleveland News:* "He could do more things and do them better than anyone else in his own times or any other time in newspaper history."

The remarks of the *New York Herald Tribune* were noncommittal: "The death removes one of the most gifted and contradictory personalities in American journalism." *The World Telegram* was openly critical: "A worshipper of success was Arthur Brisbane. He achieved what he worshipped . . . He dedicated his genius to the ends and purposes of big business . . . The measure of Arthur Brisbane's greatness was in the press run . . . He respected his father. He coveted the memory of his father. But he did not emulate him."

The funeral services, conducted Monday morning, December 28th, at New York's St. Bartholomew's Church was more in the nature of a mass meeting. More than 2,000 people jammed their way into the church edifice, while a crowd at least equally great gathered outside. It was the kind of gathering Arthur Brisbane would have wanted. A symbol of the practice of journalism as taught and practiced by Brisbane was there, too, for a candid cameraman had edged his way into the front pew, from which he snapped a complete camera account of the services. Outside were batteries of cameramen and news-reel photographers—the whole affair with a flavor of Hollywood pageantry.

The prominent persons at the funeral represented American capitalism: Winthrop W. Aldrich, president of the Chase National Bank; John D. Rockefeller, Jr.; Gerard Swope, of General Electric; Myron C. Taylor, of the United States Steel Corporation; Percy S. Strauss; Bernard Gimbel; William Randolph Hearst; Walter P. Chrysler; Herbert Fleishhacker, San Francisco financier; W. S. Knudsen, of General Motors, and a host of others. Also William Green, president of the American Federation of Labor, was there.

At the close of the services the black mahogany coffin, draped in a blanket of violets, began its slow and solemn journey across busy Manhattan to the estate at Allaire, New Jersey. There, near a high tower where Brisbane had written so many columns, on a high knoll overlooking the sea, the body of the world's highest paid journalist was placed to rest in a steel vault. "Today" was ended.

"My father taught me" Arthur Brisbane used to say "that if I died without doing something to help the lot of the common people my life would have been a failure and the hottest place in hell would be too good for me."

The degree to which he obeyed his father's injunction has already been suggested. In his private charities Brisbane was kind and generous to many individuals—especially to old women and young children. Rarely a day passed that he failed to slip a dollar bill into the hands of some astonished youngster or aged person. Close friends and relatives received assistance. Once he gave some of his land in New Jersey for a Boy Scout camp and in 1935 he gave a substantial gift of money to build two playgrounds for the children of the Tallulah Falls School, located in a remote section of the north Georgia mountains.

That completes the public record. No founder of schools, he left no scholarships, he gave no parks, or art galleries or museums, nor were any provided for in his will. Only one of his several faithful secretaries received a small legacy. The others were forgotten. Such good as he himself might have accomplished by his huge fortune (estimated at from $25,000,000 to $30,000,000) was left to be done by New Jersey state officials making use of the inheritance tax on his estate. At a public hearing, February 24, 1937, in Trenton, with reference to the proposed diversion of $8,000,000 from the state highway funds for relief purposes, the Secretary of the New Jersey Farm Bureau proposed it be taken from the Brisbane estate. "This is a case of Santa Claus visiting the state of New Jersey, and we, . . . want to see this money used for unemployment relief purposes and not for unnecessary appropriations."

For all his dealings in high finance, Arthur Brisbane was a nervously economical man. He would save bits of string, paper, blotters, and the wide assortment of odds and ends. Once he bought a great quantity of army cots from Camp Dix, "at a bargain" though he had no use for them. Because of his power as an editor, he would ask for (and get) blocks of tickets to theaters, the opera, or other entertainments. Members of his staff said he never bought an automobile in his life—he had them all given to him. In his money mania, he would on occasion have old cartoons and illustrations dug up from the files of the *Journal*, use them over again, with slightly varied text, and charge the paper for the price of a new drawing.

Stanley Walker, at lunch with Brisbane one day, noted that the world's highest paid editor had ordered two lamb chops, but was able to eat only one. He looked at the second one longingly, but was too full to eat it. After considerable thought, he called the waiter.

"What happens if I don't eat this chop? Will you take it back?"

"No sir, we can't do that sir," replied the startled waiter.

"But what will you do with it?" persisted Brisbane. "Will it be thrown away?"

"Not at all, sir. We give the leftovers to poor people."

Breathing a sigh of relief, Brisbane nodded approval, and paid his check.

During the last few years of his life, Brisbane always carried a small bottle of brandy with him wherever he went; and at mealtime would conclude his repast with a cup of coffee, a lump of sugar and a bit of brandy. He said the combination of brandy and sugar was good for his heart. "It puts just a slight layer of fat around my heart, a layer just thick enough to give me the added reserve I need to help me carry on my strenuous work."

Did Brisbane have a sense of humor? Charles Edward Russell, among others, insisted he had genuine wit. His latter-day associates deny it. Even so devoted a friend as Damon Runyan wrote that "when something supposed to be funny reached him, he passed it on to TAD, Bugs Baer, or others supposed to know humor, asking: 'Is that funny?'"

Nor did he care for verse. Says Runyan: "He brought some around one day saying 'You and "Bugs" read this and see if it's any good. I don't care for poetry myself. You can always say something in prose better than in rhyme.'"

The overpowering mania for gold Brisbane denounced without being able to overcome it himself. An acquaintance of many years standing said of him:

"Brisbane had a money-greed of intense, almost hysterical proportions and there are many who feel that his immense salary covered other advantages to Hearst besides journalistic services.

"I stood with him for a few minutes overlooking one of the most beautiful landscapes in the world, the sort which cannot be recalled even in memory without emotion. I made some remarks about its character, composition, color, suggestiveness—the sort of remark any landscape amateur might make. Brisbane's reply was quick, intense, almost savage: 'Yes, and there is oil in those hills; I have scouts out in various places; I have got options here and there' and he went on to describe in glowing terms the amount of money he might make from them.

"Another time we were looking at another landscape and I spoke of some historical associations with it, to which Brisbane replied: 'Yes, and there is a big chance to make some money there; one or two of the owners are in financial difficulties, and I have got some options up there, too.' "

"All that I am I owe to my father," was a common phrase with the great editor. He would add that he did poorly what his father had done well; and whereas his father had to pay to write a column in the New York *Tribune*, he, Arthur, was well-paid for the privilege of expounding his ideas to his millions of readers.

This attitude seemed part of Arthur Brisbane's sentimentality. He had the highest respect for his own writing and intellect; and for that matter, from the point of view of mass appeal, his writings were far better than those of his father. But his writing was never inspired. He was, without doubt, an outstanding reporter of the commonplace. He told of his conversation with the barber who shaved him, or the bits of conversation he heard and the things he saw as he strolled up the Main Street of some midwestern town. He would discuss how far a flea could jump; the plight of a child with a headless doll; or what an ant thinks about as it creeps across a cobblestone. He gave his readers a superficial knowledge of the day's news, freely interspersed with saccharine inspirational messages about how far we have evolved since the days of the dinosaur.

The best analysis of his style and its success is perhaps that presented by Arthur Upham Pope:

"The success of his column 'Today' was due, it seems to me, to the adroit way in which he explained the laws of the rhythm of attention which govern the average mind. It was a 'discovery' comparable to the discovery of the sonata or the sonnet form. The sentences were just the right length and the paragraphs also. He used extremely simple words, strung them together with a rhythm that required the minimum effort of attention and, at the same time, with just enough of mild surprise to keep the attention from flagging. He left the subject just the moment before it tended to become even slightly fatiguing and sounded the note of recall at just that moment when the first impression tends to reaffirm itself. This returning tide of interest reinforced now by an agreeable sense of the familiar, floated his conclusion neatly into the dock. The column "Today" was in its form something like a work of art, and at the same time psychologically shrewd and sound."

When Albert Brisbane died in 1890, he was alone—forgotten by those whom he had tried to help. The newspapers scarcely carried an obituary notice. And he himself, dying as the month of April closed, asked only that he be allowed to live through May Day to see the rising hosts of Labor marching on to victory.

But when Arthur Brisbane died December 25, 1936, the politicians, from Roosevelt down; the captains of industry – like Ford, Schwab, and Mellon; the great merchant princes – like Gimbel, as well as the Wall Street speculators, joined in giving homage to this man who had been their friend. He had strayed far from the path of his father. He had given of his time and his talent to achieve financial success and the applause of those whom he and his father had once fought. With his mind and his body and his heart he had gone over to his father's enemies, and they claimed him as their own.

BIBLIOGRAPHY

Books and Pamphlets

Andrews, E. Benjamin: THE UNITED STATES IN OUR TIME—1870-1903 (1912)

Ayer, N. W. & Sons: DIRECTORY OF NEWSPAPERS AND PERIODICALS (1933-4)

Baker, Ray Stannard: LIFE AND LETTERS OF WOODROW WILSON (1922)

Beard, Charles and Mary: RISE OF AMERICAN CIVILIZATION (1927)

Beck, James M.: THE ENEMY WITHIN OUR GATES (1917)

Beer, Max: SOCIAL STRUGGLES AND THOUGHT (1925)

Bent, Silas: STRANGE BEDFELLOWS (1928), BALLYHOO—THE VOICE OF THE PRESS, (1927)

Bleyer, W. G.: HISTORY OF AMERICAN JOURNALISM (1927)

Brisbane, Redelia: ALBERT BRISBANE: A MENTAL BIOGRAPHY (1893)

Brisbane, Albert: SOCIAL DESTINY OF MAN (1840), A CONCISE EXPOSITION OF THE DOCTRINE OF ASSOCIATION, (1843), THEORY OF THE FUNCTIONS OF THE HUMAN PASSIONS (1851), GENERAL INTRODUCTION TO THE SOCIAL SCIENCES (1876)

Brisbane, Arthur: EDITORIALS FROM THE HEARST NEWSPAPERS (1906), MARY BAKER EDDY (1908), THE BOOK OF TODAY (1923), TODAY AND THE FUTURE DAY (1925)

Bradford, Gamaliel: AS GOD MADE THEM (1929)

Brooks, Van Wyck: THE FLOWERING OF NEW ENGLAND (1936)

Buss, W. F.: GAZETTEER AND BIOGRAPHICAL RECORD OF GENESEE COUNTY (1890)

Carlson, Oliver and Bates, Ernest Sutherland: HEARST: LORD OF SAN SIMEON (1936)

Codman, John T.: BROOK FARM (1894)

Commons, John R.; and Associates: HISTORY OF LABOR IN THE UNITED STATES (1918)

Creelman, James: ON THE GREAT HIGHWAY (1901)

Croffut, William A.: AMERICAN PROCESSION—1855-1914 (1931)

Curtis, George William: EARLY LETTERS OF GEORGE WILLIAM CURTIS TO JOHN S. DWIGHT; BROOK FARM AND CONCORD (1898)

DICTIONARY OF AMERICAN BIOGRAPHY, Vol. III

Ely, Richard T.: RECENT AMERICAN SOCIALISM (1885)

Fahrney, Ralph Ray: HORACE GREELEY AND THE TRIBUNE IN THE CIVIL WAR (1936)

Flint, Leon M.: THE CONSCIENCE OF THE NEWSPAPER (1925)

Greeley, Horace: RECOLLECTIONS OF A BUSY LIFE

Hapgood, Norman: THE CHANGING YEARS (1930)

Hawthorne, Nathaniel: AMERICAN NOTEBOOKS (1932)

Hearst, William Randolph: BRIEF TO THE PUBLIC SERVICE COMMISSION (1931), LET UNITED STATES PROMOTE THE WORLD'S PEACE (1915), OBLIGATIONS AND OPPORTUNITIES OF THE UNITED STATES IN MEXICO AND THE PHILIPPINES (1916), ON THE FOREGOING WAR DEBTS (1931), TRUTHS ABOUT THE TRUSTS (1916)

Hibben, Captain Paxton: THE PEERLESS LEADER, WILLIAM JENNINGS BRYAN (1929)

Hillquit, Morris: HISTORY OF SOCIALISM IN THE UNITED STATES (1903)

Kennedy, John: ROBERT MORRIS AND THE HOLLAND PURCHASE (1894)

Kirby, Mrs. Georgiana (Bruce): YEARS OF EXPERIENCE (1887)
Klein, Henry H.: MY LAST FIFTY YEARS (1935)
Linn, W. A.: HORACE GREELEY (1912)
Lord, C. S.: REMINISCENCES OF CHARLES A. DANA
Luhan, Mabel Dodge: MAKERS AND SHAKERS (1933-1936)
Lundberg, Ferdinand: IMPERIAL HEARST (1936)
MacGowan, Kenneth: COILED IN THE FLAG (1918)
McMaster, John B.: HISTORY OF THE PEOPLE OF THE UNITED STATES
Millis, Walter: THE MARTIAL SPIRIT (1931)
Moskowitz, Henry: ALFRED E. SMITH (1924)
Myers, Gustavus: THE HISTORY OF TAMMANY HALL
Noyes, John Humphrey: HISTORY OF AMERICAN SOCIALISMS (1870)
O'Brien, Frank M.: STORY OF THE "SUN" (1918)
Older, Mrs. Fremont: WILLIAM RANDOLPH HEARST: AMERICAN (1936)
Palmer, Frederick: WITH MY OWN EYES (1933)
Parrington, Vernon Louis: MAIN CURRENTS IN AMERICAN THOUGHT (1927)
Parry, Albert: GARRETS AND PRETENDERS
Payne, George H.: HISTORY OF JOURNALISM IN THE UNITED STATES (1920)
Pringle, Henry F.: THEODORE ROOSEVELT (1931)
Rosebault, Charles J.: WHEN DANA WAS *The Sun* (1931)
Russell, Charles Edward: BARE HANDS AND STONE WALLS (1933)
Seaver, William: HISTORICAL SKETCH OF THE VILLAGE OF BATAVIA (1849)
Seitz, Don C.: HORACE GREELEY, FOUNDER OF THE NEW YORK TRIBUNE, JOSEPH PULITZER
Seldes, Gilbert: YEARS OF THE LOCUST (1933)

Sherover, Max: FAKES IN AMERICAN JOURNALISM (1916)
Sinclair, Upton: THE BRASS CHECK
Smith, Alfred E.: UP TO NOW (1929)
Steffens, Lincoln: AUTOBIOGRAPHY OF LINCOLN STEFFENS (1931)
Sullivan, Mark: OUR TIMES (1926)
Swing, Raymond Gram: FORERUNNERS OF AMERICAN FASCISM (1935)
Symes, Lillian and Travers, Clement;: REBEL AMERICA (1934)
Thomas, Norman: WHAT'S THE MATTER WITH NEW YORK
Thompson, Charles Willis: PARTY LEADERS OF THE TIME (1906)
United States Senate, PROPAGANDA OR MONEY ALLEGED TO HAVE BEEN USED BY FOREIGN GOVERNMENTS TO INFLUENCE UNITED STATES SENATORS (1928), BREWING AND LIQUOR INTERESTS AND GERMAN AND BOLSHEVIK PROPAGANDA (1919)
Villard, Oswald Garrison: PROPHETS FALSE AND TRUE (1928), SOME NEWSPAPERS AND NEWSPAPERMEN (1926), THE PRESS TODAY (1930)
Walker, Stanley: CITY EDITOR (1934)
Werner, M. R.: TAMMANY HALL (1928), BRYAN (1929)
Wilkerson, Marcus M.: PUBLIC OPINION AND THE SPANISH-AMERICAN WAR (1932)
Wilson, J. H.: LIFE OF CHARLES DANA (1907)
Winkler, J. K.: W. R. HEARST—AN AMERICAN PHENOMENON (1928)

Magazine articles

American Mercury, Jan. 1926; May 1927; Nov. 1930.
American Magazine, June 1918.
Bookman, June 1904.

Christian Century, Oct. 15, 1930; May 10, 1933.
Collier's Weekly, Feb. 18, 1908; Mar. 4, 1908; Mar. 11, 1908; Oct. 24, 1908; June 22, 1912; Oct. 5, 1912; Dec. 30, 1922; Feb. 20, 1926.
Cosmopolitan, Sept. 1901; May 1902; Aug. 1907; Apr.-May 1908; Aug. 1908; Feb. 1909.
Current Opinion, May 1924.
Fortune, Aug. 1931; Oct. 1935.
Editor & Publisher, Jan. 2 & Jan. 9, 1937.
Harper's Weekly, May 21, 1904; Jan. 9, 1909; Apr. 26, 1913; Oct. 9, 1915.
Everybody's, Mar. 1916.
Literary Digest, Oct. 5, 1918.
North American Review, Sept. 21, 1906; Oct. 4, 1906.
Nation, Feb. 22, 1906; July 15, 1918; Mar. 28, 1923; Dec. 27, 1927; Dec. 31, 1936.
Outlook, Oct. 2, 1918.
World's Work, Apr. 1906; Oct. 1906; Oct. 1922.

Newspapers

The files of the following newspapers were checked:
New York Tribune, 1842-1872.
New York Sun, 1883-1890.
New York World, 1890-1898.
New York Journal, 1897-1916.
Washington, D. C. Times, Apr. 1917-Aug. 1919.
New York Times, 1909-1937.
Los Angeles Examiner, 1920-1937.
New York Mirror, 1934-1935.

Additional magazines

Harbinger, 1845-46.
Democratic Review, 1841-1842.

INDEX

INDEX

INDEX

INDEX

INDEX

INDEX

INDEX

INDEX

INDEX